TERESA CORRALES

Writing with a Thesis

Writing with a Thesis

A Rhetoric and Reader

Second Edition

David Skwire
Cuyahoga Community College

HOLT, RINEHART AND WINSTON
New York   Chicago   San Francisco   Atlanta   Dallas
Montreal   Toronto

An *Instructor's Manual* is available. It may be obtained
through a local Holt representative or by writing to
English Editor, Holt, Rinehart and Winston, 383 Madison
Avenue, New York, NY 10017.

Library of Congress Cataloging in Publication Data

Skwire, David.
  Writing with a thesis.

  Includes index.
  1. College readers.   2. English language—Rhetoric.
I. Title.
PE1147.S47   1979   808'.042   78–15452

ISBN 0–03–040276–X

This book is written in loving memory
of my father, Raymond Skwire,
''who tawt me awl I no.''

Contents

To the Instructor

I love the young dogs of this age: they have more wit and humor and knowledge of life than we had; but then the dogs are not so good scholars. Sir, in my early years I read very hard.

SAMUEL JOHNSON

In many respects, *Writing with a Thesis* tries to do a traditional job in a traditional way. Its readings are arranged according to traditional rhetorical patterns, one pattern per chapter. Each group of readings is preceded by a detailed discussion of the writing techniques appropriate to that pattern. Headnotes, explanatory footnotes, and questions on content and style accompany each reading. The book wholeheartedly accepts such traditional ideas about teaching composition as the value of omnivorous reading, the utility of close analysis of individual works, and the salutary influence of models.

In some other respects, *Writing with a Thesis* is less traditional, though its commitment to the job of improving writing skills remains constant.

First, the traditional reader or rhetoric-reader tends to approach each rhetorical pattern as a separate entity requiring the development of a new set of writing skills. Chapter 1 of this book presents what it calls *the persuasive principle*: the development and support of a thesis. It goes on to demonstrate how the persuasive principle underlies almost all good writing, and subsequent chapters show how the persuasive principle functions within each of the rhetorical patterns. A major unifying theme thus runs through the entire book, each pattern being viewed not as a separate entity but as the application of a permanent writing principle to varying subject matter, insights, and purposes. The concept of the persuasive principle has long been stressed in some of the most popular handbooks and rhetorics. It has not ordinarily—or ever—been the animating force behind a general reader.

Second, in addition to the standard apparatus, the book includes after each selection brief comments titled "What About *Your* Writing?" These comments, directly related to the selection just studied, attempt to teach students something extra, something beyond what they have already learned from the selection as a model for a given rhetorical pattern.

"What About *Your* Writing?" entries offer pointers and tips, quick practical lessons that students can pick up from the reading and apply to their own work. The stress generally is on style because major issues of organization are dealt with in the opening sections of each chapter, but the coverage is wide and by no means confined to style. Topics range all the way from common high school superstitions—"Can I begin a sentence with *and*?"—to such broader issues as topical references and constructive and destructive criticism.

"What About *Your* Writing?" material in no way can substitute for the handbook that will almost certainly accompany *Writing with a Thesis* as a required text. "What About *Your* Writing?" attempts to deal with topics normally ignored or slighted in handbooks; it sometimes also attempts to present familiar topics with a new slant. The entries are not and cannot be systematic because they are directly related to the readings, and no instructor ever assigned all the readings in a text. More important, the entries *should* not be systematic, either.

"What About *Your* Writing?" tries to duplicate in some fashion one of the important ways by which people improve their writing: they read, and they pick things up. What can best be taught systematically must be so taught, of course, but not everything can be. Every instructor knows the benefits that can come when a student raises a hand and says, "This doesn't have anything to do with the subject exactly, but I was just wondering . . ." As an instructor structures a lesson and a course but builds into the structure an atmosphere that welcomes the sudden, just-wondering question, *Writing with a Thesis* uses "What About *Your* Writing?" to complement the rigorously structured elements of the rest of the book.

On pages xvi–xvii, a guide to "What About *Your* Writing?" provides a convenient listing of all topics.

Finally, one of the traditional problems with many traditional texts is that they bore and scare too many students. Instructors write them for other instructors, and the students suffer. *Writing with a Thesis,* with all its traditional philosophy, is written in an informal, simple, and we hope engaging style. The reading selections themselves, although a few are deliberately long and challenging, are generally short and easy to read. Class time can be devoted primarily to showing not what the readings mean, but what they mean for the student's writing.

December 1975   D.S.

A Note on the Second Edition

The second edition of *Writing with a Thesis* contains at least one new reading selection in each chapter. Six photographs have been added to accompany certain selections—"The Spider and the Wasp" and "Who Killed Benny Paret?" for example. The photographs are not meant to be decorations or vague stimuli for vague emotions; they are meant to convey additional information about the subject matter. The extremely warm response to the first edition has made it easy to resist the temptation to indulge in massive overhauls for their own sake, but a good textbook, like any other living thing, either changes or begins to die. We hope that all our changes have been life-giving.

Acknowledgments

The comments and criticisms of Professor Richard S. Beal, to no one's surprise, combined brilliance with common sense, good instincts with good taste. I am most grateful.

In addition, I am indebted to the following, who also read the manuscript, for their valuable criticism: Professors P. Burnes, D. Dean Cantrell, Margaret Carter, Marilyn D. Fillers, Ruth E. Hoeckle, Harry V. Moore, Gretchen Niva, William J. Starr, and John Stratton.

For countless services, both great and small, I also want to thank my friends and associates at Holt, Rinehart and Winston: Susan Katz, Pamela Forcey, and Anita Baskin. Special thanks go to Harriett Prentiss, for whom superhuman effort and achievement are all in a day's work.

And, once again, to Midge.

December 1978   D.S.

To the Student

Buying textbooks is more than the dreariness of waiting in line at the bookstore. It probably also marks the only time in your life when you pay good money for books you know nothing about.

The process isn't quite as outrageous as it might seem. Your instructors already know what your courses are designed to teach and are in a solid position to decide which books will be most helpful. You can safely assume that they've spent a long time wading through piles of texts in order to make their final selections and that you wouldn't have enjoyed taking that drudgery on yourself. Still, in many ways your purchase of this book is an act of faith, and before committing yourself much further, you have a right to some information.

This book is designed to help you in several ways to become a better writer.

First, each section begins with a detailed, practical discussion of how to handle the writing assignments you are likely to get: comparison and contrast, classification, cause and effect, and so on. These assignments are based on highly artificial writing patterns. The patterns often overlap and are rarely encountered in their pure form. A paper devoted primarily to classification, for example, could easily spend a good deal of time comparing and contrasting each class. Most instructors find it valuable, however, to discuss and assign the patterns separately. Nobody ever played a set of tennis using only a forehand drive, but serious players may devote hours at a time to practicing that one shot. Similarly, a substantial piece of writing is likely to demand a combination of patterns, but each pattern is best practiced and mastered by being treated at the start as an independent unit.

Second, each section of the book contains a group of readings designed to show effective—and, once in a while, ineffective—use of the pattern under consideration. These readings can be thought of as models—but only in a general sense. Professional writers had to put ideas together in the same pattern that will be required of you, and they went about their task in such and such a way. Studying the techniques by which they achieved their success can stimulate any writer faced with similar problems— but nobody wants you to write a barren imitation of someone else's work. A tennis player can profit from studying Chris Evert's backhand without attempting to duplicate it. The writer, as well as the athlete, uses models to discover the basic principles for shaping individual strengths into an effective force, not to follow blindly some particular conception of good form.

Third, questions on each reading selection are designed to help you look closely at the means by which each writer worked. A vague impression that an essay was competently written will be of little practical benefit to your own efforts.

Fourth, in order to add to the practical emphasis of this book, each reading selection is followed by a brief comment called "What About *Your* Writing?" These comments tend to get away from the presentation of broad principles and deal instead with specific pointers and suggestions, ranging all the way from avoiding overused words like *very* to tips on how to write about controversial subjects.

Fifth, all the readings are designed to drive home a special approach to writing that runs through this book: if writing is thought of, wherever possible, as an attempt to persuade the reader of the validity of a particular point, many common problems virtually disappear or solve themselves. Chapter 1 presents this idea in detail; the following chapters show how the idea can be applied to particular writing assignments.

That's the theory. You and your instructor are the only authorities on whether the theory works for you. If it does, the book was worth the money.

Guide to "What About <u>Your</u> Writing?"

As noted in "To the Instructor" (pp. xi–xii), "What About *Your* Writing?" entries offer comments and pointers on miscellaneous matters of practical concern to the student writer, as such matters turn up in the readings. For general perspectives and quick references, the following guide is appended.

Style

Writing with a Thesis

Chapter 1

THE PERSUASIVE PRINCIPLE

This book offers you one central piece of advice: *Whenever possible, think of your writing as a form of persuasion.*

Persuasion is traditionally considered a separate branch of writing. When you write what's usually called a persuasion paper, you pick a controversial issue, tell readers what side you're on, and try to persuade them that you're correct: birth control should be made compulsory, the space program is a waste of money, Shakespeare's plays were written by his mother-in-law, required freshman English courses are an insult to human dignity. Persuasion is supposed to be based on different principles from those of other kinds of writing—description, narration, exposition, and so forth.

It isn't.

A description of a friend, an account of what you went through to get your first job, a comparison of two makes of cars—if you can approach such assignments as an effort to persuade your reader of the validity of a particular opinion or major point, you're in business as a writer. Your paper's opinion or major point is called its *thesis*. Your thesis may be that your friend is a great athlete, that getting your first job was easier than you thought it would be, that a Chevrolet is cheaper to repair than a Ford. If you have a thesis and if you select and organize your material so that it supports the thesis, a number of basic writing problems begin to solve themselves. You have built-in purpose. You have built-in organization. You have potential built-in interest. Aside from a few obvious exceptions like newspaper reports, encyclopedia articles, instruction manuals, recipes, and certain types of stories, poems, and plays, *all writing can benefit enormously from a commitment to the persuasive principle: develop a thesis, and then back it up.*

There is no better way to demonstrate the effectiveness of the persuasive principle than to take a close look at what goes on, or ought to go on, as a paper is being planned.

General Subject

"Write something worth reading about such and such." In essence, all writing assignments—for students, business executives, Nobel Prize winners, and everyone else—begin this way, though ordinarily the directions aren't that frank.

Let's start from scratch and assume that your instructor has left the choice of subject mostly up to you. You may be entirely on your own, or you may have a list of general subjects from which you must make your selection. Imagine that you have to write something worth reading about one of the following: education, sports, prejudice, politics, television.

You make your choice, if you're like the majority of people, by deciding what you're most interested in and informed about or what will go over best with your audience. Let's say you pick education. You now have a subject, and your troubles have now begun.

You have to write 500 words or so on a subject to which tens of thousands of books have been devoted. Where do you begin? Where do you stop? Will it ever be possible to stop? What's important? What's not important? Until you *limit your subject,* you have no way of answering any of these questions. You are at the mercy of every miscellaneous thought and scrap of information that drifts into your mind.

Limited Subject

Narrow down your subject. Then narrow it down some more. Narrow it down until you have a subject that can be treated effectively in the assigned length. In many respects, the narrower your subject, the better off you are, as long as you still have something to say about it. With a properly limited subject, you explore only a small part of your general subject, but you explore it thoroughly.

A paper of 500 words on education is doomed to be superficial at best. It might be possible, however, to write 500 words worth reading on one of your teachers, essay versus objective examinations, reasons for attending college (narrowed down to just one reason if you have enough to say), registration procedures, abolishing *F* grades, fraternities, physical education requirements, and so on.

With a sensibly limited subject, you start to have a fighting chance of producing a good paper. You are no longer doomed to superficiality. If you write a description of one of your teachers, for example, you possess immensely more knowledge of your subject than do fellow students who have not taken a course from that teacher. Certainly, you are no longer at the mercy of every thought about education that you have ever had.

General Subject	Limited Subject
Education	Professor X
Sports	The Olympics
Prejudice	Interracial marriages
Politics	Influence of the media
Television	Commercials

Your troubles are not over, though. You've limited your subject, and you've done it well, but what now? Look at the most limited of the subjects in the preceding table. You're writing a description of a teacher—Professor X. Do you tell your reader about the teacher's height, weight, age, marital status, clothing, ethnic background, religious background, educational background? Publications? Grading policy? Attendance policy? Lecture techniques? Sense of humor? Handling of difficult classroom situations? Attitude toward audiovisual aids? Knowledge of field? How, in short, do you determine what belongs in your paper and what doesn't?

The truth is that you're still at the mercy of every thought that occurs to you. This time it's every thought about Professor X, not every thought about education in general. But until you find a *thesis,* you still have trouble.

Thesis

Your thesis is the basic stand you take, the opinion you express, the point you make about your limited subject. It's your controlling idea, tying together and giving direction to all other separate elements in your paper. *Your primary purpose is to persuade the reader that your thesis is a valid one.*

You may, and probably should, have secondary purposes; you may want to amuse or alarm or issue a call to action, for instance—but unless the primary purpose is achieved, no secondary purpose stands a chance. If you want to amuse your readers by making fun of a bad movie, there's no way to do it successfully without first convincing them of the validity of your thesis that the movie *is* bad and thus *does* deserve to be laughed at.

A thesis, of course, is only a vibration in the brain until it is turned into words. The first step in creating a workable thesis is to write a one-sentence version of the thesis, which is called a *thesis statment.*

Professor X is an incompetent teacher.

Professor X is a classic absentminded professor.

Professor X's sarcasm antagonizes many students.

Professor X's colorful personality has become a campus legend.

Professor X is a great teacher.

Professor X's youthful good looks have created awkward problems in class.

If you need more than one relatively uncomplicated sentence, chances are either that the thesis isn't as unified as it ought to be or that it's too ambitious for a short paper.

Limited Subject	Thesis Statement
Professor X	Professor X is an incompetent teacher.
The Olympics	The Olympic games are hypocritical nonsense.
Interracial marriages	Hostility to interracial marriages is the prejudice least likely to die.
Influence of the media	Newspapers and television have seriously distorted American politics.
Commercials	Television commercials are great entertainment.

Writing with a thesis obviously gives a paper a sense of purpose and eliminates the problem of aimless drift. Your purpose is to back up the thesis. As a result, writing with a thesis also helps significantly in organizing the paper. You use only what enables you to accomplish your purpose. Weight problems and religion have nothing to do with Professor X's abilities as a teacher; so you don't bother with them. Most of all, writing with a thesis gives a paper an intrinsic dramatic interest. You commit yourself. You have something at stake: "This is what I believe, and this is why I'm right." You say, "Professor X is incompetent." Your reader says, "Tell me why you think so." You say, "I'll be glad to." Your reader says, "I'm listening." And you're ready to roll.

So far, then, it's been established that a thesis is the main idea that all elements in the paper should support and that you should be able to express it in a single sentence. It's been established that a thesis has several important practical benefits. That's the bird's-eye view, but the concept is important enough to demand a closer look.

What a Thesis Isn't

A thesis is not a title. A title can often give the reader some notion of what the thesis is going to be, but it is not the thesis itself. The thesis itself, as presented in the thesis statement, does not suggest the main idea—it *is* the main idea. Remember, too, that a thesis statement will always be a complete sentence; there's no other way to make a statement.

Title: Not a Thesis	Thesis Statement
The Decline of Baseball	In recent years, baseball has experienced a steady decline in popularity.
Homes and Schools	Parents ought to participate more in the education of their children.
James Cagney: Hollywood Great	James Cagney was one of the greatest actors ever to appear in movies.

A Shattering Experience	My first visit to the zoo was a shattering experience.
The Fad of Divorce	Too many people get divorced for trivial reasons.

A thesis is not an announcement of the subject. A thesis takes a stand. It expresses an attitude toward the subject. It is not the subject itself.

Announcement: Not a Thesis	Thesis Statement
My subject is the incompetence of Professor X.	Professor X is an incompetent teacher.
I want to share some thoughts with you about our space program.	Our space program is a waste of money.
The many unforeseen problems I encountered when I went camping are the topic of this theme.	I encountered many unforeseen problems when I went camping.
This paper will attempt to tell you something about the emotions I felt on viewing the Grand Canyon.	The Grand Canyon was even more magnificent than I had imagined.
The thesis of this paper is the difficulty of solving our environmental problems.	Solving our environmental problems is more difficult than many environmentalists believe.

A thesis is not a statement of absolute fact. A thesis makes a judgment or interpretation. There's no way to spend a whole paper supporting a statement that needs no support.

Fact: Not a Thesis

Jane Austen is the author of *Pride and Prejudice*.
In 1970, Ohio had a population of 10,652,017.
Suicide is the deliberate taking of one's own life.
President Lincoln's first name was Abraham.
The planet closest to the sun is Mercury.

What a Good Thesis Is

It's possible to have a one-sentence statement of an idea and still not have a thesis that can be supported effectively. What characterizes a good thesis?

A good thesis is restricted. In certain respects, devising a thesis statement as you plan your paper can sometimes be a way of limiting, or restricting, your subject even further. A paper supporting the thesis that Professor X is incompetent, besides taking a stand on its subject, has far less territory to cover than a paper on Professor X in general. Thesis statements themselves, however, may not always have been sufficiently narrowed down. A good thesis deals with restricted, bite-size issues rather than issues that would require a lifetime to discuss intelligently. The more restricted the thesis, the better the chances are for exploring it fully.

Poor	Better
The world is in a terrible mess.	Trade barriers contribute to international tensions.
People are too selfish.	Human selfishness is seen at its worst during rush hour.
Old age has many difficulties.	The worst part of being old is the boredom.
Crime must be stopped.	Our courts should hand out tougher sentences.

A good thesis is unified. The thesis expresses *one major idea* about its subject. The tight structural strength of your paper depends on its working to support that one idea. A good thesis may sometimes include a secondary idea if it is strictly subordinated to the major one, but without that subordination the writer will have too many important ideas to handle, and the structure of the paper will suffer.

Poor	Better
Detective stories are not a high form of literature, but people have always been fascinated by them, and many fine writers have experimented with them.	Detective stories appeal to the basic human desire for thrills.
The new health program is excellent, but it has several drawbacks, and it should be run only on an experimental basis for two or three years.	The new health program should be run only on an experimental basis for two or three years. *or* Despite its general excellence, the new health program should be run only on an experimental basis for two or three years.
The Columbus Cavaliers have trouble at the defensive end and linebacker positions, and front-office tensions don't help, but the team should be able to make the play-offs.	The Columbus Cavaliers should be able to make the play-offs. *or* Even granting a few troubles, the Columbus Cavaliers should be able to make the play-offs.

A good thesis is specific. A satisfactorily restricted and unified thesis may be useless if the idea it commits you to is vague. "The new World Trade Center is impressive," for example, could mean anything from impressively beautiful to impressively ugly. With a thesis statement like "Hemingway's war stories are very good," you would probably have to spend so many words defining what on earth "good" means that there would be no room for anything else. Even when there's no likelihood of confusion, vague ideas normally come through as so familiar or dull or universally accepted that the reader sees no point in paying any attention to them.

Poor	Better
The new World Trade Center is impressive.	The new World Trade Center is a monument to human folly.
Hemingway's war stories are very good.	Hemingway's war stories helped create a new prose style.
Drug addiction is a big problem.	Drug addiction has caused a huge increase in crimes of violence.
Our vacation was a tremendous experience.	Our vacation enabled us to learn the true meaning of sharing.
My parents are wonderful people.	Everything my parents do is based on their loving concern for the welfare of the family.

EXERCISES FOR REVIEW

A. Write *T* next to each thesis statement below. Write *NT* if there is no thesis statement.

   1. I want to tell you exactly what is wrong with the administration's energy program.
   2. Ty Cobb has the highest lifetime batting average of any player in baseball history.
   3. Justice delayed is justice denied.
   4. My thesis asks whether affirmative action programs are just a new form of racism.
   5. It's not only poor people who get government handouts.
   6. Typewriters: Their Maintenance and Repair
   7. This paper will examine recent programs designed to attack organized crime.
   8. My wife is a terrible cook.
   9. My wife cooks all the meals' for our family.
   10. Christmas shopping shows that the law of the jungle is still with us.

B. Write *G* next to each good thesis statement. Write *NG* next to each statement that is not sufficiently restricted, unified, or specific, and be prepared to suggest revisions.

   1. The history of the United States is dominated by lust for money.
   2. Common sense is sometimes the enemy of genius.
   3. Love is the most wonderful thing in the world.
   4. Thirst is harder to endure than hunger.
   5. Jogging is a worthwhile activity.
   6. Jogging can add years to one's life.
   7. Carpet tiles are more difficult to install than many people think.
   8. The way people shake hands can reveal something about their characters.

9. Natural beauty must be preserved, but government agencies often make foolish decisions on this matter, and jobs must also be preserved.
10. In *Moby-Dick,* Melville does a very good job.

The Thesis at Work in the Paper

The thesis statement is a tool, not an end in itself. It has two outstanding values. First, it serves as a test of whether your main idea meets the requirements we have just discussed: whether it is a firm concept that can actually be put into words or only a fuzzy notion that is not yet ready for development. Second, the thesis statement is a constant, compact reminder of the point your paper must make, and it is therefore an indispensable means of determining the relevancy or irrelevancy, the logic or lack of logic, of all the material that goes into the paper.

In itself, however, the thesis statement is a deliberately bare-bones presentation of your idea. In your paper you will attempt to deal with the idea in a far more interesting way. The thesis statement, for example, may quite likely never appear word for word in your final paper. There's not even any special rule that in the final paper you must declare the thesis in a single sentence. In some rare cases, the thesis may only be hinted at rather than stated openly. The proper places for the bare-bones thesis statement are in your mind with every word you write; on any piece of scratch paper on which you jot down the possible ingredients of your composition; and at the beginning of a formal outline, if you're ever required to construct one.

In most short papers, the thesis is presented in the first paragraph, the *introduction*. Again, no absolute rule states that this must always be the case—just as no rule demands that an introduction must always be just one paragraph—but in practice most papers do begin that way. It's simply what seems to work for most people most of the time. As a general guideline, then, it's helpful to think of the first paragraph's job as presenting the thesis in an interesting way.

The word *interesting* is important. The introduction should not ordinarily be a one-sentence paragraph consisting solely of the unadorned thesis statement. The introduction certainly should indicate clearly what the thesis is, but it also should arouse curiosity or stress the importance of the subject or establish a particular tone of humor, anger, solemnity, and so forth.

Thesis Statement	*Sample First Paragraph*
Professor X is an incompetent teacher.	Any school the size of State is probably going to get its share of incompetent teachers. I'm told that last year an elderly history professor came to class to give a final exam and then realized he'd forgotten to make one up. Professor Z tells jokes nobody understands and keeps chuckling to himself about them through the whole class period. Professor Y doesn't return term papers until the last day of class; so her students never

know how they're doing until it's too late. As far as I'm concerned, though, the biggest dud of all is Professor X.

The Olympic games are hypocritical nonsense.	The only civilized part of the Olympic games is the lighting of the flame. After that, the games turn into a tragicomedy of hypocritical nonsense. State-subsidized athletes pass themselves off as noble amateurs; blatantly biased referees and judges make the crucial decisions; international sports in which Americans excel, like golf and tennis, are deemed unworthy of Olympic status. Laugh, cry, or fly into a rage, if you like—just as long as you don't confuse the Olympics with serious athletic competition.
Hostility to interracial marriages is the prejudice least likely to die.	Progress in relations between the races often seems grotesquely slow. Looking at bundles of years instead of days, however, one can see that there has been real progress in jobs, education, and even housing. The most depressing area, the area in which there has been no progress, in which no progress is even likely, in which progress is not even discussed, is the area of interracial marriages.
Newspapers and television have seriously distorted American politics.	When politicans complain about bias in newspapers and television, I don't get too excited. I don't believe in conspiracies, and from what I've seen, the media try hard to be fair. But fair or not, intentionally or not, the media have affected politics and affected it seriously. And I think they've affected it for the worse.
Television commercials are great entertainment.	I like television commercials. It's a terrible confession. I know I'm supposed to sneer and brood and write letters to people who want to protect me, but I like commercials. They're great entertainment, and it's time somebody said so.

The function of subsequent paragraphs—paragraphs generally referred to as the *body*—is to support the thesis. All sorts of paragraph arrangements are possible. The important consideration is that the body paragraphs, individually and as a whole, must persuade your reader that your thesis makes sense.

One of the most common paragraph arrangements is worth studying at this time since it's the easiest to follow and since our concern here is with the essential connection between body paragraphs and thesis, not with fine points. This arrangement gives a separate paragraph to each supporting point and the specific evidence necessary to substantiate it. In sketchy outline form, the progression of paragraphs might look something like this:

¶1—Presentation of thesis: There are at least three good reasons for abolishing capital punishment.

Start of ¶2—First, statistics show that capital punishment is not really a deterrent . . .

Start of ¶3—Second, with capital punishment it is forever impossible to correct a mistaken conviction . . .

Start of ¶4—Third, capital punishment has traditionally been used in a discriminatory fashion against poor people and blacks . . .

Using the same form of one paragraph for each supporting idea, but abandoning the neatness of numbered points, we might find the following:

¶1—Presentation of thesis: Dieting can be dangerous.

Start of ¶2—Some diets can raise cholesterol levels alarmingly . . .

Start of ¶3—In other cases, over an extended period, some diets can lead to serious vitamin deficiencies . . .

Start of ¶4—One further danger is that already existing medical problems such as high blood pressure can be drastically aggravated . . .

Most papers also have a distinct *conclusion*, a last paragraph that provides a needed finishing touch. The conclusion can be a quick summary of your thesis and main supporting points. It can emphasize or reemphasize the importance of your thesis. It can relate a seemingly remote thesis to people's everyday lives. In one way or another, the conclusion reinforces or develops the thesis; it should never introduce a totally unrelated, brand-new idea. There are dozens of possible conclusions, but almost all papers benefit from having one. (For specific examples of different kinds of conclusions, see pages 43–44.)

The group of readings that follows shows the persuasive principle in action by offering contrasting examples of good and not-so-good writing. From short thank-you notes to essay exams and freshman English compositions, the results of writing with and without a thesis can be explored in detail. Later chapters will comment on and provide examples of the techniques appropriate for particular patterns of writing: classification, description, and so on. Patterns change depending on subjects and approaches. Principles do not change. The basic nature of good writing, as discussed in this chapter, remains constant.

Two Ads on the Community Bulletin Board

A.   BABYSITTER

Experienced high school student available, weekdays to midnight, weekends to 2 A.M. Reasonable rates. Call Sandy, 335-0000.

B.   BABYSITTER

A HIGH SCHOOL STUDENT WHO KNOWS THE THREE R'S
Ready—any weekday to midnight, weekends to 2 A.M.
Reliable—four years' experience, references available.
Reasonable—$1.50 per hour, flat fee for more than five hours.
Call Sandy, 335-0000

DISCUSSION AND QUESTIONS

Even a little "position wanted" ad can use the persuasive principle to its advantage. Two dozen high school students pin two dozen different typed or handwritten index cards to the bulletin board at the local library or supermarket. Most of the cards convey lifeless facts. One or two cards make the same facts come alive by using them to support an idea. Those are the cards that get a second look—and get their writers a phone call.

1. Which ad has a thesis?
2. Does the ad support its thesis?
3. Which ad uses more specific facts?

Two Sets of Directions

A.

How to Get from Town to Camp Wilderness

Take Freeway west to Millersville Road exit. Go north on Millersville Road to Route 256. West on 256 to Laurel Lane. North on Laurel Lane until you see our sign. Turn right, and you're there.

B.

How to Get from Town to Camp Wilderness

You'll have an easy trip if you avoid *three trouble spots*.

1. You have to take the MILLERSVILLE ROAD Exit as you go west on the Freeway, and it's a *left-hand* exit. Start bearing left as soon as you see the "Millersville 5 miles" sign.

2. After turning north (right) on Millersville Road, don't panic when you see Route 526. You want ROUTE 256, and that's 8 more miles.

3. Go west (left) on Route 256 to LAUREL LANE. The street signs are almost impossible to read, but Laurel Lane is the second road on the right after the Mobil station.

   Once on Laurel Lane, you're all set. Go 2 miles until you see our sign. Turn right, and you're there.

DISCUSSION AND QUESTIONS

Writing competent directions is a difficult task. When you are explaining something you know well, it's hard to put yourself in the place of a total novice. You may be excessively casual about some step or even forget to mention it. Directions can also be hard to read: for novices they can seem to be a series of one disconnected step after another. Writing with a thesis helps the steps come together in the readers' minds and gives them a comforting sense of security.

1. Which set of directions has a thesis?
2. Which tries to anticipate difficulties?
3. Explain the unconventional capitalization in B.

Two Thank-You Notes

A.   July 23, 1979

Dear Aunt Sally,

This isn't just one thank-you note—it's a whole lot put together.

It's thank you for being so thoughtful in the first place. It's thank you for being so generous. Not many couples start out with a Steuben vase, and Jim and I never dreamed that we would. It's thank you for the absolute beauty and rightness of your choice. It's thank you, thank you for everything.

Much love,

Ellen

B.   July 23, 1979

Dear Aunt Sally,

Thank you very much for the beautiful Steuben vase. It was very generous of you to send us such a wonderful wedding present, and Jim and I are very grateful.

Much love,

Ellen

DISCUSSION AND QUESTIONS

Back in the days before long-distance phone calls became routine, people wrote many more personal letters than they do now. For a good number of people today, the thank-you note is probably the only personal letter-writing they do, other than a cheerful "Hi, there!" on postcards or Christmas cards. Graduates, brides, new parents, and grieving widows and widowers all need to write thank-you notes. There's not much choice of subject, of course, and even most of the ideas are predetermined. How can the writer make a thank-you note sound like a sincere expression of emotion rather than mere good manners? The persuasive principle is a valuable aid.

1. Which note has a thesis?
2. How many pieces of "evidence" support the thesis?
3. How does the choice of words in the supporting evidence further reinforce the thesis?
4. Which note communicates more feeling?

Two Letters of Complaint

A.

13 Pier Street
New York, N.Y. 10016
July 23, 1979

Customer Complaints
Maybach Company
123 Fifth Avenue
New York, N.Y. 10001

Gentlemen:

I have tried calling three different times and have not received any satisfaction, so now I am going to try writing.

I have absolutely no intention of paying any $749.60. I returned my coffee table more than a month ago. One of the legs was wobbly and the top had a bad scratch. Two times the pickup men did not come on the day they said they would. I returned the first bill for the table, and now you just sent me another one, and all I get from people when I call the store is "We'll look into it."

Also the price was $74.96, not $749.60. I await your reply.

Yours very truly,

Augusta Briggs

Augusta Briggs

B.

13 Pier Street
New York, N.Y. 10016
July 23, 1979

Customer Complaints
Maybach Company
123 Fifth Avenue
New York, N.Y. 10001

Gentlemen:

When you folks make mistakes, you don't kid around. You make big ones. Phone calls haven't done me much good, so I'm hoping that this letter can clear things up.

Early last month—probably June 9 or 10—I returned a defective coffee table. Since you had no more in stock, I canceled the order.

When the bill came for the table, I returned it with a note of explanation.

Exactly one week ago, July 16, I received a second bill. To add to the fun, this second bill was for $749.60 instead of the original $74.96.

When I called the store, I was told I'd be called back by the next day at the latest. I'm still waiting.

I'm sure you agree that these are too many mistakes, and that they are big enough to be extremely annoying. Shall we get this matter settled once and for all?

Thank you for your attention.

Yours very truly,

Augusta Briggs

Augusta Briggs

DISCUSSION AND QUESTIONS

The letter to a friend may not be as common as it once was, but business writing—and business plays a role in our private lives as well as in our jobs—is as important as ever. An employee makes a good suggestion and is told to "put it into writing." When the clear and methodical statement of ideas and facts is essential, putting it into writing becomes inevitable.

The writer of a letter of complaint has two special difficulties, both of which must be resolved if the letter is to be effective. On the one hand, the writer must communicate the gravity of the complaint, or the complaint may be treated casually, perhaps even ignored. On the other hand, the writer must simultaneously come through as a rational human being calmly presenting a grievance. It's essential that the writer not be dismissed as a crackpot or crank. Letters from crackpots and cranks get shown around the office, every-one has a good laugh, and then the letter goes to the bottom of the fattest pile of unan-swered correspondence.

1. Which letter has a thesis?
2. Does the letter support the thesis with specific evidence?
3. Does the letter have a conclusion to reinforce or develop the thesis?
4. Why does the writer of Letter B say nothing specific about what was wrong with the coffee table?
5. What is the purpose of the slang ("you folks," "kid around") and humorous touches in Letter B?
6. Are there elements in Letter A that might allow the reader to dismiss the writer as a crank?
7. Why do business-letter paragraphs tend to be so short?

Two Essay Examinations

Essay topic: Near the end of *The Great Gatsby,* Nick Carraway says to Gatsby, "They're a rotten crowd. . . . You're worth the whole damn bunch put together." Explain your reasons for agreeing or disagreeing with Nick.

A.

Nick is right, just as he always is. Gatsby is worth "the whole damn bunch" because there is some purpose to his life. Gatsby wants to get back Daisy, and everything he does is related to his quest for her.

Most of the other characters have no purpose other than an idle interest in possibly finding something amusing to do. Daisy's husband, Tom, since he stopped being a football star, plays polo, read an occasional book, and engages in a halfhearted affair with Myrtle Wilson. The author says that everything in Tom's life was an "anticlimax" since he left Yale. He does anything he feels like because he doesn't feel like doing anything.

Daisy and Jordan Baker are first seen lying down lazily, being bored, and wondering what to do. There is nothing at all to do, of course, since there's no central meaning to their lives. Jordan, besides dating Nick, plays golf sometimes—and then she cheats, maybe to give her life some excitement. Daisy has a bit more in the way of good instincts than Jordan and Tom, but basically she too spends her time "wherever people were rich together," and she leaves it to others to "clean up the mess." She once loved Gatsby and his raw vitality, but having felt a strong emotion, she is unable to sustain it. Even her disgust with her meaningless life—"Sophisticated, God, I'm sophisticated"—is not so much a strong emotion as a casual effort to make herself seem sensitive and interesting to Nick.

The guests at Gatsby's parties have no purpose other than getting drunk, spotting celebrities, and gossiping about their host.

Gatsby's life is devoted to recapturing Daisy. Daisy isn't worth it, and that's why the book is tragic—but the parties, the shady deals, and all the showing off are meant to make Gatsby become "somebody," somebody who will be worthy of the "golden girl" he has created in his mind. Gatsby's passion and energy and capacity to care make him a character we, like Nick, can respect. We disapprove of him, like Nick, but we respect him too. He pursues an ideal. There is something in his life to which he has given himself fully.

B.

Jay Gatsby, whose real name was James Gatz, was born in North Dakota. The author of *The Great Gatsby,* F. Scott Fitzgerald, shows how Gatsby joined the army and first met and fell in love with Daisy.

During their separation in the war, their engagement broke off, and Daisy married Tom Buchanan of Chicago. When the war is over, Gatsby tries to become rich through associating with people like Meyer Wolfsheim, who fixed the World Series. His money enables him to throw wild parties at West Egg, Long Island, to try to attract people's attention.

Nick Carraway, a Midwesterner who came to New York to learn to be a stockbroker, meets Gatsby and arranges for him to meet Daisy again. Daisy's husband is having an affair, and Daisy is very unhappy. Nick really wants no part of any of this, but something about Gatsby appeals to him. He tries to warn Gatsby to stay away from Daisy, but Gatsby pays no attention. "Of course you can repeat the past," Gatsby says.

Nick thinks Gatsby is worth "the whole damn bunch." Gatsby has worked hard and spent much money to make a good impression, and his reward is having Daisy turn her back on him and getting killed through a misunderstanding. At the end of the novel, Nick returns to the Midwest because he cannot stand the corruption he has seen in the East.

DISCUSSION AND QUESTIONS

Students sometimes say it's easy to bluff on an essay exam. Maybe so, but most teachers are as aware of the hazards as anyone else and make a special effort to spot bluffing.

A good essay on an exam, especially on a "What's-your-opinion?" question, can go in many different directions, but it always displays the following characteristics:

1. It discusses the subject assigned, not the one the student wishes had been assigned. Inexperienced or nervous students might see the title *The Great Gatsby* and start haphazardly writing everything they have ever heard or thought about the book. *Stick to the subject.*
2. It uses specific details to support its thesis. The teacher wants an essay from someone who has read and remembered and understood the book, not from someone who, from all the essay shows, has merely turned up in class and gotten the general drift of what the book must be about.
3. In a literature exam, it does not get sidetracked into a plot summary. Any references to the plot should support a thesis, not tell the story all over again.

1. Which essay has a thesis?
2. Is the thesis supported with specific details?
3. Which essay is mostly a plot summary?
4. Compare first sentences. Which is more directly related to the assignment?
5. Does the writer of the essay that has a thesis keep the thesis in mind throughout, or are there some digressions?
6. Can the merits of both essays be judged with some accuracy even by a reader unfamiliar with *The Great Gatsby*?

Two "How I Spent My Summer Vacation" Themes

(In-Class Assignment)

A.

I couldn't find a job this summer, and it's hard to write much about my summer vacation.

Every morning I would get up between 8:30 and 9:00. My breakfast would usually be juice, toast, and coffee, though sometimes I would have eggs, too.

For a couple of weeks, after breakfast I would mow some neighbors' lawns, but after a while I got bored with that, and mostly I just hung around. Usually I read the paper and then straightened up my room.

For lunch I had a sandwich and a glass of milk. I remember once my mother and I had a real argument because there wasn't anything for a sandwich.

After lunch, if my mother didn't need the car, I'd usually drive over to the big shopping center with some of my friends. We'd walk around to see what was happening, and sometimes we'd try to pick up some girls. Mostly, we'd just look at the girls. Sometimes, instead of going to the shopping center, we'd go swimming.

After supper, it was usually television or a movie. Television is mostly reruns in the summer, and it was a bad scene. Some of the movies were okay, but nothing sensational.

In the middle of the summer, my older sister and her family came to visit from out of town. That was fun because I like my two little nephews a lot, and we fooled around in the backyard. My brother-in-law kept asking what I was doing with my time, and my mother said at least I was staying out of trouble.

B.

I couldn't find a job this summer, and most people would probably say that I spent my summer doing nothing. In fact, I spent most of my summer practicing very hard to be a pest.

To start with, I developed hanging around the house into an art. It drove my mother crazy. After breakfast, I'd read the paper, spreading it out over the entire living room, and then take my midmorning nap. Refreshed by my rest, I'd then ask my mother what was available for lunch. Once when there was no Italian salami left and the bread was a little stale, I looked at her sadly and sighed a lot and kept opening and closing the refrigerator. She didn't take my suffering too well. As I recall, the expression she used was "no good bum" or something of that order. In the evenings, I'd sigh a lot over having to watch television reruns. When my mother asked me why I watched if I didn't enjoy myself, I sighed some more.

The other main center for my activities as a pest was at the big shopping center a short drive from home. My friends and I—we figured we needed protection—would stand in people's way on the mall and make them walk around us. We'd try on clothes we had no intention of buying and complain about the price. We'd make eyes, and gestures, and offensive remarks at any pretty girls. We'd practice swaggering and strutting and any other means of looking obnoxious that occurred to us.

Miscellaneous other activities during the summer included splashing people at the beach, laughing in the wrong places at movies, and honking the car horn madly at pedestrians as they started to cross the street. These are small-time adventures, I realize, but difficult to do with real style.

Basically, I had myself a good summer. It's always a pleasure to master a set of skills, and I think I've come close to being an expert pest. I wonder what new thrills lie in wait next summer.

DISCUSSION AND QUESTIONS

Here, in all its mythic tiresomeness, is the worst of all possible subjects: "How I Spent My Summer Vacation." Students boo. The *Peanuts* comic strip makes fun of the subject. Even teachers laugh about it. That's why it's been chosen for this book.

The subject is deadly. To make matters worse, here are two students who spent a remarkably uneventful summer. One blunders along and writes a frightful paper. The other develops a thesis, supports it, and ends with an appealing little paper. It's no candidate for a prize, but it's an appealing little paper. Enough said.

1. In Theme A, is "it's hard to write much about my summer vacation" a thesis? Is it a good thesis? Does the writer support it?
2. If both themes have a thesis, are the theses basically the same?
3. What topics mentioned in Theme A are not mentioned in Theme B? Why?
4. Which theme has a conclusion? Is it effective?
5. Both themes use many specific details. Which uses them better? Why?
6. Which theme has better developed paragraphs?
7. Which paragraphs in Theme A do not have topic sentences? Do all the paragraphs in Theme B have topic sentences?
8. Which theme handles the argument about lunch better? Why?

Chapter 2
EXAMPLES

An example is a single item drawn from a larger group or concept to which it belongs. Smog is one of many possible examples of pollution. Chicken pox is an example of a childhood disease. The egg yolk on Bill's necktie is an example of his sloppiness. The French Reign of Terror is an example of the possible dangers of violent revolution. (The preceding four sentences are examples of examples.)

Many instructors feel that writing an example theme is a sensible first assignment because it's hard to write a good paper of any kind without using at least some examples. Examples *clarify* a writer's thought by bringing remote abstractions down to earth.

The American Civil War was not all the romantic valor we read about in storybooks. It was the horrors of trench warfare, the medical nightmare of wholesale amputations, and for the South, at least, the agony of slow starvation.

Examples also *add interest*: the most humdrum generalization can take on new life if supported by effective examples. Specific details described in specific language are at the heart of almost all good writing, and examples by their very nature are specific.

Professor Smathers's course in Shakespeare was the worst I have ever taken. Once we spent a whole week listening to students recite—or mumble—sonnets they had been forced to memorize. Another time Professor Smathers devoted an entire period to attacking one of the footnotes in our edition of *Hamlet*. And I never understood the true meaning of boredom until the great day that I heard him discourse on Shakespeare's preference for daisies over roses.

Examples help *persuade*. Without the help of examples, many perfectly valid statements can come across as dismal echoes of ideas the author has heard somewhere but has never thought about seriously. If the writer of the following paragraph had omitted the examples, there would be no way of evaluating the merits of the complaint.

Routine city services are in a terrible state. The freeway from West 50th Street to the Downtown exit has been filled with gaping chuckholes since early Spring. Rat-infested, condemned, and abandoned buildings still line Water Street despite three-year-old promises to tear them down. Last week the papers reported the story of a man who called the police about a burglar entering his home—and got a busy signal.

An example theme is one that relies entirely on examples to support its thesis. The ordinary pattern for an example theme is elementary, though bear in mind that no pattern should be followed blindly. A first paragraph presents the thesis. A varying number of paragraphs—depending on the subject, complexity of thesis, and material available to the writer—then establishes through examples the validity of the thesis. A concluding paragraph reinforces or advances the thesis. The pattern seems simple, and it is.

What isn't quite so simple is seeing to it that all the examples are relevant and persuasive.

Are there enough examples to support your thesis? Three examples may sometimes be enough. A hundred may often be too few (and in that case you've made a poor choice of thesis for an example theme). Common sense is your best guide. Three in-depth examples of sickeningly sentimental deathbed scenes from Dickens's novels may be enough to establish that Dickens had trouble with deathbed scenes. A hundred examples of middle-aged men with protruding stomachs will not even begin to establish that most middle-aged men have potbellies. As a general rule for a paper of 500 words or so, choose a thesis that can be supported adequately with no more than fifteen examples, unless your instructor tells you otherwise. Don't use fewer than three examples unless you're extremely confident about the virtues of your paper. (One of the reading selections in this section of the book uses only two examples.) Remember, too, that the fewer examples, the more fully each should be developed.

Are the examples fairly chosen? Your reader must be convinced that the examples represent a reasonable cross section of the group you're dealing with. Choose typical examples. Anyone can load the dice. You may have an imposing number of dramatic examples showing that the downtown business area of a city is deserted and dying, but if you drew all the examples from only one street or from visiting the area on a Sunday afternoon, you would not have played fair. Plan your paper with the notion of a cross section constantly in mind. If you're generalizing about teachers in your school, try to pick examples from different departments, age groups, sexes, and so on. If you're attacking television commercials, make sure your examples include significantly different products; otherwise, you might wind up convincing your reader that only ads for soaps and detergents are bad.

Have you stuck to your thesis? One way of losing sight of your thesis has just been described. Poorly selected examples, besides creating an impression of unfairness, may support only part of the thesis: one writer demonstrates that only a single block is deserted and dying, not the whole downtown area; another shows that commercials directed toward housewives are offensive, not commercials in general.

A second, but equally common, way of drifting off is to forget about writing an example paper. A writer starts out well by providing examples establishing the idea that "routine city services are in a terrible state." Halfway through the paper, the writer gets sidetracked into a discussion of the causes for this condition and the steps the average citizen can take to remedy it. The writer thus manages to produce a paper that is 50 percent irrelevant to the declared thesis.

Have you arranged your examples to produce the greatest impact? In planning your paper, you've limited your subject, developed a thesis, and jotted down lots of examples. You've eliminated irrelevant and illogical examples. Now how do you handle those that are left? Which comes first? Which comes last?

Unless you're superhuman, some of the examples you're going to use will be clearly superior to others. As a general principle, try to start off with a bang. Grab the attention of your reader as soon as possible with your most dramatic or shocking or amusing or disturbing example. If you have two unusually effective examples, so much the better. Save one for last: try to end with a bang, too.

An exceptionally strong example can also lead to a common variation on the orthodox pattern of devoting the first paragraph to a presentation of the thesis. Use the first paragraph instead to present the strong example. (Humorous anecdotes often work particularly well.) Stimulate curiosity. Arouse interest. Then present the thesis in the second paragraph before going on to the other examples.

Paragraphing itself is important throughout the theme to help the reader understand the nature of your material and the logic of your argument. With a few well-developed examples, there's no problem. Each should get a paragraph to itself. With a great number of examples, however, there's some potential for difficulties. Each example will probably be short—one or two sentences, let's say—because you're writing a theme of only a few hundred words, not a term paper. If each of these short examples gets a separate paragraph, the paper is likely to be extremely awkward and choppy to read.

But even without that burden, the physical appearance alone of the page can be guaranteed to bother most readers: before ever getting to the actual process of reading, they will have begun to think of the paper as a collection of separate sentences and thoughts rather than as a unified composition.

The solution to this paragraphing problem is to gather the many examples together into a few logical groups and write a paragraph for each group, not for each example. Suppose you have fifteen good examples of declining city services. Instead of writing fifteen one-sentence paragraphs, you observe that four examples involve transportation; five, safety; three, housing; and the rest, pollution and sanitation. Your paragraphing problems are over.

¶1 Thesis: Routine city services are in a terrible state.

¶2 Transportation
  Example 1—higher fares for same or worse service
  Example 2—no parking facilities
  Example 3—poor snow removal
  Example 4—refusal to synchronize traffic lights downtown

¶3 Safety
  Example 1—unrepaired chuckholes
  Example 2—unrepaired traffic lights
  Example 3—busy signals at police station
  Example 4—slow response when police do come
  Example 5—releasing of dangerous criminals because of overcrowding at city jail

¶4 Housing
  Example 1—decaying public projects
  Example 2—abandoned buildings not torn down
  Example 3—housing codes not enforced in slums

¶5 Pollution and Sanitation
  Example 1—flooded basements
  Example 2—litter in public parks
  Example 3—increase in rats

¶6 Conclusion

WRITING SUGGESTIONS FOR EXAMPLE THEMES

Write an example theme supporting one of the following statements or a related statement of your own.

1. Life in .... (your town) is not as bad as it's cracked up to be.
2. Some teachers try too hard to identify with their students.
3. Female bosses are too pushy.
4. Corruption is part of the American way of life.
5. Teen-age marriages are likely to end unhappily.
6. People express their personalities through the clothes they wear.
7. The generation gap is a myth.

8. Children's television programs display too much violence.
9. A student's life is not a happy one.
10. Nuns and/or priests are complex human beings, not plaster saints.
11. You can tell a lot from what a person eats.
12. Student government is a farce.
13. Apparent nonconformists are sometimes the worst conformists.
14. Everyone loves to gossip.

The Honest Repairman— A Vanishing American?

KEN W. PURDY

Best known for his writings about automobiles past and present, Ken W. Purdy (1913–1972) also wrote some distinguished mystery and suspense fiction. His books include *Motorcars of the Golden Past* (1966), *Young People and Driving* (1967), and *Ken Purdy's Book of Automobiles* (1972). In "The Honest Repairman—A Vanishing American?" Purdy uses specific examples to give fresh interest and immediacy to a familiar complaint.

A few weeks ago I took a Minox camera into a New York shop for repairs. The trouble seemed simple enough: I couldn't load it, the film cassette wouldn't go in. The clerk told me it needed cleaning and lubrication, one week, $6.50. When I came back the camera was taken out of a drawer in an elaborately wrapped, stamped, tagged package. I paid the $6.50. It didn't *look* any cleaner than it had been, but I thought the important work had been done on the inside. 1

I bought a cassette of film. It wouldn't go in. Amazement and bafflement were registered by the clerk. He tried to load it. Another clerk tried. Another. No use, it would have to "go back to the shop." Ten days. Right. 2

Next time, when the Minox was taken out of its official-looking wrapping, I realized I was being hustled: when I told the clerk I wanted to see if it would take film there was a pregnant pause. I pointed to an open cassette on a nearby shelf. It was "new" and I couldn't use it. . . . I used it anyway. It wouldn't go in, as everybody in the shop had known it would not. 3

I raised the roof. I made a phone call to a famous New York photographer who knew the president of the Minox importing company. Unpleasantness followed, and by next day I could prove that the camera had been nowhere near the repair shop and that it had not even been dusted off, much less cleaned and lubricated. The store returned my $6.50 without a word of argument or defense. The Minox company cleaned, lubricated and practi- 4 cally rebuilt the camera for me without charge, entirely as a courtesy, since the company itself had been in no way involved. But this happy ending came about only because I knew whom to call. Most customers being deliberately cheated are helpless.

5   Unless he's lucky the cheated customer may never find out. I took my daughter's expensive watch, made by an internationally known company, to a shop displaying the company's dealership sign. The watch had been running badly. It needed, the man said, a complete cleaning and adjustment, $20. He was an old-world-craftsman-type, with just a trace of accent, probably fake Swiss, and he looked as trustworthy as your grandmother. When I came back for the watch he said he needed "another three days for checking, just to be sure." I returned, gave him the $20 and took the watch. It stopped dead four days later. Even in my rage, I had to admire the subtlety of his technique. Who could suspect a man who wanted three extra days just to be sure he'd done a great job?

6   I went to the U.S. headquarters of the company. A woman clerk in the elaborate and luxurious repair department took the watch away, brought it back and told me it needed a complete cleaning and adjustment, $30, ready in 12 weeks.

7   I told her that since the watch had just come from one of its dealerships, I required to know its precise condition.

8   "We don't give out that information," she said.

9   I explained the position more fully: somebody, I said, was a liar and a cheat. After a considerable discussion, and one more trip to consult with the technicians in the back room, she was able to say that the work did in fact need to be done, and that, yes, that indicated pretty clearly that it certainly had not been done by the little old watchmaker with the winning ways.

10   I entered a complaint with an official of the company, but he chose to make no comment.

11   It used to be that occasionally one would find repair work had been badly done. Now it seems to me that more and more one finds it hasn't been done at all. I suspected that a garage was cheating me. I took a car in for gearbox adjustment, but I sealed the gear-box lid. It could be opened easily enough, but it would show. When the car came back, with a bill for over $30, the seal hadn't been broken. Nobody had even looked into the gearbox, much less adjusted anything. I screamed. I refused to pay. I let it come to suit and settled for 50 percent. So, after a great deal of trouble, I came out only half-cheated.

12   Legally to prove a case of non-service, Better Business Bureau officials say, the customer must be expert or sophisticated or lucky or all three. Probably for this reason, and also because often the customer doesn't know he's been victimized, non-service complaints are uncommon. What is *not* uncommon are complaints about incompetent or careless service and repair, or fraudulent guarantees, or "hijacking," the technique of enticing a customer with a promise of a low-cost minor job, then hitting him with expensive, unnecessary work—which may or may not be done at all.

"We just don't have enough people to go out and thoroughly investigate   13
non-service complaints," the Metropolitan New York Better Business Bureau says. "Often it's a case of one man's judgment or opinion. And it's
very difficult to get people to testify. One mechanic bills a customer $189
for new transmission parts, let's say. A week later another mechanic, one
whom the customer knows and trusts, tells him that no such work has been
done. But will he make an affidavit, or testify in court? No, he won't.
Almost never.

"All we can tell people is to deal with reputable stores and shops, and   14
get written guarantees for work and parts clearly spelled out on the bill.
Beware of come-ons, of big bargains. Today it's hard enough to get something for something; you certainly aren't going to get something for nothing."

There is no doubt that the standard of morality has dropped sharply in   15
recent years (shoplifting and cheating by customers is booming, too) and
there are probably many repairmen who consider themselves honest because they don't do anything worse than persuade a customer to buy something he doesn't need. After all, if the customer actually gets the part or the
service he paid for, that's not stealing, is it?

The TV and radio field, which used to be rich ground for swindlers, has   16
been notably cleaned up. Most manufacturers now maintain factory service
or use authorized service agencies which are tightly checked and super-
vised. A service agency with a good company is lucrative, it's well worth
having, and smart operators won't risk losing it for the sake of a couple of
hundred dollars on the side. If a shop does start to cheat, the word soon
gets out. The BBB recently took a Bronx repairman to court when he billed
a customer $47.50 on a TV "repair." The set was a plant, in perfect order
except for a $7 tube. It was taken straight from the crooked shop to a
reputable one, where it was established that $40.50 of the bill was over-
charge.

A current gold-mine for crooked repairmen is the air-conditioner field.   17
The BBB says that there are no authorized service agencies for air condi-
tioners. A standard ploy begins with a baited offer to recondition your
machine for $8.95 or so. The repairman arrives and goes into a well-re-
hearsed act: your freon is missing, the frattistat valve is completely shot,
you could be asphyxiated in your sleep, the conditioner has to go into the
shop. The next bulletin is that the bill won't be $8.95, it will be $34.95. You
still want the $8.95 special? Well, there's a trucking charge of $7.50 and the
conditioner is now all taken apart, it will have to be put together again . . . most
people finally authorize the $34.95 overhaul.

Some mechanics find woman customers irresistible targets. Mrs. Anita   18
Lemberg of Brooklyn went to a muffler shop for a while-you-wait replace-
ment. When her car was on the hoist, the mechanic told her a horror story
about the condition of her steering system, it was so dangerous she shouldn't
drive another foot, and so on. In only two hours, he said, he could "replace
all the bushings" and perform other wonders. The bill was $51. Her regular
mechanic, doing a lube job a week later, showed her that the grease and

grime on her steering system was a year old if it was a minute. She went back to the muffler shop, where she was told that her mechanic was a liar.

19 An Ellenville, N.Y., woman, Mrs. Marian Talken, had trouble with her clothes dryer. The repairman told her it needed a new drive-shaft and bearings. The bill was $72, and when the original trouble recurred, he wouldn't come back. Another repairman charged $13 to take the dryer apart and show Mrs. Talken that the same old drive-shaft was still in business at the same old spot. He would not, however, be her witness. "I don't want to get involved," he said. "You'll have to settle it yourself."

20 Doesn't anything *good* ever happen? Well, yes. A few months ago a friend of mine asked a jeweler how much he would charge to fix an old watch. The man said he didn't like to work on anything but brand-new watches. A second watchmaker said, reluctantly, that he'd do it, for around $150. My friend kept shopping around until he got a better price—$7.20— and a prompt, superb job. How? That part was a little tricky: he asked a friendly airline pilot to take it to a shop in London. But even that is not a guaranteed solution. A London jeweler charged me twice the list price for a wrist-watch crystal three years ago, probably because I had an American accent.

21 Maybe the answer is to do it yourself, or forget it.

WHAT DID THE WRITER SAY, AND WHAT DID YOU THINK?

1. Express the thesis in one sentence.
2. Does the author overstate his case, or does he play fair? Does he acknowledge that some honest and competent people still make repairs? Does he recognize any improvements that have been made?
3. Does the author provide any suggestions for remedying the bad situation? If not, should he?
4. What is the difference between incompetence and cheating? Does the author make the distinction? Does it matter to the consumer?
5. Are any consumer products exceptions to the rule? Can you think of any for which repairs are generally cheap and effective?
6. Have you or people you know ever paid more to purchase a product from a dealer because of the dealer's reputation for service after the purchase?
7. The article was written about ten years ago. Has the repair problem become better, worsened, or stayed the same? Have consumer protection movements had any effect?
8. What accounts for the bad situation? Have people simply become increasingly dishonest, or are more complex causes at work?

HOW DID THE WRITER SAY IT?

1. Is the thesis ever stated directly? If not, should it have been?
2. How many examples are used? Are they enough to support the thesis?

3. Are the examples distributed over a wide enough range of products?
4. The article has two watch-repair examples and two car-repair examples. Are they repetitious? Would the article have been stronger if the second example in each case had dealt with a different product?
5. In paragraph 17, *frattistat* is a nonsense word invented by the author. What is the purpose of this invention?
6. Does the conclusion begin with paragraph 20 or with the one sentence of paragraph 21? Is the conclusion effective or ineffective?
7. Vocabulary: *affidavit, lucrative, freon, ploy, asphyxiated, bushings.*

WHAT ABOUT <u>YOUR</u> WRITING?

"The Honest Repairman—A Vanishing American?" is a good example of why-didn't-I-think-of-saying-that writing. Who doesn't grumble about being cheated by repairmen? Who doesn't have a few spectacular stories to tell? Apart from the interview with the Better Business Bureau, many readers probably see in the Purdy article material they are as familiar with as the author, read insights they themselves have probably had, and mutter, "Why didn't I think of saying that?" Maybe they didn't think of it because they were too busy lamenting that they didn't have anything to write about. More likely, they had drifted into the habit of not taking their own ideas seriously.

In "Self-Reliance," Ralph Waldo Emerson presents this moral more memorably when he complains of the person who "dismisses without notice his thought, because it is his. In every work of genius we recognize our own rejected thoughts: they come back to us with a certain alienated majesty." You don't have to believe that Purdy's article is a work of genius to agree with Emerson's conclusion: We "should learn to detect and watch that gleam of light which flashes across the mind . . . Else, tomorrow a stranger will say with masterly good sense precisely what we have thought and felt all the time, and we shall be forced to take with shame our own opinion from another."

The Case of the Flying Ashtray: A Story with a Moral

HAIM G. GINOTT

Dr. Haim G. Ginott's *Between Parent and Child* (1965), from which "The Case of the Flying Ashtray" is taken, was an enormously successful book, remaining on the best-seller list for more than a year. Commenting on the book, the *Christian Science Monitor* observed, "It is a great relief to hear from enlightened professionals who have practical illustrated advice." Dr. Ginott (1922–1973) also wrote *Between Parent and Teenager* (1969) and *Teacher and Child* (1972).

Ask yourself what ingredients in content and style might help explain Ginott's great popular success. What audience did he have in mind as he wrote? How realistically do his examples relate to your own experiences as a child or parent?

Reprinted by permission of Dr. Alice Ginott.

1   It was early in the morning, the Monday after Thanksgiving weekend. The woman on the telephone sounded frantic. "Figure this out," she said, "if you can. Here we are in the car, the whole family. We drove four hundred miles from Pittsburgh to New York. In the back of the car, Ivan behaved like an angel, quiet and deep in thought. I said to myself, 'He deserves some praise.' We were just entering the Lincoln Tunnel[1] when I turned to him and said, 'You are such a good boy, Ivan. You behaved so well. I am proud of you.'

2   "A minute later the sky fell on us. Ivan pulled out an ashtray and spilled its contents all over us. The ashes, the cigarette butts, and the smoke kept coming, like atomic fallout. We were in the tunnel, in heavy traffic, and we were choking. I could have killed him. If it were not for the other cars around us, I would have murdered him on the spot. And what burned me up most was that I had just praised him so sincerely. Isn't praise good for children any more?"

3   Weeks later Ivan himself revealed the cause of the explosion. All the way home he had been wondering how he could get rid of his younger brother, who was snuggled up between mother and father in the front of the car. Finally the idea occurred to him that if their car were jackknifed in the middle, he and his parents would be safe, but the baby would be cut in two. Just then mother had congratulated him on his goodness. The praise made him feel guilty, and he wanted desperately to show that he did not deserve it. He looked around, saw the ashtray, and the rest had followed instantly.

Praising Accomplishments or Personality?

4   Most people believe that praise builds up a child's confidence and makes him feel secure. In actuality, praise may result in tension and misbehavior. Why? Many children have, from time to time, destructive wishes about members of their family. When parents tell a child, "You are such a good boy," he may not be able to accept it because his own picture of himself is quite different. In his own eyes, he cannot be "good" when only recently he wished that his mother had a zipper on her mouth or that his brother would spend next weekend in the hospital. In fact, the more he is praised, the more he misbehaves in order to show his "true self." Parents frequently report that just after praising a child for good deportment, he starts to act wild, as though to disprove their compliment. It is possible that "acting-up" is the child's way of communicating his private reservations about his public image.

5   *Desirable and undesirable praise.*—Does this mean that praise is now "out"? Not at all. It does mean, however, that praise, like penicillin, must not be administered haphazardly. There are rules and cautions that govern the handling of potent medicines—rules about timing and dosage, cautions

---

[1] Tunnel connecting New Jersey and New York City.

about possible allergic reactions. There are similar regulations about the administration of emotional medicine. The single most important rule is that praise deal only with the child's efforts and accomplishments, *not* with his character and personality.

When a boy cleans up the yard, it is only natural to comment on how   6 hard he has worked, and on how good the yard looks. It is highly unrelated, and inappropriate, to tell him how good he is. Words of praise should mirror for the child a *realistic* picture of his *accomplishments,* not a Madison Avenue[2] image of his personality.

The following example illustrates desirable praise: Jim, age eight, did a   7 good job cleaning up the yard. He raked the leaves, removed the garbage, and rearranged the tools. Mother was impressed and expressed her appreciation of his efforts and achievements:

MOTHER: The yard was so dirty. I didn't believe it could be cleaned up in one day.

JIM: I did it!

MOTHER: It was full of leaves and garbage and things.

JIM: I cleaned it all up.

MOTHER: What a job!

JIM: Yeah, it sure was.

MOTHER: The yard is so clean now, it is a pleasure to look at it.

JIM: It's nice.

MOTHER: Thank you, son.

JIM (*with a mile-wide smile*): You are welcome.

Mother's words made Jim feel glad of his efforts and proud of his accomplishments. That evening he could not wait for his father to come home in   8 order to show him the cleaned-up yard and again to feel within himself the pride of a task well done.

In contrast, the following words of praise addressed to the child's personality are unhelpful: 9

"You are such a wonderful child."

"You are truly mother's little helper."

"What would mother do without you?"

Such comments may threaten a child and cause him anxiety.[3] He may   10 feel that he is far from being wonderful and that he is unable to live up to this label. So, instead of fearfully waiting to be exposed as a fraud, he may decide to lessen his burden immediately by a confession of misbehavior.

Direct praise of personality, like direct sunlight, is uncomfortable and   11 blinding. It is embarrassing for a person to be told that he is wonderful, angelic, generous, and humble. He feels called upon to deny at least part of the praise. Publicly, he cannot stand up and say, "Thank you, I accept

---

[2] Street in New York City, associated with the advertising industry.

[3] Praise may also be threatening to adults. In "Robert Frost Confronts Khrushchev," F. D. Reeve states: "The honors Frost received made him nervous, for honors . . . may be terrifying: it may mean you have to do something better next time, something which you fear will fail." *Atlantic Monthly* (September, 1963), p. 38. [Ginott's note]

your words that I am wonderful.'' Privately, too, he must reject such praise. He cannot honestly say to himself, ''I am wonderful. I am good and strong and generous and humble.''

12   He may not only reject the praise but may have some second thoughts about those who have praised him: ''If they find me so great, they cannot be so smart.''

Our Words and the Child's Inferences

13   Praise should deal, not with the child's personality attributes, but with his efforts and achievements. Our comments should be so phrased that the child draws from them positive inferences about his personality. Kenny, age ten, helped his father fix up the basement. In the process he had to move heavy furniture.

FATHER: The workbench is so heavy. It is hard to move.
KENNY (*with pride*): But I did it.
FATHER: It takes a lot of strength.
KENNY (*flexing his muscles*): I am strong.

14   In this example, father commented on the difficulty of the task. It was the child himself who drew the inference about his personal power. Had his father said, ''You are so strong, son,'' Kenny might have replied, ''No, I am not. There are stronger boys than I in my class.'' A fruitless, if not bitter, argument might have followed.

Silent Statements and Self-Image

15   Praise has two parts: our words and the child's inferences. Our words should state clearly that we appreciate the child's effort, work, achievement, help, consideration, or creation. Our words should be so framed that the child will almost inevitably draw from them a realistic conclusion about his personality. Our words should be like a magic canvas upon which a child cannot help but paint a positive picture of himself. The following examples illustrate this point:

Helpful praise: Thank you for washing the car, it looks new again.
Possible inference: I did a good job. My work is appreciated.
(Unhelpful praise: You are an angel.)

Helpful praise: I liked your get-well card. It was so pretty and witty.
Possible inference: I have good taste, I can rely on my choices.
(Unhelpful praise: You are *always* so considerate.)

Helpful praise: Your poem spoke to my heart.
Possible inference: I am glad I can write poems.
(Unhelpful praise: You are a good poet for your age.)

Helpful praise: The bookcase that you built looks beautiful.
Possible inference: I am capable.
(Unhelpful praise: You are such a good carpenter.)

Helpful praise: Your letter brought me great joy.
Possible inference: I can bring happiness to others.
(Unhelpful praise: When it comes to letters, you are wonderful.)

Helpful praise: I appreciate greatly your washing the dishes today.
Possible inference: I am helpful.
(Unhelpful praise: You did a better job than the maid.)

Helpful praise: Thanks for telling me that I overpaid you. I appreciate
  it very much.
Possible inference: I'm glad I was honest.
(Unhelpful praise: You are such an honest child.)

Helpful praise: Your composition gave me several new ideas.
Possible inference: I can be original.
(Unhelpful praise: You write well for your grade. Of course, you still
  have a lot to learn.)

Such descriptive statements and the child's positive conclusions are the   16
building blocks of mental health. What he concludes about himself in response to our words, the child later restates silently to himself. Realistic
positive statements repeated inwardly by the child determine to a large
extent his good opinion of himself and the world around him.

WHAT DID THE WRITER SAY, AND WHAT DID YOU THINK?

1. Try to summarize the author's main point about praising children in one sentence of
   your own.
2. What assumptions about the basic nature of children—and grownups—serve as background for the author's comments?
3. Does the author give an unrealistically rosy picture of the good results that will be
   achieved by following his methods?
4. Does he give an unrealistically bleak picture of the bad effects of other methods?
5. What elements make the author's message appealing to parents?

HOW DID THE WRITER SAY IT?

1. Where does Ginott first state his thesis? Does he ever repeat it? Where?
2. Ginott begins with a striking example—the flying ashtray story. Why does he bother
   to tell us about such apparent trivia as when and where the event took place ("the
   Monday after Thanksgiving weekend," "just entering the Lincoln Tunnel," and so on)?
3. How does the title, "The Case of the Flying Ashtray," add to reader interest? Why is
   it appropriate?
4. Does the author provide enough examples to support his thesis?
5. How effective is the author's choice of examples? Do the examples present a reasonable cross section of likely situations? Are they distributed among different age
   groups? Do too many of them deal with one particular kind of activity?

6. How good is Ginott's use of dialogue? Do the people speak like human beings? If not, how significant is this failing?
7. Do the various headings and subheadings make a positive contribution to the selection? Explain.
8. Vocabulary: *inference.*

WHAT ABOUT <u>YOUR</u> WRITING?

One cause for the commercial success of Ginott's book may have been the ecstasy many people felt at coming across a book on psychology that they could bear to read. Psychology, sociology, education, government, economics, the armed forces—virtually every area of human activitiy has its own *jargon,* specialized terminology and trade talk that is all but incomprehensible to outsiders. So much material, allegedly written for general audiences, has been filled with jargon that in addition to its meaning as specialized terminology the word has come to be synonymous with pompous double-talk, offensive to outsiders and insiders alike. Except possibly for his use of "self-image" (he could just have written "how we see ourselves"), Ginott is excellent at avoiding jargon.

You'll be writing for a general audience, too, in your composition course. It's almost always possible to turn the high-sounding mumbo jumbo of jargon into everyday English. Be extremely careful about picking subjects in which it's not possible: tuning an engine, sailing a boat, performing a chemical analysis. If you decide to go ahead anyway, be sure to provide simple definitions for any unfamiliar terms.

OFFENSIVE JARGON	EVERYDAY ENGLISH
Maximum utilization of vehicular resources . . .	Making the best use of transportation . . .
Furtherance of interpersonal communications between disparate socioeconomic units . . .	Getting people of different backgrounds to talk more with each other . . .
Bilateral accommodation is imperative.	Both sides will have to compromise.
The classroom situation is geared to the fostering of meaningful, democratic decision-making opportunities by the student population.	Students have a voice in determining what happens in class.

from The Great Bridge
DAVID McCULLOUGH

David McCullough has served as a writer and editor on *Time, American Heritage,* and other magazines. His first book, *The Johnstown Flood,* was published in 1968. *The Great Bridge* (1972), according to historian Bruce Catton, ''sheds fresh light on a whole era in American history. . . . Additionally it is an excellent study in the technical problems involved in the construction project and in the human price that was part of the solution.'' McCullough's most recent work is *The Path Between the*

Seas (1977), an account of the construction of the Panama Canal that won the National Book Award for history.

Some background information should be helpful. The reading comes from the "Epilogue" of *The Great Bridge*. Having described the building of the Brooklyn Bridge in lavish detail, McCullough is ready to summarize and evaluate.

Universally acknowledged today as an engineering and artistic masterpiece, the Brooklyn Bridge, completed in 1883 after thirteen years of labor, is 1595½ feet long. It was conceived and designed by John Roebling, a German immigrant, who died before construction could get under way and was succeeded by his son, Washington. During most of the construction, Washington Roebling lived in hideous physical pain from "the bends," a disease caused by too rapid decrease in air pressure after staying in the compressed-air atmosphere of underwater construction caissons. Brooklyn Bridge, remodeled not long ago, is still a heavily traveled link over the East River between Manhattan and Brooklyn.

1   The bridge remained a subject of endless fascination for almost everybody who saw it. For the millions of immigrants arriving in New York through the 1880's and 1890's and on into the new century, it was one of the first things to be seen of the New World as they came up the bay. It was one of the landmarks they all looked for, the great world-famous symbol of the faith that was literally moving mountains. And the fact that it had been designed by an immigrant and built largely by immigrant workers did much naturally to enhance its appeal.

2   In truth there is really no end to the number of things the bridge meant to people. For whole generations growing up in New York and Brooklyn it was simply a large, dominant, and generally beloved part of the natural order of things. The river without the bridge or Brooklyn without the bridge would have been unthinkable and year after year people went to it on especially fine days, or at moments of personal stress or joy, the way people go to a mountain or walk beside the sea.

3   For countless people their first walk on the bridge would remain one of childhood's earliest memories. Countless others would tell how it was the place where they fell in love. No doubt it very often was. Al Smith[1] was among those who loved to sing "Danny by My Side," the opening line of which runs "The Brooklyn Bridge on Sunday is known as lovers' lane."

4   In *A Tree Grows in Brooklyn,* the most popular of the many novels to be written with a Brooklyn setting, a young World War I soldier from Pennsylvania says, "I thought if ever I got to New York, I'd like to walk across the Brooklyn Bridge." It was something felt by whole generations of Americans before and since. They would come from every part of the country, take photographs of it and from it with one of the new Kodak cameras introduced not long after the bridge was finished, or buy some of the stereopticon views that sold by the millions. They would ride bicycles across, take honeymoon strolls by moonlight, carry newborn babies proudly down the promenade, or scatter the ashes of the dearly departed from the middle of the main span.

[1] Governor of New York; Democratic candidate for president, 1928.

The Brooklyn Bridge and the New York City skyline: "one of the two or three most soul-stirring spots in America, like standing at the rim of the Grand Canyon." (Photo: Kenneth Karp)

It was a place to go on stifling summer evenings, to take some exercise   5
to and from work, to walk the baby, to watch the gulls, to find relief from
the city. Its promenade was and would remain one of the most exhilarating
walks on the continent. To be on the promenade of the Brooklyn Bridge on
a fine day, about halfway between the two towers, looking over the harbor
and the city skyline, was to be at one of the two or three most soul-stirring
spots in America, like standing at the rim of the Grand Canyon.

Just why this bridge, more than all others, has had such a hold on people   6
is very hard to pin down. But in the years since it opened it has been the
subject of more paintings, engravings, etchings, lithographs, and photographs than any man-made structure in America. There are probably a
thousand paintings and lithographs of the bridge by well-known artists
alone.[2] It has been the setting for scenes in films, for Maxwell Anderson's
Winterset, and for all kinds of advertising. (It would seem that a whole
chronological display of female fashions in America, since the advent of
photography, could be assembled just from pictures posed on the bridge
year after year.) It has been used repeatedly on postcards, Christmas cards,
book jackets, posters, record jackets. It has been the symbol for a New
York television network and for a popular Italian chewing gum.

There have been songs about the bridge, besides the one Al Smith liked,   7
and a great many poems, nearly all of which have been less than memorable.
The one notable exception is *The Bridge* by Hart Crane, who, in the 1920's,
to identify as closely as possible with his subject, moved into Washington
Roebling's old house at 110 Columbia Heights. In Crane's powerful but not
altogether coherent masterpiece, the bridge is seen as a shining symbol of
affirmation at the end of an epic search through the American past. It is the
"Tall Vision-of-the-Voyage," spare, "silver-paced," and all-redeeming.

The finest thing written at the time the bridge was opened appeared in   8
Harper's Weekly. The author was a newspaperman named Montgomery
Schuyler and his article, "The Bridge as a Monument," was not only the
first critical review of the great work, but a bugle call, as Lewis Mumford
would say, for serious architectural criticism in America. Schuyler did not
think much of the bridge as a work of art. Still, everything considered, he
judged it "one of the greatest and most characteristic" structures of his
century. "It so happens," he wrote, "that the work which is likely to be
our most durable monument, and to convey some knowledge of us to the
most remote posterity, is a work of bare utility; not a shrine, not a fortress,
not a palace, but a bridge."

The towers, he believed, would outlast everything else on either shore,   9
and he asked his readers to imagine some future archaeologist surveying the
ruins of New York, "a mastless river and a dispeopled land." The cables

---

[2] Joseph Pennell, Joseph Stella, John Marin, Childe Hassam, Georgia O'Keeffe, O. Louis
Guglielmi, Raoul Dufy, Ludwig Bemelmans, Lyonel Feininger, Albert Gleizes, and Max
Weber are some of the artists who have taken the bridge as their subject. Several, such as
Marin and Stella, have gone back to it many times. Stella's powerful abstraction *The Bridge*
(1918) is probably the best known of all the paintings. [McCullough's note]

and roadway would have long since disintegrated, he said. The Roeblings would be as forgotten as the builders of the Pyramids. Only the towers of the Great Bridge would remain standing and the archaeologist would have "no other means of reconstructing our civilization." "What will his judgment of us be?"

10   Henry James, writing soon after the turn of the century, would see something darkly ominous in the looming silhouette of the bridge and its shuttling trains. New York for him had become a "steel-souled machine room," the end product of which was "merciless multiplications" and the bridge was a "monstrous organism," marking the beginning of a new age. For James the prospect was chilling.

11   By the 1920's, however, the bridge was a unique source of "joy and inspiration" for the critic Lewis Mumford.

> The stone plays against the steel; the heavy granite in compression, the spidery steel in tension. In this structure, the architecture of the past, massive and protective, meets the architecture of the future, light, aerial, open to sunlight, an architecture of voids rather than solids.

12   The bridge proved, he said, that industrialism need not be synonymous with ugliness. It was something done exceedingly well by Victorian America. "All that the age had just cause for pride in—its advances in science, its skill in handling iron, its personal heroism in the face of dangerous industrial processes, its willingness to attempt the untried and the impossible—came to a head in Brooklyn Bridge."

13   Others, later, would see it as a symbol of liberation, of release from the "howling chaos" on either shore. It would be said that at heart it was a monumental embodiment of the open road, the highway call, the abiding rootlessness that runs in the American grain—"not so much linking places as leaving them and shooting untrammeled across the sky." And an age that can no longer regard it as an engineering marvel has declared it a work of art. One prominent contemporary American architect has gone so far as to say it is one of the two works of architecture in New York of any real importance, the other one being Central Park.

14   It has also, of course, been taken quite for granted by millions who use it regularly and quite sentimentally by some. It can be seen as merely one of a number of different ways to get to or from Brooklyn or as the grandest sort of memento of a New York that was, a serene, aspiring emblem rising out of an exhilarating and confident age too often remembered solely for its corruption and gimcrackery. It can be seen as the beginning of modern New York—of monumental scale, of structural steel—or the end of old Brooklyn. It is all these. And possibly its enduring appeal may rest on its physical solidity and permanence, the very reverse of rootlessness. It says, perhaps, as does nothing else built by Americans before or since, that we had come to stay.

WHAT DID THE WRITER SAY, AND WHAT DID YOU THINK?

1. The thesis is simple and utterly noncontroversial, but there is a thesis, and every example is related to it. What is the thesis?
2. What sentence states the thesis? What sentence restates it?
3. In his conclusion, the author tries to go beyond his relatively bland and general thesis by indicating his own response to the Brooklyn Bridge. Express that response in your own words.
4. Are there other man-made structures that register on people's minds with the same power as the Brooklyn Bridge? The Statue of Liberty? The Roman Coliseum?
5. Aside from the last paragraph, what indicates that the author is himself a great admirer of the Brooklyn Bridge?

HOW DID THE WRITER SAY IT?

1. McCullough often bunches related short examples into single paragraphs. Cite instances.
2. Would paragraph 5 have been more logical if placed between paragraphs 2 and 3?
3. Why are two separate paragraphs given to Schuyler's article, "The Bridge as a Monument"?
4. How would you evaluate this selection for number of examples? For presenting a reasonable cross section of examples?
5. What is the basic principle of organization in paragraph 6?
6. Vocabulary: *stereopticon, etching, lithograph, gimcrackery.*

WHAT ABOUT YOUR WRITING?

Some students tend to think that the necessity of developing a thesis makes demands on intellectual powers they do not possess. The selection from *The Great Bridge* demonstrates that if you have plenty of interesting material, you can view your thesis primarily as an organizational device for tying things together, not as a blazing new insight or philosophical revelation. Don't ignore great ideas when they happen to pop up, but first-rate papers have been built around theses no more profound than "There are two sharply conflicting ways of approaching such and such a subject," "Thomas Hardy's reputation as a poet is still a matter of controversy," "Solving the problems of pollution is more complicated than it looks," and so on.

Professions for Women

VIRGINIA WOOLF

Virginia Woolf (1882–1941) was one of the most original and ingenious modern British novelists, contributing significantly to the development and refinement of stream-of-consciousness techniques. Her novels include *Jacob's Room* (1922), *Mrs. Dalloway* (1925), *To the Lighthouse* (1927), *Orlando* (1928), and *The Years* (1937). Virginia Woolf also established a substantial reputation as a critic and essayist in such volumes as *The Common Reader* (1925), *A Room of One's Own* (1929), *The Second Common Reader* (1933), and *The Death of the Moth* (1942), from which the following speech comes. The outbreak of World War II accentuated her personal torments, and she committed suicide in 1941.

Paragraphs 3 and 5 are a bit tricky because the author relies heavily on figures of speech to describe her experiences. Don't try to rush through these paragraphs. They'll reward your attention.

1   When your secretary invited me to come here, she told me that your Society is concerned with the employment of women and she suggested that I might tell you something about my own professional experiences. It is true I am a woman; it is true I am employed; but what professional experiences have I had? It is difficult to say. My profession is literature; and in that profession there are fewer experiences for women than in any other, with the exception of the stage—fewer, I mean, that are peculiar to women. For the road was cut many years ago—by Fanny Burney, by Aphra Behn, by Harriet Martineau, by Jane Austen, by George Eliot—many famous women, and many more unknown and forgotten, have been before me, making the path smooth, and regulating my steps. Thus, when I came to write, there were very few material obstacles in my way. Writing was a reputable and harmless occupation. The family peace was not broken by the scratching of a pen. No demand was made upon the family purse. For ten and sixpence one can buy paper enough to write all the plays of Shakespeare—if one has a mind that way. Pianos and models, Paris, Vienna and Berlin, masters and mistresses, are not needed by a writer. The cheapness of writing paper is, of course, the reason why women have succeeded as writers before they have succeeded in the other professions.

2   But to tell you my story—it is a simple one. You have only got to figure to yourselves a girl in a bedroom with a pen in her hand. She had only to move that pen from left to right—from ten o'clock to one. Then it occurred to her to do what is simple and cheap enough after all—to slip a few of those pages into an envelope, fix a penny stamp in the corner, and drop the envelope into the red box at the corner. It was thus that I became a journalist; and my effort was rewarded on the first day of the following month— a very glorious day it was for me—by a letter from an editor containing a cheque for one pound ten shillings and sixpence. But to show you how little

I deserve to be called a professional woman, how little I know of the struggles and difficulties of such lives, I have to admit that instead of spending that sum upon bread and butter, rent, shoes and stockings, or butcher's bills, I went out and bought a cat—a beautiful cat, a Persian cat, which very soon involved me in bitter disputes with my neighbours.

What could be easier than to write articles and to buy Persian cats with the profits? But wait a moment. Articles have to be about something. Mine, I seem to remember, was about a novel by a famous man. And while I was writing this review, I discovered that if I were going to review books I should need to do battle with a certain phantom. And the phantom was a woman, and when I came to know her better I called her after the heroine of a famous poem, The Angel in the House. It was she who used to come between me and my paper when I was writing reviews. It was she who bothered me and wasted my time and so tormented me that at last I killed her. You who come of a younger and happier generation may not have heard of her—you may not know what I mean by the Angel in the House. I will describe her as shortly as I can. She was intensely sympathetic. She was immensely charming. She was utterly unselfish. She excelled in the difficult arts of family life. She sacrificed herself daily. If there was chicken, she took the leg; if there was a draught she sat in it—in short she was so constituted that she never had a mind or a wish of her own, but preferred to sympathize always with the minds and wishes of others. Above all—I need not say it—she was pure. Her purity was supposed to be her chief beauty—her blushes, her great grace. In those days—the last of Queen Victoria—every house had its Angel. And when I came to write I encountered her with the very first words. The shadow of her wings fell on my page; I heard the rustling of her skirts in the room. Directly,[1] that is to say, I took my pen in hand to review that novel by a famous man, she slipped behind me and whispered: "My dear, you are a young woman. You are writing about a book that has been written by a man. Be sympathetic; be tender; flatter; deceive; use all the arts and wiles of our sex. Never let anybody guess that you have a mind of your own. Above all, be pure." And she made as if to guide my pen. I now record the one act for which I take some credit to myself, though the credit rightly belongs to some excellent ancestors of mine who left me a certain sum of money—shall we say five hundred pounds a year?—so that it was not necessary for me to depend solely on charm for my living. I turned upon her and caught her by the throat. I did my best to kill her. My excuse, if I were to be had up in a court of law, would be that I acted in self-defense. Had I not killed her she would have killed me. She would have plucked the heart out of my writing. For, as I found, directly I put pen to paper, you cannot review even a novel without having a mind of your own, without expressing what you think to be the truth about human relations, morality, sex. And all these questions, according to the Angel in the House, cannot be dealt with freely and openly by women; they must charm, they must conciliate, they must—to put it

3

---

[1] As soon as.

bluntly—tell lies if they are to succeed. Thus, whenever I felt the shadow of her wing or the radiance of her halo upon my page, I took up the inkpot and flung it at her. She died hard. Her fictitious nature was of great assistance to her. It is far harder to kill a phantom than a reality. She was always creeping back when I thought I had despatched her. Though I flatter myself that I killed her in the end, the struggle was severe; it took much time that had better have been spent upon learning Greek grammar; or in roaming the world in search of adventures. But it was a real experience; it was an experience that was bound to befall all women writers at that time. Killing the Angel in the House was part of the occupation of a woman writer.

4   But to continue my story. The Angel was dead; what then remained? You may say that what remained was a simple and common object—a young woman in a bedroom with an inkpot. In other words, now that she had rid herself of falsehood, that young woman had only to be herself. Ah, but what is "herself"? I mean, what is a woman? I assure you, I do not know. I do not believe that you know. I do not believe that anybody can know until she has expressed herself in all the arts and professions open to human skill. That indeed is one of the reasons why I have come here—out of respect for you, who are in process of showing us by your experiments what a woman is, who are in process of providing us, by your failures and successes, with that extremely important piece of information.

5   But to continue the story of my professional experiences. I made one pound ten and six by my first review; and I bought a Persian cat with the proceeds. Then I grew ambitious. A Persian cat is all very well, I said; but a Persian cat is not enough. I must have a motor car. And it was thus that I became a novelist—for it is a very strange thing that people will give you a motor car if you will tell them a story. It is a still stranger thing that there is nothing so delightful in the world as telling stories. It is far pleasanter than writing reviews of famous novels. And yet, if I am to obey your secretary and tell you my professional experiences as a novelist, I must tell you about a very strange experience that befell me as a novelist. And to understand it you must try first to imagine a novelist's state of mind. I hope I am not giving away professional secrets if I say that a novelist's chief desire is to be as unconscious as possible. He has to induce in himself a state of perpetual lethargy. He wants life to proceed with the utmost quiet and regularity. He wants to see the same faces, to read the same books, to do the same things day after day, month after month, while he is writing, so that nothing may break the illusion in which he is living—so that nothing may disturb or disquiet the mysterious nosings about, feelings round, darts, dashes and sudden discoveries of that very shy and illusive spirit, the imagination. I suspect that this state is the same both for men and women. Be that as it may, I want you to imagine me writing a novel in a state of trance. I want you to figure to yourselves a girl sitting with a pen in her hand, which for minutes, and indeed for hours, she never dips into the inkpot. The image that comes to my mind when I think of this girl is the image of a fisherman

lying sunk in dreams on the verge of a deep lake with a rod held out over the water. She was letting her imagination sweep unchecked round every rock and cranny of the world that lies submerged in the depths of our unconscious being. Now came the experience, the experience that I believe to be far commoner with women writers than with men. The line raced through the girl's fingers. Her imagination had rushed away. It had sought the pools, the depths, the dark places where the largest fish slumber. And then there was a smash. There was an explosion. There was foam and confusion. The imagination had dashed itself against something hard. The girl was roused from her dream. She was indeed in a state of the most acute and difficult distress. To speak without figure[2] she had thought of something, something about the body, about the passions which it was unfitting for her as a woman to say. Men, her reason told her, would be shocked. The consciousness of what men will say of a woman who speaks the truth about her passions had roused her from her artist's state of unconsciousness. She could write no more. The trance was over. Her imagination could work no longer. This I believe to be a very common experience with women writers—they are impeded by the extreme conventionality of the other sex. For though men sensibly allow themselves great freedom in these respects, I doubt that they realize or can control the extreme severity with which they condemn such freedom in women.

These then were two very genuine experiences of my own. These were two of the adventures of my professional life. The first—killing the Angel in the House—I think I solved. She died. But the second, telling the truth about my own experiences as a body, I do not think I solved. I doubt that any woman has solved it yet. The obstacles against her are still immensely powerful—and yet they are very difficult to define. Outwardly, what is simpler than to write books? Outwardly, what obstacles are there for a woman rather than for a man? Inwardly, I think, the case is very different; she has still many ghosts to fight, many prejudices to overcome. Indeed it will be a long time still, I think, before a woman can sit down to write a book without finding a phantom to be slain, a rock to be dashed against. And if this is so in literature, the freest of all professions for women, how is it in the new professions which you are now for the first time entering?   6

Those are the questions that I should like, had I time, to ask you. And indeed, if I have laid stress upon these professional experiences of mine, it is because I believe that they are, though in different forms, yours also. Even when the path is nominally open—when there is nothing to prevent a woman from being a doctor, a lawyer, a civil servant—there are many phantoms and obstacles, as I believe, looming in her way. To discuss and define them is I think of great value and importance; for thus only can the labour be shared, the difficulties be solved. But besides this, it is necessary also to discuss the ends and the aims for which we are fighting, for which   7

[2] Without a figure of speech: metaphor, simile, and so on.

we are doing battle with these formidable obstacles. Those aims cannot be taken for granted; they must be perpetually questioned and examined. The whole position, as I see it—here in this hall surrounded by women practicing for the first time in history I know not how many different professions—is one of extraordinary interest and importance. You have won rooms of your own in the house hitherto exclusively owned by men. You are able, though not without great labour and effort, to pay the rent. You are earning your five hundred pounds a year. But this freedom is only a beginning; the room is your own, but it is still bare. It has to be furnished; it has to be decorated; it has to be shared. How are you going to furnish it, how are you going to decorate it? With whom are you going to share it, and upon what terms? These, I think are questions of the utmost importance and interest. For the first time in history you are able to ask them; for the first time you are able to decide for yourselves what the answers should be. Willingly would I stay and discuss those questions and answers—but not tonight. My time is up; and I must cease.

WHAT DID THE WRITER SAY, AND WHAT DID YOU THINK?

1. What can you determine about the nature of the group being addressed?
2. What is the thesis? Is it ever stated directly?
3. How does it strengthen rather than weaken Woolf's comments about the problems women face when a literary career is wide open to them?
4. What does the "Angel" symbolize?
5. What does the fishing scene symbolize? What is represented by the "smash . . . explosion . . . foam and confusion"?
6. What is meant by "killing" the Angel? What is meant by "I acted in self-defense"? Does the author feel guilty about killing the Angel?
7. How would you describe the author's attitude toward men?
8. Are two examples enough to support the thesis adequately?

HOW DID THE WRITER SAY IT?

1. What elements show that "Professions for Women" was originally a speech?
2. The author makes some sharp complaints about the problems women face. Like any writer, she must be careful that her complaints do not sound like mere crankiness. What does she do to establish an atmosphere of reason and common sense?
3. Point out some of the author's touches of humor. What purposes do they serve?
4. Does the author seem too modest or apologetic about herself?
5. The passages about the Angel and the fishing may add slightly to reading difficulty, but they also have many advantages over flat, direct statements. What are those advantages?
6. "Professions for Women" is the author's title. The selection has also appeared as "The Angel in the House." Which title is superior?

7. Paragraph 4 begins, "But to continue my story." Paragraph 5 begins, "But to continue the story of my professional experiences." Do these sentences show some obvious sloppiness in the organization of ideas?
8. Vocabulary: *conciliate, lethargy.*

WHAT ABOUT <u>YOUR</u> WRITING?

"Willingly would I stay and discuss those questions and answers—but not tonight. My time is up; and I must cease." Let's grant the many differences between giving a speech and writing a paper for class. For all we know, the person in charge of the meeting might have been signaling frantically to Virginia Woolf because the hour was late and a half dozen speakers were yet to be heard. Still, those last two sentences of "Professions for Women" will strike most readers, correctly, as a weak conclusion to an otherwise polished and even beautiful piece of work. The sentences make it seem as if the speaker has a bus to catch or as if, having collected her fee and spoken for the agreed-upon twenty minutes, she doesn't want to be bothered any more. What would you think of a student paper that ended with "There is more to say on this subject, but I have written the specified 500 words, and I must cease"?

Your conclusion must be related to, must grow out of, what has come before. It is your last chance to remind your reader of your main idea and to drive home its importance. It is not the place to introduce irrelevant or trivial new topics. It is not the place to worry about counting words or missing a bus. The words of your conclusion are the last ones your reader will see, and they ought to be good words.

Beyond these observations, unfortunately, there are no tidy rules governing the writing of conclusions. Too many different kinds of conclusions exist to be wrapped into one neat package. Your best bet for writing a good conclusion is to keep the various choices in mind so they'll be available when you need them—and then to trust your instincts and common sense.

The following list suggests a few of the most useful kinds of conclusions:

SUMMARY

We can see, then, that for many people divorce has become the preferred method of settling marital problems. Liberalized grounds for divorce, the increased social acceptance of those who have been divorced, and the loosening of religious taboos have all contributed to the dramatic increase in the divorce rate.

Note: Summaries run the risk of dullness. If your conclusion is a summary, try at least not to make it a word-for-word repetition of language used earlier in the paper. Summaries work best in long papers. The shorter the paper, the more you should consider another kind of conclusion.

CALL FOR ACTION

As this paper has shown, the divorced man gets sympathy and attention and lots of dinner invitations. The divorced woman generally just gets propositioned. It's time she got some sympathy, too. She's not asking for special favors, but it's time to stop treating her like a social outcast.

PREDICTION

And so it goes. Divorce becomes more common every day. Eventually it may become so common that it will stop mattering much. Then, perhaps, we will find people boasting about their former marriages the way our quaint old grandparents used to boast about shipping on a tramp steamer, or winning first prize for apple pie at the county fair, or—their voices soft with pride and joy and love—staying happily married for forty or fifty years.

QUESTION

The increasing divorce rate is not merely a colorful statistic. It raises disturbing questions. How great is the damage done to children? Does divorce solve a problem or only run away from it? Is marriage itself a dying institution? Can a society of broken homes be a healthy society? These and other questions will trouble this nation for years to come.

QUOTATION

All in all, there seems little any one person or group can do about the increasing number of broken marriages except to start taking seriously the century-old wisecrack of *Punch* magazine: "Advice to those about to marry: Don't."

ANECDOTE

Yes, everybody's doing it, The tragedy has gone from divorce. It's now an official part of the natural cycle. Last week one of the churches in my town had a divorce service. It was a big dress-up occasion. Friends and relatives got invited. Music. Prayers, Lots of lofty sentiments about change and growth and stages. It was just like getting married. It was just like dying.

RESTATEMENT OF IMPORTANCE OF THE TOPIC

At a time when newsmagazines and television specials go into weekly panics about gas mileage and electric bills, about the balance of payments and inflation, about disarmament and dictator-ships, it may seem almost frivolous to start brooding about how many people are getting divorced. In an age of revolution, it may seem almost irresponsible to create a new panic by studying statistics at the county courthouse. In the long run, however, nothing may be less frivolous or more thoroughly revolutionary for American civilization than the frightening basic truths revealed by the divorce figures of our turbulent society.

Chapter 3

PROCESS

In its most familiar form, writing about a process provides instructions. This kind of process paper tells readers the series of steps they must perform to achieve a particular result. At its simplest level, the process paper is thus a "how-to-do-it" paper: how to cook Beef Wellington, how to drive from town to Camp Wilderness (see pp. 11–12), how to install wall paneling, how to operate an IBM 1400 or Polaroid SX 70, how to put together a child's bike on Christmas morning. Writing simple, clear instructions makes many demands on a writer, and people who are good at it often earn excellent salaries. Ask the parents struggling with the bike on Christmas morning how many dollars they would offer for easy-to-read and easy-to-follow instructions.

The conventional how-to-do-it paper sometimes can lend itself to humor, as when a writer deliberately gives instructions on what no one wants to learn: how to flunk out of school, how to have a heart attack, and so forth. Besides drawing on the appeal of humor, such papers can also have serious instructional purposes by telling the reader, between the lines, how to do well in school or how to avoid coronaries. Other humorous pieces give instructions on what many people do want to learn but don't usually want to acknowledge; *How to Succeed in Business Without Really Trying* and *Gamesmanship, or The Art of Winning Games Without Actually Cheating* are the titles of two successful books.

Several other variations on the how-to-do-it paper are also fairly common. A "how-it-works" paper explains the functioning of anything from an electric toothbrush to the system for ratifying a new constitutional amendment.

A "how-it-*was*-done" paper might trace the process by which Stonehenge or the Pyramids were built or of how the chase scenes in the old Keystone Kops movies were filmed. A "how-*not*-to-do-it" paper might trace the process by which the writer did everything wrong in reshingling the roof or buying a used car.

At a more advanced level, process papers can study the course of social, political, scientific, and cultural developments: the process that led to the discovery of the smallpox vaccine, the decision of Napoleon to invade Russia, the spread of Christianity, Franklin D. Roosevelt's proposal to increase the membership of the Supreme Court. Process writing can also be a powerful instrument of literary analysis: the process by which Frederic Henry in *A Farewell to Arms* comes to desert the army, or Captain Ahab in *Moby-Dick* associates the white whale with evil, or Iago persuades Othello that Desdemona has been unfaithful.

How does the persuasive principle apply to process writing? If you're writing a straightforward how-to-do-it paper, for example, why not simply list the steps and forget about a thesis? You don't have a "point" to make as such, do you? Aren't you saying only that here are the things one must do to paint a room or change a flat tire or study for an exam? So why not just list them?

These questions are legitimate, and it's certainly possible to write a process paper without a thesis. In most cases, though, the paper won't be as good as it could be and ought to be. Apart from the advantages of writing with a thesis as described in Chapter 1, you're writing a how-to-do-it paper, after all, for people who don't yet know "how to do it." (If they knew, they'd have no reason to read the paper.) A mere long list of things to do, each step considered separately, can both madden readers with boredom and overwhelm them with confusion. A thesis helps readers get solidly oriented at the outset and enables them to see each separate step as part of a coherent pattern.

But what kind of thesis makes sense in the humble little paper on how to paint a room? All kinds.

Painting a room is much easier than it seems.

Painting a room is much harder than it seems.

Painting a room is great fun.

Painting a room is horrible drudgery.

Painting a room is easy compared to preparing the room to be painted.

Painting a room takes less time than most people suppose.

Painting a room takes more time than most people suppose.

Any one of these ideas, not to mention many more imaginative ones, could give unity and interest to a how-to-do-it paper. The writer, in addition to making each step convey the necessary raw information, would connect each step or group of related steps to the thesis.

¶1—Presentation of thesis: Painting a room is much easier than it seems.

Start of ¶2—To prepare the room, you need only a dust cloth, lots of masking tape, and spackling paste . . .

Start of ¶3—If preparing the room was easy, the painting itself is child's play . . .

Start of ¶4—Cleaning up is the easiest part of all . . .

With the desirability of a thesis in mind, it's no massive project to think up promising theses for some of the other process paper subjects already mentioned.

Every step of the way, Napoleon's decision to invade Russia was based on foolish overconfidence.

Frankin D. Roosevelt's proposal to pack the Supreme Court came in response to a long series of legislative frustrations.

Frederic Henry's desertion of the army in *A Farewell to Arms* is the last step in a gradually accelerating process of disillusionment.

The dramatic discovery of the smallpox vaccine came as the result of a coldly logical, totally undramatic scientific process.

The seemingly spontaneous, mad chase scenes in Keystone Kops movies were actually the product of careful planning of every detail.

The process by which the Pyramids were built shows an astonishing knowledge of the laws of modern physics.

Once you set up a thesis, the signficant issues are the mechanics of writing about the process itself.

Be sure you are writing about a process. The words "How to" or "How" in your title guarantee nothing. A process is a series, a sequence, an orderly progression. One step or event follows another: first this, then that, then something else. A happy-go-lucky collection of handy hints is not a process. Chapter 1 of this book followed a necessary sequence in the description of the process of *first* starting with a general subject, *then* limiting the subject, *then* devising a thesis and thesis statement, *then* incorporating the thesis into the whole paper. Chapter 2, on the other hand, while telling "how to" write an example paper, presented a bundle of miscellaneous suggestions on what to think about.in looking over the examples; the suggestions were in no particularly rigid order and therefore did not constitute a real process.

Follow strict chronological order. The rule to follow strict.chronological order seems obvious, but in fact it is unique to process writing. In other patterns, you try to begin with your most important or dramatic or amusing material. In process writing, you begin with step one. You try to make all the steps of the process as interesting as possible to your reader, but you have no choice about the order in which you discuss them.

Before describing the first step of the process, indicate any special ingredients or equipment that will be needed. Recipes, for example, almost always begin with a list of ingredients.

Be sure the process is complete. In a how-to-do-it paper, you're describing a process that you probably can do automatically, and it's easy to omit some obvious steps because you don't consciously think about them at all. They're not so obvious to your reader. If you're telling the reader how to change a flat tire, for instance, don't forget to have the poor soul set the parking brake before jacking up the car.

Try to anticipate difficulties. First, warn the reader in advance if a notably tough step is coming up:

Now comes the hard part.
The next step is a bit tricky.
Be extremely careful here.

Second, advise the reader of what can be done to make the process easier or more pleasant. You're an insider, and you have an insider's information. The process of changing a flat tire does not require anyone to put the lugs into the inverted hubcap so they won't get lost, but it's a technique insiders use to head off trouble before it starts. Painting a room does not require anyone to wear an old hat, but your mentioning the advisability of an old hat might be appreciated.

Third, tell the reader what to do if something goes wrong. Don't terrify the reader, but be frank about common foul-ups:

If any paint should get onto the window . . .
If the hubcap is hard to replace . . .

If you need to handle many separate steps, arrange them into groups when possible. Even a simple process may involve a large number of steps. The process paper is far less intimidating if the steps are presented in manageable bunches. On page 47 the writer divided the process of painting a room into preparation, painting, and cleaning up. Each division received a paragraph, and the reader got the impression of having only three major areas to worry about instead of fifty separate steps. Even as uninspired a grouping of steps as Phase I, Phase II, Phase III, or Beginning, Middle, End is preferable to none at all. The more steps in the process, of course, the more essential it becomes to collect them into groups.

Define unfamiliar terms. Definitions of unfamiliar terms are needed in all writing, but they're especially important in the how-to-do-it paper because the instructions are for an audience that must be assumed to know nothing about the subject.

Two final recommendations about your choice of topics are worth brief notes:

Avoid highly technical processes. Because you must define all unfamiliar terms, you don't want to choose an obscure scientific subject with such a specialized vocabulary that most of your energies will be spent providing definitions rather than presenting a process.

Avoid subjects for which pictures work better than words. Some processes, often but not always the highly technical ones, can best be explained with a few diagrams and almost as few words. Depending solely or almost solely on words would create pointless trouble for the writer and confusion for the reader. Since you are in a writing class, not an art class, you should avoid such processes.

WRITING SUGGESTIONS FOR PROCESS THEMES

Many topics have already been mentioned in this chapter. The suggestions here are designed to provide some further inspiration. Suggestions have been divided into two categories: general areas for exploration (with examples) and specific topics.

General Areas for Exploration

1. Do-it-yourself repairs: bikes, cars, radios, television sets, broken windows.
2. Routine chores: gardening, cooking, shopping.
3. School and business: studying, taking notes, registering, applying to colleges, applying for jobs, creating a good impression at job interviews.
4. Sports, games, and other recreational activities: how to win at poker, bridge, Monopoly; how to watch a football game, throw Frisbees, water ski; how to plan a trip.
5. Finances: budgeting, borrowing, investing.
6. Hobbies: how to start a stamp, coin, tropical fish collection; how to work at a particular art or craft; how a magic trick is performed.
7. Children and pets: baby sitting, toilet training, safety, housebreaking, traveling.
8. Personal care: grooming, breaking a bad habit, treating a cold, curing a hangover.
9. Humor: how to be a bore, worrywart, nag; how to get out of housework, butter up teachers, call in sick; how to die at thirty.
10. How-it-works: power steering, air conditioning, instant photography, zippers.
11. The past: how a battle was fought, a crime was committed, a structure was built, a law was passed, a disease was conquered.
12. Literature: how an author prepares the reader for a surprise ending, how a character makes a crucial decision, and so on.

Specific Topics

1. What to do if arrested.
2. What to do in a car accident.
3. How to find a rich husband or wife.
4. How to diet.
5. How to exercise.
6. How to drive defensively.
7. How to apply first aid for snake bites.

8. How to protect oneself in a natural disaster (tornado, hurricane, flood).
9. How to waste time.
10. How to plan for a holiday or other special occasion: Thanksgiving dinner, Passover seder, birthday party, bar mitzvah or confirmation party, Easter egg hunt, wedding.
11. How to live on nothing a year.
12. How to pack a suitcase.
13. How to stop smoking.
14. How to hitch a ride.
15. How to give oneself a perfect shave.

Drownproofing

CARLA STEPHENS

Carla Stephens specializes in producing popularly written self-help and how-to-do-it articles. In ''Drownproofing,'' she introduces a new technique for staying afloat in the water. Note the way in which she arranges the separate steps of the process into logical groups.

1   If your warm-weather plans include water sports, there's one thing you should do to make this summer safe as well as enjoyable for your family: Drownproof them!

2   Drowning is the second leading cause of accidental death for people between the ages of 4 and 44, according to the American National Red Cross. Twenty-eight percent of those drowned are children under 15 years old. Seven out of ten of them are boys.

3   Even more shocking is the fact that many of the seven thousand annual drowning victims *know how to swim*. In fact, swimmers face several hazards that non-swimmers don't. First, they may overexert themselves—especially in May and June when they're likely to expect out-of-condition bodies to perform as well as in summers past. They may also get into a situation beyond their skills. If panic takes over, tragedy may follow.

4   With drownproofing, on the other hand, a poor swimmer or even a non-swimmer can survive in the water twelve hours or more—even when fully clothed and in rough water.

5   Developed by the late Fred Lanoue, drownproofing relies on the body's ability to float when air fills the lungs. Picture yourself bobbing restfully just under the surface of the water. With a few easy movements you come up to breathe as often as necessary. That's the basic idea of drownproofing, a technique endorsed by the Red Cross, the National Safety Council and the

YMCA. It's easy to learn, even for some three-year-olds. You can teach yourself and your family.

Here's how it's done: First, take a breath through your mouth. Then, holding your breath, put your face into the water and float vertically with your arms and legs dangling. Don't try to keep your head up; it weighs fifteen pounds. 6

When you're ready for another breath, slowly raise your arms to shoulder height. At the same time bring one leg a little forward and the other back into a position somewhat like the scissors kick. (If injury makes it necessary, drownproofing can be done with either the arm or the leg movements.) Then gently press your arms down to your sides (not backward) and bring your legs together. Keep your eyes open and raise your head until your mouth is out of the water. Exhale through your nose, your mouth or both. 7

Inhale through your mouth while continuing to press your arms down. But don't press too hard, for you want to keep your chin at, not above, the surface of the water. Finally, return to the resting position with your face in the water. If you sink too far, a small kick or a slight downward push of your arms will return you to the surface. 8

When teaching your children, it's advisable to stand with them in shoulder-deep water. Have them bend forward to practice the breathing and arm movements. If they swallow water, be patient and encourage them to try again. Once they're comfortable with the procedure, move into deeper water near the side of the pool to coordinate the floating, breathing and body movements. Water just deep enough for them to go under is sufficient. Remember, all movements should be easy and relaxed. 9

10   If your child needs to work at the vertical float, let him practice at the side of a pool or some other spot where he'll be able to hold on. At first you might even help hold him up by placing a hand just beneath his shoulder. Have him take a breath, put his face into the water and then remove his hands from the side. As soon as he has some experience in floating remove your hand and watch.

11   While practicing, youngsters usually spend only about three seconds under water at first. That time should gradually increase—depending, of course, on their age. Older children may reach ten seconds, the period recommended for adults.

12   With a little practice your family will be drownproofed and truly ready for fun in the water.

WHAT DID THE WRITER SAY, AND WHAT DID YOU THINK?

1. This reading selection was published in *Woman's Day*, a mass-circulation magazine distributed in supermarkets. Why would the publishers of the magazine be likely to think that the article would interest their readers? What other magazines would be interested in an article of this kind?
2. The author actually describes two related processes. What is the second process?
3. What is the thesis and where is it stated? (The thesis is *not* a self-evident idea like "Drowning is hazardous to your health" or "Many people die from drowning.")
4. Does the author explain why inhaling should be done through the mouth rather than the nose? If not, would an explanation be desirable?

HOW DID THE WRITER SAY IT?

1. Where does the introduction stop and the body begin? Is the introduction too short, too long, or about right?
2. Does the body of the article support the thesis?
3. How important are the illustrations? Would most readers be able to understand the process without them? Does the article ignore this book's recommendation on page 49 to "Avoid subjects for which pictures work better than words"?
4. In paragraph 7, should "scissors kick" have been defined?
5. In the first sentence of paragraph 11, why is a comma necessary after "practicing"?
6. Is the conclusion too abrupt, too short? Would a summary have been appropriate?
7. Vocabulary: *hazards, vertically.*

WHAT ABOUT <u>YOUR</u> WRITING?

Your instructors are captive audiences. They may often enjoy their captivity and be eager to read your work, but in fact they have no choice. In the mood or not, they have to read it. That's their job. Fret all you want about their grading—you'll never find such soft touches again. Your future, noncaptive audiences will be infinitely tougher. They don't use red ink, but they don't need any. All they need is a wastebasket. And every good writer respects and fears wastebaskets.

Like Carla Stephens in "Drownproofing," the professional writer of a magazine article or advertisement suffers from, and benefits tremendously from, one problem that more writers ought to feel. *How do I get my reader's attention?* Nobody starts to read a magazine wondering what Carla Stephens or the Jones and Smith Company has to say that day. The author or the company has to make the reader stop turning the pages. The soft-touch instructor may sometimes comment, "This essay starts slowly but gets better as it goes along." The other folks out there just keep turning the pages.

Think about your readers. They're rooting strongly for you, if only because they want their own reading experience to be pleasurable, but they need your help. Here are three specific suggestions for making a good start.

First, try for a strong title. You won't find the word "drownproofing" in the dictionary: the author made it up. It's original and catchy, a term that can easily stimulate a reader's curiosity. (For a more detailed discussion of titles, see p. 56.)

Second, spare the reader such unpromising first sentences as "In this composition I will try to show . . ." or "My theme has as its thesis . . ." or "According to Webster's Dictionary . . ." You needn't go overboard—there's no virtue in being self-consciously cute or eccentric. (Stephens' opening sentence, for example, is mostly a simple, straightforward statement, though it ends with a dramatic two-word exclamation.) Still, a well-calculated touch of show biz now and then never hurt anyone and can sometimes work miracles. Consider these first sentences from three essays by George Orwell:

> As I write, highly civilised human beings are flying overhead, trying to kill me.

> Soon after I arrived at Crossgates (not immediately, but after a week or two, just when I seemed to be settling into the routine of school life) I began wetting my bed.

> In Moulmein, in Lower Burma, I was hated by large numbers of people—the only time in my life that I have been important enough for this to happen to me.

Third, and most important, remember that there's a real person reading what you've written. Writing isn't just self-expression—it's communication. If self-expression were the whole story, you'd be better off doodling or singing in the shower or making funny noises while you run through the nearest meadow. Whenever you can—and that will be most of the time—give your reader an immediate reason for paying attention to you. In "Drownproofing," the author employs the oldest, and still most effective, technique in the writer's trade: from the first sentence on, *she appeals to the reader's self-interest.* She's not writing abstractly about an interesting new method of staying afloat; she's writing about saving the lives of the reader's family. Naturally, you won't always be writing about life-and-death issues, but you can almost always give your reader a reason to care.

A writer is at one end and a reader at the other. And unless the reader is your instructor, that reader has a wastebasket.

How to Write a Rotten Poem with Almost No Effort

RICHARD HOWEY

Part-owner of a bookstore and copywriter for a Cleveland advertising agency,
Richard Howey has published a number of humorous free-lance articles. Beneath the
humor in this selection, however, you should be alert to a few serious comments that
sneak in from time to time. The test of the author's skill in process writing will come
when you take five minutes (or less) and see whether by following his instructions
you, too, can produce a truly rotten poem.

1   So you want to write a poem. You've had a rotten day or an astounding
thought or a car accident or a squalid love affair and you want to record it
for all time. You want to organize those emotions that are pounding through
your veins. You have something to communicate via a poem but you don't
know where to start.

2   This, of course, is the problem with poetry. Most people find it difficult
to write a poem so they don't even try. What's worse, they don't bother
reading any poems either. Poetry has become an almost totally foreign art
form to many of us. As a result, serious poets either starve or work as
account executives.[1] There is no middle ground. Good poets and poems are
lost forever simply because there is no market for them, no people who
write their own verse and seek out further inspiration from other bards.

3   Fortunately, there is a solution for this problem, as there are for all imponderables. The answer is to make it easy for everyone to write at least
one poem in his life. Once a person has written a poem, of whatever quality,
he will feel comradeship with fellow poets and, hopefully, read their works.
Ideally, there would evolve a veritable society of poet-citizens, which would
elevate the quality of life worldwide. Not only that, good poets could make
a living for a change.

4   So, to begin. Have your paper ready. You must first understand that the
poem you write here will not be brilliant. It won't even be mediocre. But
it will be better than 50% of all song lyrics and at least equal to one of Rod
McKuen's best efforts. You will be instructed how to write a four-line poem
but the basic structure can be repeated at will to create works of epic length.

5   The first line of your poem should start and end with these words: "In
the ———— of my mind." The middle word of this line is optional. Any word
will do. It would be best not to use a word that has been overdone, such
as "windmills" or "gardens" or "playground." Just think of as many nouns
as you can and see what fits best. The rule of thumb is to pick a noun that
seems totally out of context, such as "filing cabinet" or "radiator" or
"parking lot." Just remember, the more unusual the noun, the more profound the image.

From *The Plain Dealer,* Cleveland, February 11, 1975. Reprinted by permission of *The Plain
Dealer.*

[1] Upper-level positions in advertising agencies.

The second line should use two or more of the human senses[2] in a con- 6
flicting manner, as per the famous, "listen to the warm." This is a sure way
to conjure up "poetic" feeling and atmosphere. Since there are five different
senses, the possibilities are endless. A couple that come to mind are "see
the noise" and "touch the sound." If more complexity is desired other
senses can be added, as in "taste the color of my hearing," or "I cuddled
your sight in the aroma of the night." Rhyming, of course, is optional.

The third line should be just a simple statement. This is used to break up 7
the insightful images that have been presented in the first two lines. This
line should be as prosaic as possible to give a "down-to-earth" mood to the
poem. An example would be "she gave me juice and toast that morning,"
or perhaps "I left for work next day on the 8:30 bus." The content of this
line may or may not relate to what has gone before.

The last line of your poem should deal with the future in some way. This 8
gives the poem a forward thrust that is always helpful. A possibility might
be, "tomorrow will be a better day," or "I'll find someone sometime," or
"maybe we'll meet again in July." This future-oriented ending lends an aura
of hope and yet need not be grossly optimistic.

By following the above structure, anyone can write a poem. For example, 9
if I select one each of my sample lines, I come up with:

> In the parking lot of my mind,
>   I cuddled your sight in the aroma of the night.
> I left for work next day on the 8:30 bus.
>   Maybe we'll meet again in July.

Now that poem (like yours, when you're finished) is rotten. But at least 10
it's a poem and you've written it, which is an accomplishment that relatively
few people can claim.

Now that you're a poet, feel free to read poetry by some of your more 11
accomplished brothers and sisters in verse. Chances are, you'll find their
offerings stimulating and refreshing. You might even try writing some more
of your own poems, now that you've broken the ice. Observe others' emotions and experience your own—that's what poetry is all about.

Incidentally, if you find it impossible to sell the poem you write to Bobby 12
Goldsboro or John Denver, burn it. It will look terrible as the first page of
your anthology when it's published.

WHAT DID THE WRITER SAY, AND WHAT DID YOU THINK?

1. Is the author making fun of poetry in general or only of bad poetry?
2. What are the alleged benefits of learning to write a rotten poem? Are we meant to take these benefits seriously?
3. Do the author's instructions follow the rules of process writing presented in this chapter?

[2] The five senses are taste, touch, smell, hearing, and sight.

4. What is the thesis? Is there more than one?
5. Why is a poem written according to the instructions inevitably going to be a rotten one? Does the author ever suggest what is required to make good poetry?

HOW DID THE WRITER SAY IT?

1. How much of the article is actually devoted to giving instructions?
2. With what issues does the rest of the article concern itself? Are the concerns helpful to the article or are they mostly distracting?
3. Why is *rotten* a better word choice than *poor* or *bad*?
4. Vocabulary: *squalid, via, bards, imponderables, veritable, conjure, prosaic, aura, grossly.*

WHAT ABOUT YOUR WRITING?

Howey's unusual, witty title serves to put the reader on his side. The reader senses that Howey may have written a lively article for a general audience on a subject too often treated with solemnity or sentimentality. The rest of the article may be worth a look.

A good title is worth fussing about. It helps identify your subject and sometimes your attitude towards the subject. Thus, it enables the reader to become properly oriented even before looking at your opening sentence. A good title also stimulates curiosity: it makes the reader willing to bother with your opening sentence in the first place. A good title won't save a bad piece of writing, and a bad title won't destroy good writing, but good titles help, and writers shouldn't be shy about accepting all the help they can get.

BORING TITLE	BETTER TITLE
The Making of the Constitution	A More Perfect Union
My Trip to Niagara Falls	Honeymoon Heaven, Honeymoon Hell
Three Kinds of Teachers	Teach, Teacher, and Sir
Great Vampire Movies	Fangs for the Memory
The New Father	Have a Baby, My Wife Just Had a Cigar

To Make Them Stand in Fear

KENNETH M. STAMPP

Kenneth M. Stampp is professor of American history at the University of California in Berkeley. In addition to *The Peculiar Institution* (1956), his works include *And the War Came* (1950) and *The Era of Reconstruction* (1965).

Note the extraordinary versatility of process writing as it is applied to historical analysis in this selection.

A wise master did not take seriously the belief that Negroes were natural-born slaves. He knew better. He knew that Negroes freshly imported from Africa had to be broken in to bondage; that each succeeding generation had to be carefully trained. This was no easy task, for the bondsman rarely submitted willingly. Moreover, he rarely submitted completely. In most cases there was no end to the need for control—at least not until old age reduced the slave to a condition of helplessness.

Masters revealed the qualities they sought to develop in slaves when they singled out certain ones for special commendation. A small Mississippi planter mourned the death of his "faithful and dearly beloved servant" Jack: "Since I have owned him he has been true to me in all respects. He was an obedient trusty servant. . . . I never knew him to steal nor lie and he ever set a moral and industrious example to those around him. . . . I shall ever cherish his memory." A Louisiana sugar planter lost a "very valuable Boy" through an accident: "His life was a very great one. I have always found him willing and obedient and never knew him to fail to do anything he was put to do." These were "ideal" slaves, the models slaveholders had in mind as they trained and governed their workers.

How might this ideal be approached? The first step, advised those who wrote discourses on the management of slaves, was to establish and maintain strict discipline. An Arkansas master suggested the adoption of the "Army Regulations as to the discipline in Forts." "They must obey at all times, and under all circumstances, cheerfully and with alacrity," affirmed a Virginia slaveholder. "It greatly impairs the happiness of a negro, to be allowed to cultivate an insubordinate temper. Unconditional submission is the only footing upon which slavery should be placed. It is precisely similar to the attitude of a minor to his parent, or a soldier to his general." A South Carolinian limned a perfect relationship between a slave and his master: "that the slave should know that his master is to govern absolutely, and he is to obey implicitly. That he is never for a moment to exercise either his will or judgment in opposition to a positive order."

The second step was to implant in the bondsmen themselves a consciousness of personal inferiority. They had "to know and keep their places," to "feel the difference between master and slave," to understand that bondage was their natural status. They had to feel that African ancestry tainted them,

1

2

3

4

that their color was a badge of degradation. In the country they were to show respect for even their master's nonslaveholding neighbors; in the towns they were to give way on the streets to the most wretched white man. The line between the races must never be crossed, for familiarity caused slaves to forget their lowly station and to become "impudent."

5   Frederick Douglass[1] explained that a slave might commit the offense of impudence in various ways: "in the tone of an answer; in answering at all; in not answering; in the expression of countenance; in the motion of the head; in the gait, manner and bearing of the slave." Any of these acts, in some subtle way, might indicate the absence of proper subordination. "In a well regulated community," wrote a Texan, "a negro takes off his hat in addressing a white man. . . . Where this is not enforced, we may always look for impudent and rebellious negroes."

6   The third step in the training of slaves was to awe them with a sense of their master's enormous power. The only principle upon which slavery could be maintained, reported a group of Charlestonians, was the "principle of fear." In his defense of slavery James H. Hammond admitted that this, unfortunately, was true but put the responsibility upon the abolitionists. Antislavery agitation had forced masters to strengthen their authority: "We have to rely more and more on the power of fear. . . . We are determined to continue masters, and to do so we have to draw the rein tighter and tighter day by day to be assured that we hold them in complete check." A North Carolina mistress, after subduing a troublesome domestic, realized that it was essential "to make them stand in fear"!

7   In this the slaveholders had considerable success. Frederick Douglass believed that most slaves stood "in awe" of white men; few could free themselves altogether from the notion that their masters were "invested with a sort of sacredness." Olmsted[2] saw a small white girl stop a slave on the road and boldly order him to return to his plantation. The slave fearfully obeyed her command. A visitor in Mississippi claimed that a master, armed only with a whip or cane, could throw himself among a score of bondsmen and cause them to "flee with terror." He accomplished this by the "peculiar tone of authority" with which he spoke. "Fear, awe, and obedience . . . are interwoven into the very nature of the slave."

8   The fourth step was to persuade the bondsmen to take an interest in the master's enterprise and to accept his standards of good conduct. A South Carolina planter explained: "The master should make it his business to show his slaves, that the advancement of his individual interest, is at the same time an advancement of theirs. Once they feel this, it will require but little compulsion to make them act as it becomes them." Though slave-

---

[1] Escaped slave and abolitionist leader, Douglass (c. 1817–1895) later became a government official and ended his career as U.S. ambassador to Haiti. His moving *Narrative of the Life of Frederick Douglass* was published in 1845.

[2] Frederick Law Olmsted (1822–1903), most famous as the designer of New York's Central Park, first became known as the Northern author of books about the South: *A Journey in the Seaboard Slave States* (1856), *A Journey Through Texas* (1857), *A Journey in the Back Country* (1860), and *Journeys and Explorations in the Cotton Kingdom* (1861).

holders induced only a few chattels to respond to this appeal, these few were useful examples for others.

The final step was to impress Negroes with their helplessness, to create   9
in them "a habit of perfect dependence" upon their masters. Many believed it dangerous to train slaves to be skilled artisans in the towns, because they tended to become self-reliant. Some thought it equally dangerous to hire them to factory owners. In the Richmond tobacco factories they were alarmingly independent and "insolent." A Virginian was dismayed to find that his bondsmen, while working at an iron furnace, "got a habit of roaming about and *taking care of themselves.*" Permitting them to hire their own time produced even worse results. "No higher evidence can be furnished of its baneful effects," wrote a Charlestonian, "than the unwillingness it produces in the slave, to return to the regular life and domestic control of the master."

A spirit of independence was less likely to develop among slaves kept on   10
the land, where most of them became accustomed to having their master provide their basic needs, and where they might be taught that they were unfit to look out for themselves. Slaves then directed their energies to the attainment of mere "temporary ease and enjoyment." "Their masters," Olmsted believed, "calculated on it in them—do not wish to cure it—and by constant practice encourage it."

Here, then, was the way to produce the perfect slave: accustom him to   11
rigid discipline, demand from him unconditional submission, impress upon him his innate inferiority, develop in him a paralyzing fear of white men, train him to adopt the master's code of good behavior, and instill in him a sense of complete dependence. This, at least, was the goal.

But the goal was seldom reached. Every master knew that the average   12
slave was only an imperfect copy of the model. He knew that some bondsmen yielded only to superior power—and yielded reluctantly. This complicated his problem of control.

WHAT DID THE WRITER SAY, AND WHAT DID YOU THINK?

1. Summarize the thesis in one sentence.
2. Where does the author state the thesis?
3. A process usually brings about a product of some kind: a car, a cake, a room with a fresh coat of paint. What is the desired product of the process dealt with in this selection? Where is it described?
4. How many steps are in the process?
5. Is the order of the steps important? Could the order be reversed? Could the steps occur simultaneously?
6. Does the author indicate whether the process was generally successful or unsuccessful? In what circumstances was it least successful, and why?
7. Why is so much of this selection quoted material (all quotes were footnoted in the original, by the way)? Did you feel there were too many quotes?
8. What are the sources of most of the quotes? Why?

9. How would a slaveholder define *impudence*?
10. Does the author anywhere indicate his personal feelings?
11. To what extent does this selection help shed light on current black and white tensions?

HOW DID THE WRITER SAY IT?

1. Does the title "To Make Them Stand in Fear" adequately suggest the content of this selection?
2. Each new step is clearly indicated. Identify the phrases that do the job.
3. Which steps get the most attention and which the least? Explain.
4. The author repeats his main points in the conclusion. What else does he do to keep the conclusion from being mere repetition?
5. Vocabulary: *limned, alacrity, chattels, baneful.*

WHAT ABOUT YOUR WRITING?

One of the most impressive characteristics of this selection is that Stampp lets the facts speak for themselves. His thesis is an interpretation or comment on the facts, of course, but essentially he lets the facts speaks for themselves. Writing about one of the ultimate horrors in American history, he does not rant or preach or hurl around angry exclamation points. The facts are there—complete with documentation in the original book—and the horror comes through.

In your own writing, when you have a strong case, let the facts speak for themselves. Don't yell. Don't wail and weep. Your case will be stronger. If a top sergeant or a college bureaucrat or a rich relative is a small-minded tyrant, don't waste time calling names. Give your reader the facts, the persuasive specific details that textbooks on writing keep asking for, and your reader will do the name-calling without any extra encouragement.

The Spider and the Wasp
ALEXANDER PETRUNKEVITCH

> Alexander Petrunkevitch (1875–1964) was one of the world's leading authorities on spiders. Born in Russia, he taught at various American universities. His wide range of skills and interests is suggested by his translations of English (to Russian) and Russian (to English) poetry and by such titles as *Index Catalogue of Spiders of North, Central, and South America* (1911), *Choice and Responsibility* (1947), and *Principles of Classification* (1952).

1   In the feeding and safeguarding of their progeny insects and spiders exhibit some interesting analogies to reasoning and some crass examples of

blind instinct. The case I propose to describe here is that of the tarantula spiders and their archenemy, the digger wasps of the genus Pepsis. It is a classic example of what looks like intelligence pitted against instinct—a strange situation in which the victim, though fully able to defend itself, submits unwittingly to its destruction.

Most tarantulas live in the tropics, but several species occur in the temperate zone and a few are common in the southern U.S. Some varieties are large and have powerful fangs with which they can inflict a deep wound. These formidable looking spiders do not, however, attack man; you can hold one in your hand, if you are gentle, without being bitten. Their bite is dangerous only to insects and small mammals such as mice; for a man it is no worse than a hornet's sting.

Tarantulas customarily live in deep cylindrical burrows, from which they emerge at dusk and into which they retire at dawn. Mature males wander about after dark in search of females and occasionally stray into houses. After mating, the male dies in a few weeks, but a female lives much longer and can mate several years in succession. In a Paris museum is a tropical specimen which is said to have been living in captivity for 25 years.

A fertilized female tarantula lays from 200 to 400 eggs at a time; thus it is possible for a single tarantula to produce several thousand young. She takes no care of them beyond weaving a cocoon of silk to enclose the eggs. After\they hatch, the young walk away, find convenient places in which to dig their burrows and spend the rest of their lives in solitude. The eyesight of tarantulas is poor, being limited to a sensing of change in the intensity of light and to the perception of moving objects. They apparently have little or no sense of hearing, for a hungry tarantula will pay no attention to a loudly chirping cricket placed in its cage unless the ¡nsect happens to touch one of its legs.

But all spiders, and especially hairy ones, have an extremely delicate sense of touch. Laboratory experiments prove that tarantulas can distinguish three types of touch: pressure against the body wall, stroking of the body hair, and riffling of certain very fine hairs on the legs called trichobothria. Pressure against the body, by the finger or the end of a pencil, causes the tarantula to move off slowly for a short distance. The touch excites no defensive response unless the approach is from above where the spider can see the motion, in which case it rises on its hind legs, lifts its front legs, opens its fangs and holds this threatening posture as long as the object continues to move.

The entire body of a tarantula, especially its legs, is thickly clothed with hair. Some of it is short and wooly, some long and stiff. Touching this body hair produces one of two distinct reactions. When the spider is hungry, it responds with an immediate and swift attack. At the touch of a cricket's antennae the tarantula seizes the insect so swiftly that a motion picture taken at the rate of 64 frames per second shows only the result and not the process of capture. But when the spider is not hungry, the stimulation of its hairs merely causes it to shake the touched limb. An insect can walk under its hairy belly unharmed.

"... intelligence pitted against instinct." (Photo: G. D. Dodge and D. R. Thompson)

The trichobothria, very fine hairs growing from disclike membranes on   7
the legs, are sensitive only to air movement. A light breeze makes them
vibrate slowly, without disturbing the common hair. When one blows gently
on the trichobothria, the tarantula reacts with a quick jerk of its four front
legs. If the front and hind legs are stimulated at the same time, the spider
makes a sudden jump. This reaction is quite independent of the state of its
appetite.

These three tactile responses—to pressure on the body wall, to moving   8
of the common hair, and to flexing of the trichobothria—are so different
from one another that there is no possibility of confusing them. They serve
the tarantula adequately for most of its needs and enable it to avoid most
annoyances and dangers. But they fail the spider completely when it meets
its deadly enemy, the digger wasp Pepsis.

These solitary wasps are beautiful and formidable creatures. Most species   9
are either a deep shiny blue all over, or deep blue with rusty wings. The
largest have a wing span of about four inches. They live on nectar. When
excited, they give off a pungent odor—a warning that they are ready to
attack. The sting is much worse than that of a bee or common wasp, and
the pain and swelling last longer. In the adult stage the wasp lives only a
few months. The female produces but a few eggs, one at a time at intervals
of two or three days. For each egg the mother must provide one adult
tarantula, alive but paralyzed. The mother wasp attaches the egg to the
paralyzed spider's abdomen. Upon hatching from the egg, the larva is many
hundreds of times smaller than its living but helpless victim. It eats no other
food and drinks no water. By the time it has finished its single Gargantuan
meal and become ready for wasphood, nothing remains of the tarantula but
its indigestible chitinous skeleton.

The mother wasp goes tarantula-hunting when the egg in her ovary is   10
almost ready to be laid. Flying low over the ground late on a sunny afternoon, the wasp looks for its victim or for the mouth of a tarantula burrow,
a round hole edged by a bit of silk. The sex of the spider makes no difference, but the mother is highly discriminating as to species. Each species of
Pepsis requires a certain species of tarantula, and the wasp will not attack
the wrong species. In a cage with a tarantula which is not its normal prey,
the wasp avoids the spider and is usually killed by it in the night.

Yet when a wasp finds the correct species, it is the other way about. To   11
identify the species the wasp apparently must explore the spider with her
antennae. The tarantula shows an amazing tolerance to this exploration.
The wasp crawls under it and walks over it without evoking any hostile
response. The molestation is so great and so persistent that the tarantula
often rises on all eight legs, as if it were on stilts. It may stand this way for
several minutes. Meanwhile the wasp, having satisfied itself that the victim
is of the right species, moves off a few inches to dig the spider's grave.
Working vigorously with legs and jaws, it excavates a hole 8 to 10 inches
deep with a diameter slightly larger than the spider's girth. Now and again
the wasp pops out of the hole to make sure that the spider is still there.

12   When the grave is finished, the wasp returns to the tarantula to complete her ghastly enterprise. First she feels it all over once more with her antennae. Then her behavior becomes more aggressive. She bends her abdomen, protruding her sting, and searches for the soft membrane at the point where the spider's legs join its body—the only spot where she can penetrate the horny skeleton. From time to time, as the exasperated spider slowly shifts ground, the wasp turns on her back and slides along with the aid of her wings, trying to get under the tarantula for a shot at the vital spot. During all this maneuvering, which can last for several minutes, the tarantula makes no move to save itself. Finally the wasp corners it against some obstruction and grasps one of its legs in her powerful jaws. Now at last the harassed spider tries a desperate but vain defense. The two contestants roll over and over on the ground. It is a terrifying sight and the outcome is always the same. The wasp finally manages to thrust her sting into the soft spot and holds it there for a few seconds while she pumps in the poison. Almost immediately the tarantula falls paralyzed on its back. Its legs stop twitching, its heart stops beating. Yet it is not dead, as is shown by the fact that if taken from the wasp it can be restored to some sensitivity by being kept in a moist chamber for several months.

13   After paralyzing the tarantula, the wasp cleans herself by dragging her body along the ground and rubbing her feet, sucks the drop of blood oozing from the wound in the spider's abdomen, then grabs a leg of the flabby, helpless animal in her jaws and drags it down to the bottom of the grave. She stays there for many minutes, sometimes for several hours, and what she does all that time in the dark we do not know. Eventually she lays her egg and attaches it to the side of the spider's abdomen with a sticky secretion. Then she emerges, fills the grave with soil carried bit by bit in her jaws, and finally tramples the ground all around to hide any trace of the grave from prowlers. Then she flies away, leaving her descendant safely started in life.

14   In all this the behavior of the wasp evidently is qualitatively different from that of the spider. The wasp acts like an intelligent animal. This is not to say that instinct plays no part or that she reasons as man does. But her actions are to the point; they are not automatic and can be modified to fit the situation. We do not know for certain how she identifies the tarantula—probably it is by some olfactory or chemo-tactile sense—but she does it purposefully and does not blindly tackle a wrong species.

15   On the other hand, the tarantula's behavior shows only confusion. Evidently the wasp's pawing gives it no pleasure, for it tries to move away. That the wasp is not simulating sexual stimulation is certain, because male and female tarantulas react in the same way to its advances. That the spider is not anesthetized by some odorless secretion is easily shown by blowing lightly at the tarantula and making it jump suddenly. What, then, makes the tarantula behave as stupidly as it does?

16   No clear, simple answer is available. Possibly the stimulation by the wasp's antennae is masked by a heavier pressure on the spider's body, so

that it reacts as when prodded by a pencil. But the explanation may be much more complex. Initiative in attack is not in the nature of tarantulas; most species fight only when cornered so that escape is impossible. Their inherited patterns of behavior apparently prompt them to avoid problems rather than attack them. For example, spiders always weave their webs in three dimensions, and when a spider finds that there is insufficient space to attach certain threads in the third dimension, it leaves the place and seeks another, instead of finishing the web in a single plane. This urge to escape seems to arise under all circumstances, in all phases of life, and to take the place of reasoning. For a spider to change the pattern of its web is as impossible as for an inexperienced man to build a bridge across a chasm obstructing his way.

In a way the instinctive urge to escape is not only easier but often more   17 efficient than reasoning. The tarantula does exactly what is most efficient in all cases except in an encounter with a ruthless and determined attacker dependent for the existence of her own species on killing as many tarantulas as she can lay eggs. Perhaps in this case the spider follows its usual pattern of trying to escape, instead of seizing and killing the wasp, because it is not aware of its danger. In any case, the survival of the tarantula species as a whole is protected by the fact that the spider is much more fertile than the wasp.

WHAT DID THE WRITER SAY, AND WHAT DID YOU THINK?

1. A primary thesis tells why the process is worth discussing. What is the thesis, and where does it appear?
2. A secondary thesis tries to explain why the process happens as it does. What is the thesis, and where does it appear?
3. Does the author acknowledge alternate explanations?
4. What makes the behavior of the spider so puzzling?
5. Where does the author suggest his own emotional reaction to the process?
6. Is the reader meant to take sides, to root for the spider or wasp?
7. People who think they are totally indifferent to nature and science often become deeply involved in "The Spider and the Wasp." Can you suggest why?
8. Can you think of certain types of human beings whose behavior corresponds to the spider's? The wasp's?

HOW DID THE WRITER SAY IT?

1. Who is the intended audience for this selection?
2. The description of the process does not begin until paragraph 10, though paragraph 9 presents a summary of the process. What has the author been doing until then?
3. Are all obscure scientific terms defined?
4. Consult the table of contents. What patterns of writing are in this selection besides *process*?

5. Does the author gather the many separate steps into groups? If so, into how many groups?
6. "The mother wasp goes tarantula-hunting . . ." Does this phrase seem too informal, almost slangy, for a scientific article? Are there other unusually informal words or phrases? Are they justified?
7. Vocabulary: *progeny, archenemy, unwittingly, tactile, nectar, pungent, chitinous, girth, secretion, olfactory, simulating.*

WHAT ABOUT YOUR WRITING?

Nobody reads "The Spider and the Wasp" as an interesting little essay on the strange behavior of some strange little creatures. Most readers respond because the essay reaches them at a deep emotional level, because it appeals dramatically to some permanent human concerns: in this case, life and death, care of "progeny," survival of the fittest, and so on.

You may have read with an amused smile the note at the start of this selection that Petrunkevitch was "one of the world's leading authorities on spiders." But don't you have an esoteric little specialty that you can relate to universal human concerns? If you're an enthusiastic player of pinball games, you have a beautiful piece on man versus machine that's waiting to be written. If you own tropical fish and have seen adult fish eating their own young, you have the potential for a powerful cruelty-of-nature essay that takes a different approach from Petrunkevitch's. In a sense, you're a specialist on anything that has ever hit you hard. If you ever waited week after week as a child for a "free offer" after you sent in a box top, aren't you "one of the world's leading authorities" on what waiting can do to the soul? Don't shy off from specialties because you're afraid that people won't be interested. Show how the specialty is related to a universal issue, and make them interested.

Chapter 4

COMPARISON AND CONTRAST

A comparison-and-contrast paper is one of the most common kinds of writing assignments because it reflects one of the most common kinds of thinking, the kind of thinking on which most practical decisions are probably based. Comparison and contrast often dominates thought in choosing a college, a major field, a career, a job. We compare and contrast doctors and dentists; husbands and wives (actual and potential) and children; homes, neighborhoods, and cities; breakfast foods, pizza joints, and brands of soda pop. The comparison-and-contrast assignment on an essay exam or composition in an English class is not a remote intellectual exercise but a natural extension of the role played by comparison and contrast in human life.

Just as comparison-and-contrast thinking aims at a decision or judgment—the school I attend, the job offer I accept, the horse I bet on, the toothpaste I buy—so comparison-and-contrast writing must add up to something. Without a thesis, comparison-and-contrast writing is a pointless game in a never-never land where the only activity people engage in is devising elaborate lists of "similarities and differences" or "advantages and disadvantages." The comparison-and-contrast paper must commit itself firmly to the persuasive principle:

The Ford Pinto is a better buy than the Volkswagen Rabbit.

Late Dickens novels express a far more pessimistic view of life than early Dickens novels.

Boston is a more exciting city than San Francisco.

The community college can sometimes offer a number of benefits unknown at the four-year college.

McDonald's service is superior to Burger King's.

Sexual discrimination is harder to fight against than racial discrimination.

There is no logical way of determining whether Babe Ruth or Henry Aaron was the better home-run hitter.

Three quick pointers:

1. As a matter of common sense and convenience, stick to two units for comparison and contrast. No regulation prohibits three or more units, but two are far easier to manage.

2. Avoid vague, what-else-is-new theses like "There are many similarities between Smith and Jones." The same statement could be made of any two people and is therefore worthless.

3. Don't feel that you need to pay equal attention to comparisons and contrasts. In practice, most papers give much greater weight to similarities (comparisons) *or* to differences (contrasts). Some papers may deal entirely with one or the other; their whole point may be that two seemingly similar items are, in fact, very different or that two seemingly different items are very similar. Check with your instructor whether an all-contrast or all-comparison paper is acceptable. In any event, theses like "Despite obvious differences, drug addiction and alcoholism present strikingly similar psychological problems" are quite common and quite workable. In a paper with that thesis, the "obvious differences" could be taken care of in the introduction, and the rest of the paper would deal solely with the similarities.

Patterns

Comparison-and-contrast papers can use one of two patterns, both highly structured. A long paper can sometimes shift patterns from one distinct division of the paper to another, but most papers should stick to one pattern.

Pattern A

In the first pattern, the writer discusses one unit in its entirety before going on to the other.

Thesis statement: Boston is a more exciting city than San Francisco.

    I. Boston
       A. Cultural opportunities
       B. Recreational opportunities
       C. Sense of history
       D. Physical beauty
    II. San Francisco
       A. Cultural opportunities
       B. Recreational opportunities
       C. Sense of history
       D. Physical beauty

Thesis statement: The community college can sometimes offer a number of benefits unknown at the four-year college.

  I. Community college
    A. Cost
    B. Convenience
    C. Instructors
    D. Training for a vocation
 II. Four-year college
    A. Cost
    B. Convenience
    C. Instructors
    D. Lack of training for a vocation

Notice that in these sample outlines we could easily reverse the order of the major topics. Rather than concluding with negative comments about San Francisco or four-year colleges, some writers may want to stress the positive by ending with praise of Boston or community colleges. Which comes first is up to the writer.

The danger built into Pattern A is that the writer can end with two separate essays instead of one unified comparison-and-contrast essay. To insure unity, take note of the following guidelines:

Each subtopic in Part I must also be discussed in Part II. Bring up Boston's cultural opportunities only if you have something to say about San Francisco's cultural opportunities or lack of them. Boston's cultural opportunities must be compared with or contrasted to something; in comparison-and-contrast writing, they are not significant in themselves.

Subtopics should be discussed in the same order in both parts. If cost and convenience are the first two subtopics you consider for community colleges, they should be the first two subtopics when you turn to four-year colleges.

Paragraphing should be similar in both parts. A paper with only one or two sentences for each subtopic under "Boston" will probably gather the subtopics together into one good-sized "Boston" paragraph. A paper with a lot to say on each Boston subtopic will probably give a separate paragraph to each. Whatever paragraph arrangement is appropriate for Boston should usually be maintained for San Francisco.

Subtopics in Part II should generally include reminders of the point made about the same subtopic in Part I. Since in Pattern A you consider the first unit (Boston, community colleges) before moving on to the second one (San Francisco, four-year colleges), your readers may experience some memory lapses by the time they finally reach Part II. Their memories need refreshing. Above all, they should not be allowed to forget that they are reading a single comparison-and-contrast paper rather than two separate essays. In the paragraph outlines that follow, note the *italicized* reminders:

¶1—Presentation of thesis: Boston is a more exciting city than San Francisco.

Start of ¶2—Boston's cultural opportunities are unrivaled anywhere in the country . . .

Start of ¶3—Recreational opportunities in Boston are every bit as impressive . . .

Start of ¶4—The sense of a rich, still vital past adds to the excitement of Boston . . .

Start of ¶5—Finally, Boston is a surprising delight to the eye . . .

Start of ¶6—When we look at San Francisco, we find a cultural scene that, *in sharp contrast to Boston's* . . .

Start of ¶7—San Francisco's recreational opportunities, though plentiful, also *suffer when placed against the something-for-everyone of Boston* . . .

Start of ¶8—The sense of a living history in San Francisco *seems bland and shallow when we think of Boston* . . .

Start of ¶9—Even in its overwhelming physical beauty, San Francisco *fails to surpass the breathtaking charm of Boston* . . .

¶1—Presentation of thesis: The community college can sometimes offer a number of benefits unknown at the four-year college.

Start of ¶2—First, community colleges are cheap . . .

Start of ¶3—Second, they are incredibly convenient . . .

Start of ¶4—Third, most instructors are likely to be extremely skillful and friendly . . .

Start of ¶5—Last, community colleges offer the practical education most students want . . .

Start of ¶6—At many four-year colleges, the cost of attending is so *astronomically greater than at community colleges* that . . .

Start of ¶7—*Contrasting dramatically to the convenience of a community college,* a four-year college . . .

Start of ¶8—*Instead of meeting competent and concerned teachers,* the beginning student at a four-year college will more probably . . .

Start of ¶9—Finally, many four-year colleges are still fighting against *the vocational trends in education that the community colleges have welcomed* . . .

Pattern B

Pattern B can be thought of as a seesaw. It swings back and forth between its two subjects.

Thesis statement: Boston is a more exciting city than San Francisco.

I. Cultural opportunities
   A. Boston
   B. San Francisco
II. Recreational opportunities
   A. Boston
   B. San Francisco
III. Sense of history
   A. Boston
   B. San Francisco
IV. Physical beauty
   A. Boston
   B. San Francisco

Thesis statement: The community college can sometimes offer a number of benefits unknown at the four-year college.

I. Cost
   A. Community college
   B. Four-year college
II. Convenience
   A. Community college
   B. Four-year college
III. Instructors
   A. Community college
   B. Four-year college
IV. Training for a vocation
   A. Community college
   B. Four-year college

Most of the principles applicable to Pattern A still hold. You still say something about both subjects for each issue considered; you still use a consistent order (observe how "Boston" and "Community college" always come first); you still make a consistent arrangement of paragraphs. The major difference is that reminders are not nearly as important as in Pattern A. Instead of getting to San Francisco's cultural opportunities one or two pages after dealing with Boston's cultural opportunities, you'll be getting to them in the very next sentences.

Which Pattern?

Both patterns enable you to write what you want. Both patterns cover the same territory, though in different order. In many cases, you can probably do a good job with either pattern; so your decision may be more a matter of taste than anything else. It is possible, however, to make some distinctions between patterns, and for whatever the distinctions are worth, here are a couple to keep in mind:

Pattern A tends to work better for short papers; Pattern B, for long papers. In short papers, Pattern B can sometimes bounce back and forth between subjects too frequently to let anything settle in the reader's mind. In long papers, Pattern A can put too much of a burden on the reader's memory: the reader should not have to wonder on page 7 what it was that you said on page 2, and you may be forced to spend a disproportionate amount of time and words on reminders.

Pattern A tends to work better with few subtopics; Pattern B, with many. With only a few subtopics, the reader should have no difficulty keeping track of them. You can safely make your four points about Boston and then go on to San Francisco. The seesaw, back-and-forth movement of Pattern B could be somewhat distracting. With many subtopics, Pattern B is probably safest; if you had a dozen or more elements to consider about Boston and San Francisco, for example, discussing each city one after the other within each element would make the comparison-and-contrast relationship immediately clear. Pattern A could again put a fierce strain on the reader's memory and patience.

WRITING SUGGESTIONS FOR COMPARISON-AND-CONTRAST THEMES

Comparison-and-contrast writing offers almost endless variations in choice of subject. The subjects listed here may be less valuable for themselves than for bringing other subjects to your mind. In any event, don't forget the necessity for a thesis and for sticking to one of the two patterns of organization.

1. Two members of your family.
2. Life in a city versus life in a suburb; life in two cities or two suburbs.
3. Two commercial products: razor blades, hair sprays, tires, breakfast foods.
4. Two department stores or discount stores.
5. Contrasting fates of two married couples.
6. Two athletes: Bill Walton and Wilt Chamberlain; Jim Brown and O. J. Simpson; Chris Evert and Virginia Wade; and so on.
7. Two clergymen or two churches.
8. Two movies or television programs (should be of same basic type: westerns, horror movies, situation comedies).
9. Two politicians.
10. Two musicians or singers.
11. Conflicting viewpoints on controversial subjects: capital punishment, abortions, and so on.
12. Two character traits or emotions that can be confused: courage and recklessness, love and infatuation.
13. Two high schools or two colleges; high school versus college.
14. Two teachers with contrasting educational philosophies.
15. Dogs versus cats.
16. Attitude you had as a child versus attitude you have now toward parents, religion, sex, and so on.

17. Contrast between advertising claims and reality.
18. Two "dates."
19. Two tourist attractions.
20. Two employers.

Discrimination

ERMA BOMBECK

Erma Bombeck's lighthearted reflections on the burdens of family life appear in
hundreds of newspapers. Some of her writing has been collected in *At Wit's End*
(1967), *"Just Wait Till You Have Children of Your Own!"* (1971), *I Lost Everything
in the Post-Natal Depression* (1973), *The Grass Is Always Greener over the Septic
Tank* (1976), and *If Life Is a Bowl of Cherries—What Am I Doing in the Pits?* (1978).

As a woman who thinks a needle is something you take out splinters with 1
and step on in your bare feet, I have always been annoyed with the in-
equality of alterations.

Why is it when a man buys a suit, his alterations come free, but when a 2
woman buys an outfit of equal or more value, she pays extra?

I was with my husband a few years ago when he bought a $49.95 suit 3
(with a vest, two contrasting pairs of slacks, a matching tam, and a set of
dishes). Not only was it a cheap suit (the label said, "Made in Occupied
Guadalcanal:[1] Fashion Capital of the World") but it hung on him like an
ugly blind date.

"I don't like the way it breaks across the shoulders," he said, twisting 4
before his three-way mirror. "And the sleeves—I like them short enough
to count my fingers. Maybe you can reset them."

"No problem," smiled the salesman. 5

"There's too much slack in the seat and the waistband seems a little loose 6
. . . maybe a tuck or two."

"Of course," grinned the salesman. "Let me summon a tailor." 7

The tailor spent thirty-five minutes chalking up my husband's anatomy. 8
The suit looked like a steer being divided for two freezers—all at no charge.

The other day I tried on a dress of comparable value. 9

"It bags a little in front," I said, looking sideways into the mirror. 10

"There are operations to correct that, honey," she yawned. "Or we'll 11
alter it for three dollars."

"And the sleeves. They hang so long." 12

"That'll be two-fifty or you can roll 'em up and keep your elbows bent." 13

[1] Island in the Pacific. Scene of major battle in World War II.

14   "I don't know," I pondered. "Maybe a knit isn't for me. It clings so."

15   "Tell you what," she said, "if you want to save two dollars, just block it yourself by stretching it over a chair for a couple of days . . . or a sofa depending on how loose you want it."

16   "How much to shorten it?"

17   "Four dollars," she said, "but it'll be worth it. This dress will look like it's been made for you. Here, let me help you with the zipper."

18   "How much for helping me with my zipper?" I chided.

19   "I'll throw it in," she said. "I feel sorry for you."

WHAT DID THE WRITER SAY, AND WHAT DID YOU THINK?

1. Are any comparisons and contrasts made besides the one of charge versus no charge?
2. Does the writer expect the situation to change?
3. Consider the writer's attitude. Is she amused, angry, resigned, or what?
4. Is it true that almost all alterations on men's clothing are free?
5. Does the title adequately suggest the content of the article?

HOW DID THE WRITER SAY IT?

1. The author presents a contrast by dramatizing two scenes instead of using more conventional techniques. Why is this method so successful here? In what kinds of writing would it be risky?
2. The author has fun with wisecracks: "As a woman who thinks a needle is something you take out splinters with . . . ," "Made in Occupied Guadalcanal," and so on. Are the wisecracks purely for laughs, or do they lend support to the thesis?
3. "The other day I tried on a dress of comparable value" is a transition between the two parts of the body of this article. What would be the effect of omitting "of comparable value"?
4 Why is no conclusion necessary?
5. Does the author use Pattern A or Pattern B?

WHAT ABOUT YOUR WRITING?

One of the superstitions about writing beloved by fussbudgets is that criticism must be constructive. "Don't tear down without building up." "If you don't have something nice to say, don't say anything at all." As writing superstitions go, it's way up there with the ones about never ending a sentence with a preposition and never beginning a sentence with *but* or *and*. (See p. 110 for comments on *and*.)

Constructive criticism has its place, of course, and it's an important place. Pointing out a stupidity or evil, for example, and then telling people how to eliminate it is fine—if you know how. But nothing is wrong with just pointing out the evil, either, especially when nobody else has done it or done it well.

Erma Bombeck has no plan for changing the discrimination in altering clothing. Something irritates her, and she wants to hold forth. Why not? Pet gripes can be rich sources of material for your own writing, too. And don't feel threatened by goody-goody calls for constructive criticism.

Witchdoctors and the Universality of Healing

E. FULLER TORREY

E. Fuller Torrey, M.D., was trained in psychiatry at Stanford University and is now associated with St. Elizabeth's Hospital, Washington. The reading selection serves as a model for an "all-comparison" paper. The author quickly disposes of a few obvious contrasts in the second paragraph and then devotes all his energies to showing the surprising similarities between two groups of people who are normally considered opposites.

Witchdoctors and psychiatrists perform essentially the same function in   1
their respective cultures. They are both therapists; both treat patients, using similar techniques; and both get similar results. Recognition of this should not downgrade psychiatrists—rather it should upgrade witchdoctors.

The term "witchdoctor" is Western in origin, imposed on healers of the   2
Third World[1] by 18th and 19th century explorers. The world was simpler then, and the newly discovered cultures were quickly assigned their proper status in the Order of Things. We were white, they were black. We were civilized, they were primitive. We were Christian, they were pagan. We used science, they used magic. We had doctors, they had witchdoctors.

American psychiatrists have much to learn from therapists in other cul-   3
tures. My own experience observing and working with them includes two years in Ethiopia and briefer periods in Sarawak, Bali, Hong Kong, Colombia, and with Alaskan Indians, Puerto Ricans, and Mexican-Americans in this country. What I learned from these doctor-healers was that I, as a psychiatrist, was using the same mechanisms for curing my patients as they were—and, not surprisingly, I was getting about the same results. The mechanisms can be classified under four categories.

The first is the naming process. A psychiatrist or witchdoctor can work   4
magic by telling a patient what is wrong with him. It conveys to the patient

From *The Mind Game: Witchdoctors and Psychiatrists* by E. Fuller Torrey, M.D. Published by Emerson Hall, 1972. Copyright © 1972 by E. Fuller Torrey. Reprinted by permission of the author.

[1] Current term referring to nations, often "emerging" or "developing," unaligned with the United States or the Soviet Union.

that someone—usually a man of considerable status—understands. And since his problem can be understood, then, implicitly, it can be cured. A psychiatrist who tells an illiterate African that his phobia is related to a fear of failure, or a witchdoctor who tells an American tourist that his phobia is related to possession by an ancestral spirit, will be met by equally blank stares. And as therapists they will be equally ineffective. This is a major reason for the failure of most attempts at cross-cultural psychotherapy. Since a shared world-view is necessary for the naming process to be effective, then it is reasonable to expect that the best therapist–patient relationships will be those where both come from the same culture or subculture. The implications for our mental health programs are obvious.

5   The second healing component used by therapists everywhere is their personality characteristics. An increasing amount of research shows that certain personal qualities of the therapist—accurate empathy, nonpossessive warmth, genuineness—are of crucial importance in producing effective psychotherapy. Clearly, more studies are needed in this area, but if they substantiate the emerging trend, then radical changes in the selection of therapists will be in order. Rather than selecting therapists because they can memorize facts and achieve high grades, we should be selecting them on the basis of their personality. Therapists in other cultures are selected more often for their personality characteristics; the fact that they have not studied biochemistry is not considered important.

6   The third component of the healing process that appears to be universal is the patients' expectations. Healers all over the world use many ways to raise the expectations of their patients. The first way is the trip itself to the healer. It is a common observation that the farther a person goes to be healed, the greater are the chances that he will be healed. This is called the pilgrimage. Thus, sick people in Topeka go to the Leahy Clinic in Boston. The resulting therapeutic effects of the trip are exactly the same as have been operating for centuries at Delphi or Lourdes.[2] The next way to raise patients' expectations is the building used for the healing. The more impressive it is, the greater will be the patients' expectations. This has been called the edifice complex. Therapists in different cultures use certain paraphernalia to increase patient expectations. In Western cultures nonpsychiatric healers have their stethoscope and psychotherapists are supposed to have their couch. Therapists in other cultures have their counterpart trademark, often a special drum, mask or amulet. Another aspect of patients' expectations rests upon the therapist's training. Some sort of training program is found for healers in almost all cultures. Blackfoot Indians, for instance, had to complete a seven-year period of training in order to qualify as medicine men.

7   Finally, the same techniques of therapy are used by healers all over the world. Let me provide a few examples: Drugs are one of the techniques of

---

[2] In Ancient Greece, the oracle at Delphi counseled, cured, and prophesied. Lourdes, in southwestern France, is the site of a religious shrine to which thousands of pilgrims come every year hoping for miraculous cures.

Western therapy of which we are most proud. However, drugs are used by healers in other cultures as well. Rauwulfia root, for example, which was introduced into Western psychiatry in the 1950s as reserpine, a major tranquilizer, has been used in India for centuries as a tranquilizer, and has also been in wide use in West Africa for many years. Another example is shock therapy. When electric shock therapy was introduced by Cerletti in the 1930s, he was not aware that it had been used in some cultures for up to 4000 years. The technique of applying electric eels to the head of the patient is referred to in the writings of Aristotle, Pliny, and Plutarch.[3]

What kind of results do therapists in other cultures—witchdoctors— achieve? A Canadian psychiatrist, Dr. Raymond Prince, spent 17 months studying 46 Nigerian witchdoctors, and judged that the therapeutic results were about equal to those obtained in North American clinics and hospitals.   8

It would appear, then, that psychiatrists have much to learn from witchdoctors. We can see the components of our own therapy system in relief. We can learn why we are effective—or not effective. And we can learn to be less ethnocentric and arrogant about our own therapy and more tolerant of others. If we can learn all this from witchdoctors, then we will have learned much.   9

WHAT DID THE WRITER SAY, AND WHAT DID YOU THINK?

1. According to the author, what is the main lesson that psychiatrists can learn from witchdoctors?
2. Did the reading selection come through to you as the author hoped it would—upgrading witchdoctors rather than downgrading psychiatrists?
3. About which similarity is the author most persuasive? Were any of the similarities supported by dubious or weak evidence?
4. Can you think of professions in addition to medicine that rely heavily on the "edifice complex" and assorted "paraphernalia"?
5. How does it strike you that the author would feel about faith healing?
6. What are the obvious implications for our mental health programs to which the author refers in his discussion of "the naming process" in paragraph 4?

HOW DID THE WRITER SAY IT?

1. Does the essay follow Pattern A or Pattern B?
2. How can we tell that the author is being sarcastic in his brief discussion of contrasts in paragraph 2?
3. In paragraph 6, what does "edifice complex" mean? What common psychiatric term does it sound like?
4. Mark the topic sentence in each paragraph. In what part of the paragraphs do the topic sentences always appear? Do any paragraphs not have topic sentences?

[3] Respectively, a great philosopher, a scientist, and a famous biographer of the ancient world.

5. The author clearly thinks that "witchdoctor" is a foolish term. Can you think of a better term? Does the author himself have any suggestions?
6. Is the conclusion a simple summary, or does it add something?
7. Vocabulary: *implicitly, phobia, empathy, substantiate, edifice, paraphernalia, counterpart, amulet, ethnocentric.*

WHAT ABOUT YOUR WRITING?

In paragraph 4, Torrey writes, "A psychiatrist or witchdoctor can work magic by telling a patient what is wrong with him." Nothing is technically incorrect in this sentence. If it were written today, however, most American publishers would strongly urge the author to rewrite it—and some publishers would insist. The patient could just as easily be a woman as a man, after all. In fact, the sex of the patient is totally irrelevant to the meaning of the sentence. Isn't the use of *him* both illogical and unfair? The usage is traditional and perfectly grammatical, of course, but isn't there a way of being correct without the risk of offending some readers?

In recent years, many feminists have charged that our language echoes the sexual discrimination of society as a whole. The ease with which jokes, sometimes good ones, can be manufactured at the expense of the feminist movement probably tends to make it too easy to shrug off legitimate complaints. One may feel entitled to laugh at the insanely enlightened captain of a sinking ship who yells "Person the lifeboats" instead of "Man the lifeboats." One should be more hesitant, however, about laughing at the female employee of the post office who has spent an exhausting day trudging through the snow and who resents being known as a "mailman" instead of a "mail carrier." In any event, feminists have singled out for special attack the use of *he, his, him,* and *himself* when sex is unknown, mixed, or immaterial.

Whatever your personal preferences may be, most publishers of books, magazines, and newspapers have responded positively to the complaints. The *he, his, him, himself* usage is now disappearing from print, and the trend is virtually certain to continue. A sentence like *A driver needs to know how his car works* is already beginning to sound as quaint and outdated to some people as words like *icebox* and *Victrola.*

The best and easiest way to solve the *he* problem without damaging your style is to rephrase into plural forms whenever possible:

ORIGINAL	REPHRASED
A psychiatrist or witchdoctor can work magic by telling a patient what is wrong with him.	A psychiatrist or witchdoctor can work magic by telling patients what is wrong with them.
A good student turns in his assignments on time.	Good students turn in their assignments on time.
Nobody wants his friends to take him for granted.	People do not want their friends to take them for granted.
Everyone at the banquet rose from his seat to give the senator an ovation.	All the guests at the banquet rose from their seats to give the senator an ovation.

(*Note: Nobody* and *everyone,* in the original sentences, always take a singular verb and pronoun. Use of *they, them, their* in those sentences would be flatly incorrect.)

The word *one* can also be helpful at times, though it often creates an excessively formal tone. The plural approach is generally more satisfactory:

ORIGINAL

A person must concentrate on his own happiness first.

REPHRASED

One must concentrate on one's own happiness first.

ORIGINAL

Anybody can break his bad habits if he only tries.

REPHRASED

One can break one's bad habits if one only tries.

If you find yourself, for some reason, locked into a singular form, more substantial revisions may be necessary:

ORIGINAL

The reader will need to use all his attention to understand the plot.

REPHRASED

The reader will need to be extremely attentive to understand the plot.

ORIGINAL

The best policy for someone who has been arrested is to keep his mouth shut.

REPHRASED

The best policy for someone who has been arrested is to say as little as possible.

Now for two warnings. First, do what you can to avoid habitual reliance on the phrases *he or she, his or hers, him or her, himself or herself.* These expressions belong more to legal contracts than to ordinary writing, and when they have been used repeatedly, the result is often absurd.

POOR

A writer always should remember that he or she is writing for his or her audience, not just for himself or herself.

BETTER

Writers always should remember that they are writing for their audience, not just for themselves.

Second, avoid trendy, self-conscious inventions like *s/he* or *he/she.* Many readers, and most English teachers, will view them as strained efforts to show off the writer's devotion to equal rights. The devotion may deserve praise, but straining and showing off have almost never made for good writing.

from Message to the Grass Roots

MALCOLM X

Youthful criminal activities brought Malcolm X (1925–1965), born Malcolm Little, to prison on a burglary charge. After his release, he became associated with the Black Muslims, established himself as a dynamic speaker, and eventually was appointed to lead an important mosque in New York City. Breaking with the Black Muslims in 1964, he founded the Muslim Mosque, Inc. He was assassinated in 1965. Frequently at odds with civil rights leaders because of his contempt for nonviolent strategies and his advocacy of black nationalism, Malcolm X gave memorable expression to black resentments and aspirations. *The Autobiography of Malcolm X* (1965), written with Alex Haley, is still much read and much admired.

The following brief excerpt from a Malcolm X speech serves as a model for "all-contrast" writing.

1   There were two kinds of slaves, the house Negro and the field Negro. The house Negroes—they lived in the house with master, they dressed pretty good, they ate good because they ate his food—what he left. They lived in the attic or the basement, but still they lived near the master; and they loved the master more than the master loved himself. They would give their life to save the master's house—quicker than the master would. If the master said, "We got a good house here," the house Negro would say, "Yeah, we got a good house here." Whenever the master said "we," he said "we." That's how you can tell a house Negro.

2   If the master's house caught on fire, the house Negro would fight harder to put the blaze out than the master would. If the master got sick, the house Negro would say, "What's the matter, boss, *we* sick?" *We* sick! He identified himself with his master, more than his master identified with himself. And if you came to the house Negro and said, "Let's run away, let's escape, let's separate," the house Negro would look at you and say, "Man, you crazy. What you mean, separate? Where is there a better house than this? Where can I wear better clothes than this? Where can I eat better food than this?" That was that house Negro. In those days he was called a "house nigger." And that's what we call them today, because we've still got some house niggers running around here.

3   This modern house Negro loves his master. He wants to live near him. He'll pay three times as much as the house is worth just to live near his master, and then brag about "I'm the only Negro out here." "I'm the only one on my job." "I'm the only one in this school." You're nothing but a house Negro. And if someone comes to you right now and says, "Let's separate," you say the same thing that the house Negro said on the plantation. "What you mean, separate? From America, this good white man? Where you going to get a better job than you get here?" I mean, this is what you say. "I ain't left nothing in Africa," that's what you say. Why, you left your mind in Africa.

4   On that same plantation, there was the field Negro. The field Negroes— those were the masses. There were always more Negroes in the field than there were Negroes in the house. The Negro in the field caught hell. He ate leftovers. In the house they ate high up on the hog. The Negro in the field didn't get anything but what was left of the insides of the hog. They call it "chitt'lings" nowadays. In those days they called them what they were—guts. That's what you were—gut-eaters. And some of you are still gut-eaters.

5   The field Negro was beaten from morning to night; he lived in a shack, in a hut; he wore old, castoff clothes. He hated his master. I say he hated his master. He was intelligent. That house Negro loved his master, but that field Negro—remember, they were in the majority, and they hated the master. When the house caught on fire, he didn't try to put it out; that field Negro prayed for a wind, for a breeze. When the master got sick, the field Negro prayed that he'd die. If someone came to the field Negro and said,

"Let's separate, let's run," he didn't say "Where we going?" He'd say, "Any place is better than here." You've got field Negroes in America today. I'm a field Negro. The masses are the field Negroes. When they see this man's house on fire, you don't hear the little Negroes talking about *"our* government is in trouble." They say, *"The* government is in trouble." Imagine a Negro: *"Our* government"! I even heard one say *"our* astronauts." They won't even let him near the plant—and *"our* astronauts"! *"Our* Navy"—that's a Negro that is out of his mind, a Negro that is out of his mind.

Just as the slavemaster of that day used Tom, the house Negro, to keep   6 the field Negroes in check, the same old slavemaster today has Negroes who are nothing but modern Uncle Toms, twentieth-century Uncle Toms, to keep you and me in check, to keep us under control, keep us passive and peaceful and nonviolent. That's Tom making you nonviolent. It's like when you go to the dentist, and the man's going to take your tooth. You're going to fight him when he starts pulling. So he squirts some stuff in your jaw called novocaine, to make you think they're not doing anything to you. So you sit there and because you've got all of that novocaine in your jaw, you suffer—peacefully. Blood running all down your jaw, and you don't know what's happening. Because someone has taught you to suffer—peacefully.

WHAT DID THE WRITER SAY, AND WHAT DID YOU THINK?

1. The reading selection really has a two-level thesis, one about house and field Negroes, the other about contemporary times. Write a one-sentence version of each thesis.
2. Early in paragraph 5, the reference to a house on fire applies to an actual physical fire. Later in the same paragraph, the meaning of *fire* has expanded. What is the change in meaning?
3. Do you feel that the author relies too much on stereotyping great numbers of differing individuals? (Did *all* house Negroes really love their masters, for example?) Does the stereotyping seriously weaken the author's argument?
4. Where does the author appear to scold or even insult his audience? Would the audience's reaction be likely to interfere with its acceptance of the author's message?

HOW DID THE WRITER SAY IT?

1. Does the author use Pattern A or Pattern B?
2. Does the author appear to be addressing himself to a racially mixed audience or an all-black audience? How can you tell?
3. Where does the author use repetition to intensify the emotional power of the speech?
4. It is relatively rare to see any substantial amount of dialogue except in a short story or nonfiction narrative. What purpose is served by using so much dialogue in this speech?

WHAT ABOUT <u>YOUR</u> WRITING?

For all the harm done by teachers who make up rules like "Never begin a sentence with *and*" (see p. 110) or "Never use *you*" (see pp. 147–148), far greater harm is probably done by teachers who make up the silliest rule of all: "There are no rules." These teachers tend to fling around words like "creativity," "sensitivity," "feelings," and either directly or indirectly let their students believe that the serious discussion of the principles of style and organization is some sort of oppressive conspiracy directed by elderly neurotics, all of whom were educated before the Civil War. "Don't let them keep you down." "Let it all hang out." "Be yourself." You know the slogans. You'll do yourself a favor if you refuse to fall for them.

You'll have to look long and hard to find an author following all the rules of comparison-and-contrast writing more meticulously than Malcolm X in the excerpt from "Message to the Grass Roots." First he discusses the house Negro, then the field Negro. Every specific action and characteristic of the house Negro is carefully contrasted with a specific action and characteristic of the field Negro. The reading selection follows textbook patterns from start to finish, and follows them rigorously. Now ask yourself whether the rules kept the writer down or prevented him from hanging out anything that he wanted to hang out. Ask yourself if the rules kept him from expressing his feelings with all the passion of which he was capable. Ask if he was being anyone other than himself. Finally, ask if those wicked, nit-picking rules hindered him or helped him in communicating his ideas and emotions with maximum force.

The lesson for your own writing is simple. A reasonable rule puts experience and common sense into words. It can save you weeks, months, or years in discovering the best approach to a particular writing task. Far from interfering with creativity and emotion and all the other vital juices of good writing, a reasonable rule gives creativity a head start. As a contemporary author once observed, when most people let it all hang out, "it just dangles there." Is the baseball coach who orders this year's rookies to keep their eyes on the ball depriving them of their freedom to strike out or giving them, through knowledge, the freedom to become the players they want to be? Break any rule without regret, of course, when it truly does stifle creative energies—but if it's a good rule, it won't. If it's a good rule, it will help you become a better writer.

The Lowest Animal

MARK TWAIN

"All modern American literature comes from one book by Mark Twain called *Huckleberry Finn*," Ernest Hemingway once wrote. "There was nothing before. There has been nothing as good since." Mark Twain was the pen name used by Samuel L. Clemens (1835–1910). Mississippi steamboat pilot, Nevada newspaperman, novelist, publisher, lecturer, scathing social critic, brooding philosopher—Mark Twain is one of the giants.

"The Lowest Animal" is one of a group of essays, unpublished during Mark

From pp. 223–229 "The Lowest Animal" in *Mark Twain—Letters from the Earth* edited by Bernard DeVoto. Copyright © 1962 by The Mark Twain Co. Reprinted by permission of Harper & Row, Publishers, Inc.

Twain's lifetime, that has been collectively entitled *The Damned Human Race*. It was written between 1905 and 1909. The author felt that this selection was too controversial and too bitter to be accepted by the public. Do you agree?

I have been studying the traits and dispositions of the ''lower animals'' (so-called), and contrasting them with the traits and dispositions of man. I find the result humiliating to me. For it obliges me to renounce my allegiance to the Darwinian theory of the Ascent of Man from the Lower Animals; since it now seems plain to me that that theory ought to be vacated in favor of a new and truer one, this new and truer one to be named the *De*scent of Man from the Higher Animals.   1

In proceeding toward this unpleasant conclusion I have not guessed or speculated or conjectured, but have used what is commonly called the scientific method. That is to say, I have subjected every postulate that presented itself to the crucial test of actual experiment, and have adopted it or rejected it according to the result. Thus I verified and established each step of my course in its turn before advancing to the next. These experiments were made in the London Zoological Gardens, and covered many months of painstaking and fatiguing work.   2

Before particularizing any of the experiments, I wish to state one or two things which seem to more properly belong in this place than further along. This in the interest of clearness. The massed experiments established to my satisfaction certain generalizations, to wit: 3

1. That the human race is of one distinct species. It exhibits slight variations—in color, stature, mental caliber, and so on—due to climate, environment, and so forth; but it is a species by itself, and not to be confounded with any other.   4

2. That the quadrupeds are a distinct family, also. This family exhibits variations—in color, size, food preferences and so on; but it is a family by itself.   5

3. That the other families—the birds, the fishes, the insects, the reptiles, etc.—are more or less distinct, also. They are in the procession. They are links in the chain which stretches down from the higher animals to man at the bottom.   6

Some of my experiments were quite curious. In the course of my reading I had come across a case where, many years ago, some hunters on our Great Plains organized a buffalo hunt for the entertainment of an English earl—that, and to provide some fresh meat for his larder. They had charming sport. They killed seventy-two of those great animals; and ate part of one of them and left the seventy-one to rot. In order to determine the difference between an anaconda and an earl—if any—I caused seven young calves to be turned into the anaconda's cage. The grateful reptile immediately crushed one of them and swallowed it, then lay back satisfied. It showed no further interest in the calves, and no disposition to harm them. I tried this experiment with other anacondas; always with the same result. The fact stood proven that the difference between an earl and an anaconda is that the earl is cruel and the anaconda isn't; and that the earl wantonly destroys what he   7 has no use for, but the anaconda doesn't. This seemed to suggest that the anaconda was not descended from the earl. It also seemed to suggest that the earl was descended from the anaconda, and had lost a good deal in the transition.

8   I was aware that many men who have accumulated more millions of money than they can ever use have shown a rabid hunger for more, and have not scrupled to cheat the ignorant and the helpless out of their poor servings in order to partially appease that appetite. I furnished a hundred different kinds of wild and tame animals the opportunity to accumulate vast stores of food, but none of them would do it. The squirrels and bees and certain birds made accumulations, but stopped when they had gathered a winter's supply, and could not be persuaded to add to it either honestly or by chicane. In order to bolster up a tottering reputation the ant pretended to store up supplies, but I was not deceived. I know the ant. These experiments convinced me that there is this difference between man and the higher animals: he is avaricious and miserly, they are not.

9   In the course of my experiments I convinced myself that among the animals man is the only one that harbors insults and injuries, broods over them, waits till a chance offers, then takes revenge. The passion of revenge is unknown to the higher animals.

10   Roosters keep harems, but it is by consent of their concubines; therefore no wrong is done. Men keep harems, but it is by brute force, privileged by atrocious laws which the other sex were allowed no hand in making. In this matter man occupies a far lower place than the rooster.

11   Cats are loose in their morals, but not consciously so. Man, in his descent from the cat, has brought the cat's looseness with him but has left the unconsciousness behind—the saving grace which excuses the cat. The cat is innocent, man is not.

12   Indecency, vulgarity, obscenity—these are strictly confined to man; he invented them. Among the higher animals there is no trace of them. They hide nothing; they are not ashamed. Man, with his soiled mind, covers himself. He will not even enter a drawing room with his breast and back naked, so alive are he and his mates to indecent suggestion. Man is "The Animal that Laughs." But so does the monkey, as Mr. Darwin pointed out; and so does the Australian bird that is called the laughing jackass. No— Man is the Animal that Blushes. He is the only one that does it—or has occasion to.

13   At the head of this article[1] we see how "three monks were burnt to death" a few days ago, and a prior "put to death with atrocious cruelty." Do we inquire into the details? No; or we should find out that the prior was subjected to unprintable mutilations. Man—when he is a North American Indian—gouges out his prisoner's eyes; when he is King John, with a

---

[1] The author had intended to begin the article with excerpts from newspaper reports about religious persecution in Crete.

nephew to render untroublesome, he uses a red-hot iron; when he is a religious zealot dealing with heretics in the Middle Ages, he skins his captive alive and scatters salt on his back; in the first Richard's time he shuts up a multitude of Jew families in a tower and sets fire to it; in Columbus's time he captures a family of Spanish Jews and—but *that* is not printable; in our day in England a man is fined ten shillings for beating his mother nearly to death with a chair, and another man is fined forty shillings for having four pheasant eggs in his possession without being able to satisfactorily explain how he got them. Of all the animals, man is the only one that is cruel. He is the only one that inflicts pain for the pleasure of doing it. It is a trait that is not known to the higher animals. The cat plays with the frightened mouse; but she has this excuse, that she does not know that the mouse is suffering. The cat is moderate—unhumanly moderate: she only scares the mouse, she does not hurt it; she doesn't dig out its eyes, or tear off its skin, or drive splinters under its nails—man-fashion; when she is done playing with it she makes a sudden meal of it and puts it out of its trouble. Man is the Cruel Animal. He is alone in that distinction.

The higher animals engage in individual fights, but never in organized   14
masses. Man is the only animal that deals in that atrocity of atrocities, War. He is the only one that gathers his brethren about him and goes forth in cold blood and with calm pulse to exterminate his kind. He is the only animal that for sordid wages will march out, as the Hessians did in our Revolution, and as the boyish Prince Napoleon did in the Zulu war, and help to slaughter strangers of his own species who have done him no harm and with whom he has no quarrel.

Man is the only animal that robs his helpless fellow of his country—takes   15
possession of it and drives him out of it or destroys him. Man has done this in all the ages. There is not an acre of ground on the globe that is in possession of its rightful owner, or that has not been taken away from owner after owner, cycle after cycle, by force and bloodshed.

Man is the only Slave. And he is the only animal who enslaves. He has   16
always been a slave in one form or another, and has always held other slaves in bondage under him in one way or another. In our day he is always some man's slave for wages, and does that man's work; and this slave has other slaves under him for minor wages, and they do *his* work. The higher animals are the only ones who exclusively do their own work and provide their own living.

Man is the only Patriot. He sets himself apart in his own country, under   17
his own flag, and sneers at the other nations, and keeps multitudinous uniformed assassins on hand at heavy expense to grab slices of other people's countries, and keep *them* from grabbing slices of *his*. And in the intervals between campaigns he washes the blood off his hands and works for "the universal brotherhood of man"—with his mouth.

Man is the Religious Animal. He is the only Religious Animal. He is the   18
only animal that has the True Religion—several of them. He is the only animal that loves his neighbor as himself, and cuts his throat if his theology

isn't straight. He has made a graveyard of the globe in trying his honest best to smooth his brother's path to happiness and heaven. He was at it in the time of the Caesars, he was at it in Mahomet's time, he was at it in the time of the Inquisition, he was at it in France a couple of centuries, he was at it in England in Mary's day, he has been at it ever since he first saw the light, he is at it today in Crete—as per the telegrams quoted above—he will be at it somewhere else tomorrow. The higher animals have no religion. And we are told that they are going to be left out, in the Hereafter. I wonder why? It seems questionable taste.

19   Man is the Reasoning Animal. Such is the claim. I think it is open to dispute. Indeed, my experiments have proven to me that he is the Unreasoning Animal. Note his history, as sketched above. It seems plain to me that whatever he is he is *not* a reasoning animal. His record is the fantastic record of a maniac. I consider that the strongest count against his intelligence is the fact that with that record back of him he blandly sets himself up as the head animal of the lot: whereas by his own standards he is the bottom one.

20   In truth, man is incurably foolish. Simple things which the other animals easily learn, he is incapable of learning. Among my experiments was this. In an hour I taught a cat and a dog to be friends. I put them in a cage. In another hour I taught them to be friends with a rabbit. In the course of two days I was able to add a fox, a goose, a squirrel and some doves. Finally a monkey. They lived together in peace; even affectionately.

21   Next, in another cage I confined an Irish Catholic from Tipperary, and as soon as he seemed tame I added a Scotch Presbyterian from Aberdeen. Next a Turk from Constantinople; a Greek Christian from Crete; an Armenian; a Methodist from the wilds of Arkansas; a Buddhist from China; a Brahman from Benares. Finally, a Salvation Army Colonel from Wapping. Then I stayed away two whole days. When I came back to note results, the cage of Higher Animals was all right, but in the other there was but a chaos of gory odds and ends of turbans and fezzes and plaids and bones and flesh—not a specimen left alive. These Reasoning Animals had disagreed on a theological detail and carried the matter to a Higher Court.

22   One is obliged to concede that in true loftiness of character, Man cannot claim to approach even the meanest of the Higher Animals. It is plain that he is constitutionally incapable of approaching that altitude; that he is constitutionally afflicted with a Defect which must make such approach forever impossible, for it is manifest that this defect is permanent in him, indestructible, ineradicable.

23   I find this Defect to be *the Moral Sense*. He is the only animal that has it. It is the secret of his degradation. It is the quality *which enables him to do wrong*. It has no other office. It is incapable of performing any other function. It could never have been intended to perform any other. Without it, man could do no wrong. He would rise at once to the level of the Higher Animals.

24   Since the Moral Sense has but the one office, the one capacity—to enable man to do wrong—it is plainly without value to him. It is as valueless to

him as is disease. In fact, it manifestly *is* a disease. *Rabies* is bad, but it is not so bad as this disease. Rabies enables a man to do a thing which he could not do when in a healthy state: kill his neighbor with a poisonous bite. No one is the better man for having rabies. The Moral Sense enables a man to do wrong. It enables him to do wrong in a thousand ways. Rabies is an innocent disease, compared to the Moral Sense. No one, then, can be the better man for having the Moral Sense. What, now, do we find the Primal Curse to have been? Plainly what it was in the beginning: the infliction upon man of the Moral Sense; the ability to distinguish good from evil; and with it, necessarily, the ability to *do* evil; for there can be no evil act without the presence of consciousness of it in the doer of it.

And so I find that we have descended and degenerated, from some far   25
ancestor—some microscopic atom wandering at its pleasure between the mighty horizons of a drop of water perchance—insect by insect, animal by animal, reptile by reptile, down the long highway of smirchless innocence, till we have reached the bottom stage of development—namable as the Human Being. Below us—nothing. Nothing but the Frenchman. *hah!*

WHAT DID THE WRITER SAY, AND WHAT DID YOU THINK?

1. What meaning of *descent* did Darwin have in mind in his book *The Descent of Man*? What meaning does Mark Twain use?
2. The author attributes human inferiority to the "Moral Sense." How would he define it?
3. Mark Twain delivers a profoundly bleak message about human nature. Why doesn't he seem to be especially depressed?
4. Who are the "uniformed assassins" in paragraph 17?
5. In what sense is the cat "innocent" in its sexual behavior and torturing of the mouse?
6. Are the comments on religion primarily an attack on religion or on human attitudes toward religion? If the latter, can an attack on religion itself be implied?
7. If you wanted to criticize the author's position, would you concentrate on the case he presents or bring up matters he leaves out?
8. Does the author sentimentalize the behavior of animals?
9. What is the point in the last sentence of the remark about the French, or is the remark nothing but an irrelevant wisecrack?

HOW DID THE WRITER SAY IT?

1. In paragraph 7 the author uses the example of the earl and the anaconda to establish human cruelty. After discussing some other issues, he uses examples of torture in paragraph 13 to show human cruelty. Is he repeating himself? Is the organization weak? If you think so, how might the author defend himself?
2. Which instances of humor strike you as most successful? Which are least successful?
3. Mark Twain is a great maker of phrases: "Man is the Animal that Blushes," for instance. Can you find some other examples?

4. The language is sometimes quite formal ("Note his history, as sketched above") and sometimes quite informal (the repetitions and variations of "he was at it" in paragraph 18). Explain why this mixture is effective or ineffective.
5. Does the writer rely on Pattern A or Pattern B (see pp. 68–71) to develop his ideas?
6. There are more "Vocabulary" entries for this selection than for many others. How do you account for this selection's still being fairly easy to read?
7. Vocabulary: *conjectured, postulate, quadrupeds, anaconda, scrupled, chicane, concubines, prior, zealot, multitudinous, ineradicable.*

WHAT ABOUT YOUR WRITING?

According to Mary Poppins, "A spoonful of sugar makes the medicine go down." Think of humor as sugar. When you are dealing with intrinsically stodgy material or presenting a point of view toward which many readers might feel hostile, nothing can get your audience on your side faster than a few touches of humor. That's what Mark Twain knew throughout his career. For humor, readers will pardon a stretch of dullness, accept or at least bear with a point they strongly oppose, and generally let the writer get away with more than the writer would ever think of asking for.

There are dangers, of course. You don't want your readers to feel that your point isn't important, that beneath the humor you yourself don't take it seriously. You don't want to distract your reader from the significant intellectual content of your work. You don't want to come through as a crude smart aleck. With all these warnings, however, humor is a major resource for many good writers. Be cautious with it, but don't be shy.

Football Red and Baseball Green
MURRAY ROSS

"Football Red and Baseball Green" is one of the more demanding essays in this book; so it needs to be read slowly and carefully. Its demands on the reader come not from obscurity in thought and style as much as from the author's taking with total seriousness a subject generally reserved for casual bull sessions. Murray Ross argues in his introduction that football and baseball are popular sports because they appeal to their audiences at deeply rooted and "uniquely American" psychological and cultural levels. The nature of the contrasting appeals constitutes the body of the essay.

1   The Super Bowl, the final game of the professional football season, draws a larger television audience than any of the moon walks. . . . This revelation is one way of indicating just how popular spectator sports are in this country. Americans, or American men anyway, seem to care about the games they watch as much as the Elizabethans cared about their plays, and I

"Football Red and Baseball Green" by Murray Ross, copyright © 1971 by *Chicago Review*, in vol. 22:2 and vol. 22:3 (double issue), pp. 30–40.

suspect for some of the same reasons. There is, in sport, some of the rudimentary drama found in popular theater: familiar plots, type characters, heroic and comic action spiced with new and unpredictable variations. And common to watching both activities is the sense of participation in a shared tradition and in shared fantasies. If sport exploits these fantasies without significantly transcending them, it seems no less satisfying for all that.

It is my guess that sport spectating involves something more than the vicarious pleasures of identifying with athletic prowess. I suspect that each sport contains a fundamental myth which it elaborates for its fans, and that our pleasure in watching such games derives in part from belonging briefly to the mythical world which the game and its players bring to life.[1] I am especially interested in baseball and football because they are so popular and so uniquely *American*; they began here and unlike basketball they have not been widely exported. Thus whatever can be said, mythically, about these games would seem to apply to our culture.

Baseball's myth may be the easier to identify since we have a greater historical perspective on the game. It was an instant success during the Industrialization, and most probably it was a reaction to the squalor, the faster pace and the dreariness of the new conditions. Baseball was old-fashioned right from the start; it seems conceived in nostalgia, in the resuscitation of the Jeffersonian dream.[2] It established an artificial rural environment, one removed from the toil of an urban life, which spectators could be admitted to and temporarily breathe in. Baseball is a *pastoral* sport,[3] and I think the game can be best understood as this kind of art. For baseball does what all good pastoral does—it creates an atmosphere in which everything exists in harmony.

Consider, for instance, the spatial organization of the game. A kind of controlled openness is created by having everything fan out from home plate, and the crowd sees the game through an arranged perspective that is rarely violated. Visually this means that the game is always seen as a constant, rather calm whole, and that the players and the playing field are viewed in relationship to each other. Each player has a certain position, a special area to tend, and the game often seems to be as much a dialogue between the fielders and the field as it is a contest between players themselves: will that ball get through the hole? Can that outfielder run under that fly? As a moral genre, pastoral asserts the virtue of communion with nature. As a competitive game, baseball asserts that the team which best relates to the playing field (by hitting the ball in the right places) will win.

I suspect baseball's space has a subliminal function too, for topographi-

2

3

4

5

---

[1] "Myth," as used by the author, refers to a story, often a fantasy, that reflects and reveals the basic beliefs and values of a people.

[2] In many moods, Jefferson was suspicious of city life and conceived of an America of small farms and small towns.

[3] A pastoral is a traditional work of art, usually literary, that celebrates the simple joys of country life.

cally it is a sentimental mirror of older America. Most of the game is played between the pitcher and the hitter in the extreme corner of the playing area. This is the busiest, most sophisticated part of the ball park, where something is always happening, and from which all subsequent action originates. From this urban corner we move to a supporting infield, active but a little less crowded, and from there we come to the vast stretches of the outfield. As is traditional in American lore, danger increases with distance, and the outfield action is often the most spectacular in the game. The long throw, the double off the wall, the leaping catch—these plays take place in remote territory, and they belong, like most legendary feats, to the frontier.

6   Having established its landscape, pastoral art operates to eliminate any reference to that bigger, more disturbing, more real world it has left behind. All games are to some extent insulated from the outside by having their own rules, but baseball has a circular structure as well which furthers its comfortable feeling of self-sufficiency. By this I mean that every motion of extension is also one of return—a ball hit outside is a *home* run, a full circle. Home—familiar, peaceful, secure—it is the beginning and end. You must go out and come back; only the completed movement is registered.

7   Time is a serious threat to any form of pastoral. The genre poses a time-less world of perpetual spring, and it does its best to silence the ticking of clocks which remind us that in time the green world fades into winter. One's sense of time is directly related to what happens in it, and baseball is so structured as to stretch out and ritualize whatever action it contains. Dra-matic moments are few, and they are almost always isolated by the routine texture of normal play. It is certainly a game of climax and drama, but it is perhaps more a game of repeated and predictable action: the foul balls, the walks, the pitcher fussing around on the mound, the lazy fly ball to center-field. This is, I think, as it should be, for baseball exists as an alternative to a world of too much action, struggle and change. It is a merciful release from a more grinding and insistent tempo, and its time, as William Carlos Williams suggests, makes a virtue out of idleness simply by providing it:

> The crowd at the ball game
> is moved uniformly
> by a spirit of uselessness
> Which delights them. . . .*

8   Within this expanded and idle time the baseball fan is at liberty to become a ceremonial participant and a lover of style. Because the action is nor-malized, how something is done becomes as important as the action itself. Thus baseball's most delicate and detailed aspects are often, to the spec-tator, the most interesting. The pitcher's windup, the anticipatory crouch of the infielders, the quick waggle of the bat as it poises for the pitch—these subtle miniature movements are as meaningful as the home runs and the strikeouts. It somehow matters in baseball that all the tiny rituals are ob-

*"At the Ball Game," from *Collected Earlier Poems of William Carlos Williams*, copyright 1938 by New Directions Publishing Corporation.

served: the shortstop must kick the dirt and the umpire must brush the plate with his pocket broom. In a sense baseball is largely a continuous series of small gestures, and I think it characteristic that the game's most treasured moment came when Babe Ruth pointed to where he subsequently hit a home run.

Baseball is a game where the little things mean a lot, and this, together with its clean serenity, its open space, and its ritualized action is enough to place it in a world of yesterday. Baseball evokes for us a past which may never have been ours, but which we believe was, and certainly that is enough. In the Second World War, supposedly, we fought for ''Baseball, Mom and Apple Pie,'' and considering what baseball means that phrase is a good one. We fought then for the right to believe in a green world of tranquility and uninterrupted contentment, where the little things would count. But now the possibilities of such a world are more remote, and it seems that while the entertainment of such a dream has an enduring appeal, it is no longer sufficient for our fantasies. I think this may be why baseball is no longer our preeminent national pastime, and why its myth is being replaced by another more appropriate to the new realities (and fantasies) of our time.

Football, especially professional football, is the embodiment of a newer myth, one which in many respects is opposed to baseball's. The fundamental difference is that football is not a pastoral game; it is a heroic one. One way of seeing the difference between the two is by the juxtaposition of Babe Ruth and Jim Brown, both legendary players in their separate genres. Ruth, baseball's most powerful hitter, was a hero maternalized (his name), an epic figure destined for a second immortality as a candy bar. His image was impressive but comfortable and altogether human: round, dressed in a baggy uniform, with a schoolboy's cap and a bat which looked tiny next to him. His spindly legs supported a Santa-sized torso, and this comic disproportion would increase when he was in motion. He ran delicately, with quick, very short steps, since he felt that stretching your stride slowed you down. This sort of superstition is typical of baseball players, and typical too is the way in which a personal quirk or mannerism mitigates their awesome skill and makes them poignant and vulnerable.

There was nothing funny about Jim Brown. His muscular and almost perfect physique was emphasized further by the uniform which armored him. Babe Ruth had a tough face, but boyish and innocent; Brown was an expressionless mask under the helmet. In action he seemed invincible, the embodiment of speed and power in an inflated human shape. One can describe Brown accurately only with superlatives, for as a player he was a kind of Superman, undisguised.

Brown and Ruth are caricatures, yet they represent their games. Baseball is part of a comic tradition which insists that its participants be humans, while football, in the heroic mode, asks that its players be more than that. Football converts men into gods, and suggests that magnificence and glory are as desirable as happiness. Football is designed, therefore, to impress its audience rather differently than baseball.

"Babe Ruth had a tough face, but boyish and innocent . . ." (Wide World Photos)

" . . . Brown was an expressionless mask under the helmet." (UPI Photo)

13   As a pastoral game, baseball attempts to close the gap between the players and the crowd. It creates the illusion, for instance, that with a lot of hard work, a little luck, and possibly some extra talent, the average spectator might well be playing; not watching. For most of us can do a few of the things the ball players do: catch a pop-up, field a ground ball, and maybe get a hit once in a while. Chance is allotted a good deal of play in the game. There is no guarantee, for instance, that a good pitch will not be looped over the infield, or that a solidly batted ball will not turn into a double play. In addition to all of this, almost every fan feels he can make the manager's decision for him, and not entirely without reason. Baseball's statistics are easily calculated and rather meaningful; and the game itself, though a subtle one, is relatively lucid and comprehendible.

14   As a heroic game football is not concerned with a shared community of near-equals. It seeks almost the opposite relationship between its spectators and players, one which stresses the distance between them. We are not allowed to identify directly with Jim Brown any more than we are with Zeus, because to do so would undercut his stature as something more than human. The players do much of the distancing themselves by their own excesses of speed, size and strength. When Bob Brown, the giant all-pro tackle, says that he could "block King Kong all day," we look at him and believe. But the game itself contributes to the players' heroic isolation. As George Plimpton has graphically illustrated in *Paper Lion,* it is almost impossible to imagine yourself in a professional football game without also considering your imminent humiliation and possible injury. There is scarcely a single play that the average spectator could hope to perform adequately, and there is even a difficulty in really understanding what is going on. In baseball what happens is what meets the eye, but in football each action is the result of eleven men acting simultaneously against eleven other men, and clearly this is too much for the eye to totally comprehend. Football has become a game of staggering complexity, and coaches are now wired in to several "spotters" during the games so they can find out what is happening.

15   If football is distanced from its fans by its intricacy and its "superhuman" play, it nonetheless remains an intense spectacle. Baseball, as I have implied, dissolves time and urgency in a green expanse, thereby creating a luxurious and peaceful sense of leisure. As is appropriate to a heroic enterprise, football reverses this procedure and converts space into time. The game is ideally played in an oval stadium, not in a "park," and the difference is the elimination of perspective. This makes football a perfect television game, because even at first hand it offers a flat, perpetually moving foreground (wherever the ball is). The eye in baseball viewing opens up; in football it zeroes in. There is no democratic vista in football, and spectators are not asked to relax, but to concentrate. You are encouraged to watch the drama, not a medley of ubiquitous gestures, and you are constantly reminded that this event is taking place in time. The third element in baseball is the field; in football this element is the clock. Traditionally heroes do reckon with time, and football players are no exceptions. Time in football

is wound up inexorably until it reaches the breaking point in the last minutes of a close game. More often than not it is the clock which emerges as the real enemy, and it is the sense of time running out that regularly produces a pitch of tension uncommon in baseball.

A further reason for football's intensity is that the game is played like a war. The idea is to win by going through, around or over the opposing team and the battle lines, quite literally, are drawn on every play. Violence is somewhere at the heart of the game, and the combat quality is reflected in football's army language ("blitz," "trap," "zone," "bomb," "trenches," etc.). Coaches often sound like generals when they discuss their strategy. Woody Hayes of Ohio State, for instance, explains his quarterback option play as if it had been conceived in the Pentagon: "You know," he says, "the most effective kind of warfare is siege. You have to attack on broad fronts. And that's all the option is—attacking on a broad front. You know General Sherman ran an option through the south."

Football like war is an arena for action, and like war football leaves little room for personal style. It seems to be a game which projects "character" more than personality, and for the most part football heroes, publicly, are a rather similar lot. They tend to become personifications rather than individuals, and, with certain exceptions, they are easily read emblematically as embodiments of heroic qualities such as "strength," "confidence," "perfection," etc.—clichés really, but forceful enough when represented by the play of a Dick Butkus, a Johnny Unitas or a Bart Starr. Perhaps this simplification of personality results in part from the heroes' total identification with their mission, to the extent that they become more characterized by their work than by what they intrinsically "are." At any rate football does not make allowances for the idiosyncrasies that baseball actually seems to encourage, and as a result there have been few football players as uniquely crazy or human as, say, Casey Stengel or Dizzy Dean.

A further reason for the underdeveloped qualities of football personalities, and one which gets us to the heart of the game's modernity, is that football is very much a game of modern technology. Football's action is largely interaction, and the game's complexity requires that its players mold themselves into a perfectly coordinated unit. Jerry Kramer, the veteran guard and author of *Instant Replay,* writes how Lombardi would work to develop such integration:

> He makes us execute the same plays over and over, a hundred times, two hundred times, until we do every little thing automatically. He works to make the kickoff team perfect, the punt-return team perfect, the field-goal team perfect. He ignores nothing. Technique, technique, technique, over and over and over, until we feel like we're going crazy. But we win.

Mike Garrett, the halfback, gives the player's version:

> After a while you train your mind like a computer—put the ideas in, and the body acts accordingly.

19   As the quotations imply, pro football is insatiably preoccupied with the smoothness and precision of play execution, and most coaches believe that the team which makes the fewest mistakes will be the team that wins. Individual identity thus comes to be associated with the team or unit that one plays for to a much greater extent than in baseball. To use a reductive analogy, it is the difference between *Bonanza* and *Mission Impossible*. Ted Williams is mostly Ted Williams, but Bart Starr is mostly the Green Bay Packers. The latter metaphor is a precise one, since football heroes stand out not because of purely individual acts, but because they epitomize the action and style of the groups they are connected to. Kramer cites the obvious if somewhat self-glorifying historical precedent: "Perhaps," he writes, "we're living in Camelot." Ideally a football team should be what Camelot was supposed to have been, a group of men who function as equal parts of a larger whole, dependent on each other for total meaning.

20   The humanized machine as hero is something very new in sport, for in baseball anything approaching a machine has always been suspect. The famous Yankee teams of the fifties were almost flawlessly perfect and never very popular. Their admirers took pains to romanticize their precision into something more natural than plain mechanics—Joe DiMaggio, for instance, was the "Yankee Clipper." Even so, most people hoped fervently the Brooklyn Dodgers (the "bums") would thrash them in every World Series. To take a more recent example, the victory of the Mets in 1969 was so compelling largely because it was at the expense of a superbly homogenized team, the Baltimore Orioles, and it was accomplished by a somewhat random collection of inspired leftovers. In baseball, machinery seems tantamount to villainy, whereas in football this smooth perfection is part of the expected integration a championship team must attain.

21   It is not surprising, really, that we should have a game which asserts the heroic function of a mechanized group, since we have become a country where collective identity is a reality. Football as a game of groups is appealing to us as a people of groups, and for this reason football is very much an "establishment" game—since it is in the corporate business and governmental structures that group America is most developed. The game comments on the culture, and vice versa:

> President Nixon, an ardent football fan, got a football team picture as an inaugural anniversary present from his cabinet. . . .
> Superimposed on the faces of real gridiron players were the faces of cabinet members. (AP)

This is not to say that football appeals only to a certain class, for group America is visible everywhere. A sign held high in the San Francisco Peace Moratorium last November read: "49er Fans against War, Poverty and the Baltimore Colts."

22   Football's collective pattern is only one aspect of the way in which it seems to echo our contemporary environment. The game, like our society, can be thought of as a cluster of people living under great tension in a state

of perpetual flux. The potential for sudden disaster or triumph is as great in football as it is in our own age, and although there is something ludicrous in equating interceptions with assassinations and long passes with moonshots, there is also something valid and appealing in the analogies. It seems to me that football does successfully reflect those salient and common conditions which affect us all, and it does so with the end of making us feel better about them and our lot. For one thing, it makes us feel that something can be released and connected in all this chaos; out of the accumulated pile of bodies something can emerge—a runner breaks into the clear or a pass finds its way to a receiver. To the spectator plays such as these are human and dazzling. They suggest to the audience what it has hoped for (and been told) all along, that technology is still a tool and not a master. Fans get living proof of this every time a long pass is completed; they see at once that it is the result of careful planning, perfect integration and an effective "pattern," but they see too that it is human and that what counts as well is man, his desire, his natural skill and his "grace under pressure." Football metaphysically yokes heroic action and technology by violence to suggest that they are mutually supportive. It's a doubtful proposition, but given how we live it has its attractions.

Football, like the space program, is a game in the grand manner, yet it is a rather sober sport and often seems to lack that positive, comic vision of which baseball's pastoral mannerisms are a part. It is a winter game, as those fans who saw the Minnesota Vikings play the Detroit Lions one Thanksgiving were graphically reminded. The two teams played in a blinding snowstorm, and except for the small flags in the corners of the end zones, and a patch of mud wherever the ball was downed, the field was totally obscured. Even through the magnified television lenses the players were difficult to identify; you saw only huge shapes come out of the gloom, thump against each other and fall in a heap. The movement was repeated endlessly and silently in a muffled stadium, interrupted once or twice by a shot of a bare-legged girl who fluttered her pompons in the cold. The spectacle was by turns pathetic, compelling and absurd; a kind of theater of oblivion. 23

Games such as this are by no means unusual, and it is not difficult to see why for many football is a gladiatorial sport of pointless bludgeoning played by armored monsters. However accurate this description may be, I still believe that even in the worst of circumstances football can be a liberating activity. In the game I have just described, for instance, there was one play, the turning point of the game, which more than compensated for the sluggishness of most of the action. Jim Marshall, the huge defensive end (who hunts on dogsleds during the off season), intercepted a pass deep in his own territory and rumbled upfield like a dinosaur through the mud, the snow, and the opposing team, lateraling at the last minute to another lineman who took the ball in for a touchdown. It was a supreme moment because Marshall's principal occupation is falling on quarterbacks, not catching the ball and running with it. His triumphant jaunt, something that went unequaled 24 during the rest of that dark afternoon, was a hearty burlesque of the entire sport, an occasion for epic laughter in bars everywhere (though especially in Minnesota), and it was more than enough to rescue the game from the snowbound limbo it was in.

25   In the end I suppose both football and baseball could be seen as varieties of decadence. In its preoccupation with mechanization, and in its own display of violence, football is the more obvious target for social moralists, but I wonder if this is finally more "corrupt" than the seductive picture of sanctuary and tranquility that baseball has so artfully drawn for us. Almost all sport is vulnerable to such criticism because it is not strictly ethical in intent, and for this reason there will always be room for puritans like the Elizabethan John Stubbes who howled at the "wanton fruits which these cursed pastimes bring forth." As a long-time dedicated fan of almost anything athletic, I confess myself out of sympathy with most of this; which is to say, I guess, that I am vulnerable to those fantasies which these games support, and that I find happiness in the company of people who feel as I do.

26   A final note. It is interesting that the heroic and pastoral conventions which underlie our most popular sports are almost classically opposed. The contrasts are familiar: city versus country, aspirations versus contentment, activity versus peace and so on. Judging from the rise of professional football we seem to be slowly relinquishing that unfettered rural vision of ourselves that baseball so beautifully mirrors, and we have come to cast ourselves in a genre more reflective of a nation confronted by constant and unavoidable challenges. Right now, like the Elizabethans, we seem to share both heroic and pastoral yearnings, and we reach out to both. Perhaps these divided needs account in part for the enormous attention we as a nation now give to spectator sports. For sport provides one place where we can have our football and our baseball too.

WHAT DID THE WRITER SAY, AND WHAT DID YOU THINK?

1. How does the relative lack of popularity of baseball and football in most other countries support the author's point?
2. Using Ross's observations as starting points, can you account for the popularity of golf in America? The relative unpopularity of soccer?
3. Both baseball and football appeal to fantasies. What are they?
4. Which fantasy strikes Ross as being more "decadent," and why?
5. Explain and comment on the validity of the comparison of baseball and football to *Bonanza* and *Mission Impossible.*
6. Do recent changes in baseball rules (designated hitters, for instance) make the game more like football?
7. Do you agree with the author that time is mostly irrelevant in baseball?
8. Did the comments on the "frontier" and "home" as represented on the baseball field seem to you significant insights or wild flights of fancy?

9. How would Ross answer the charge that his comments on American life, past and present, are extreme oversimplifications?

HOW DID THE WRITER SAY IT?

1. In an anthology of sports articles, this essay was once reprinted under the title of "Football and Baseball in America." Explain your reasons for approving or disapproving of the change.
2. In this long essay, Ross mixes the two patterns for comparison-and-contrast writing. Which pattern dominates—the seesaw or first-all-one-then-all-the-other?
3. What pattern does Ross use to compare and contrast Babe Ruth and Jim Brown?
4. Explain the meaning of the last sentence: "For sport provides one place where we can have our football and our baseball too." What common expression is echoed in this sentence?
5. Does the author consistently use specific details to back up his points? Are any points unsupported?
6. Do the author's references to himself in the first person ("I") seem uncalled for in a serious article of this kind?
7. Vocabulary: *rudimentary, transcending, vicarious, prowess, squalor, resuscitation, pastoral, spatial, genre, subliminal, topographically, mitigates, poignant, lucid, ubiquitous, insatiably, idiosyncrasies, epitomize, tantamount, salient, metaphysically, limbo.*

WHAT ABOUT <u>YOUR</u> WRITING?

Note how many words of qualification and caution are spread through the Ross essay. The author needs to demonstrate his awareness that he is dealing with matters of speculation, not scientific and mathematical truths. He can't prove his points; he can only make them seem plausible. The persuasive power of the essay depends in part on whether Ross strikes the reader as reliable, a sensible person studying complex phenomena and trying to draw reasonable inferences from them.

In the first two paragraphs alone we find phrases like "*seem* to care," "I *suspect,*" "*some* [not all] of the rudimentary drama," "I *suspect*" again, "derives *in part,*" "*seem* to apply." At strategic places in the remainder of the essay, the same or similar phrases are repeated. Ross establishes a tone of reason; more, he establishes himself as a man of reason, one with a fitting hesitation about insisting on the absolute truth of his own ideas.

When you, like Ross, are presenting ideas that will strike readers as eccentric or threatening—some of Ross's readers may be hostile to him from the start through fear that thinking about sports will interfere with enjoying them—it's good policy to use Ross's techniques of qualification and caution.

Don't go overboard, of course. Don't write *in my opinion* in every other sentence. Don't confuse being reasonable with being timid. Don't write cowardly nonsense like *I think that George Washington played an important part in the American Revolution* or *It seems to me that thalidomide is a dangerous drug.* Present the strongest case you can as strongly as you can. Ross goes all out in presenting his case, too, once he's laid the foundations. The foundations are important, however, and the wise writer will not neglect them.

These remarks don't mean that *every* time you write anything offbeat or controversial you are required to use Ross's approach. Mark Twain (pp. 82–87) uses humor, for example, to get his offbeat and controversial message listened to. There's more than one way to reach a reader. Having choices is what counts.

Chapter 5

CAUSE AND EFFECT

The school board of a nearby town has decided to ask the voters to approve a large increase in property tax assessments in order to construct a new high school. The board knows that, at best, its request will be unwelcome. It launches a vigorous campaign to make the voters more favorably inclined. Part of the campaign is the printing of a pamphlet setting forth the board's case. The pamphlet, of necessity, presents a study of cause-and-effect relationships.

The board first states the *causes* for its request. Student enrollment has more than doubled. Three years ago, the board had tried to cope with this problem by going to two sessions, but the classrooms are still too crowded for basic physical comfort as well as for optimum learning conditions. Moreover, the situation is not temporary; current enrollment in the junior high and elementary schools assures continued increases in the student population. Finally, the building is in poor physical condition: the roof leaks, the basement floods, the boiler is on its last legs. The board has investigated the possibility of remodeling and expanding the old building and has found that costs for that project would mean an average of only $35 a year less in taxes per family than if a complete new school were built.

Next, the board discusses the results, or *effects,* of voter approval. The town's leading eyesore will be replaced by a beautiful new structure in which everyone can take pride. New facilities for the most modern teaching devices will improve the quality of education. Experienced teachers will be more inclined to stay than to seek new employment. The strength of the town's educational system will be a selling point for new industries and new residents and consequently will increase property values.

The school board's pamphlet, in short, presents a thesis—the proposal for a new high school should be approved—and supports it with cause-and-effect writing.

It's worth noting here that cause-and-effect relationships can sometimes shift. In the first part of the pamphlet, for example, the proposal to build a new school is the effect that was caused by overcrowding and a decaying building. In the second part of the pamphlet, however, the approved proposal becomes the cause of such beneficial effects as beauty and improved education. A cause creates an effect, but that effect, in turn, can become the cause of another effect. No problems are likely to arise as long as the writer keeps any shifting relationships clearly in mind.

Most classroom papers are not lengthy enough to give equal weight to cause and effect and will necessarily emphasize one over the other. "Cause" papers might have theses like these:

> The rioting at last week's rock concert was mostly the fault of the police.
>
> The growth of interest in coin collecting is attributable to practical financial considerations.
>
> Government policies have made fuel shortages more severe.
>
> Iago plots against Othello because of an accumulation of petty resentments.

The introduction of the cause paper will usually contain a brief description of the *effect*—the rioting that resulted from police actions, the fuel shortages that resulted from government policies—and then the entire body of the paper will analyze the causes, giving a paragraph, perhaps, to each cause.

"Effect" papers might have theses like these:

> Passage of a national health insurance program is going to result in heavy burdens on doctors.
>
> Fear of germs made me a nervous wreck as a child.
>
> The invention of the cotton gin helped perpetuate slavery in the South.
>
> Rigid enforcement of holding penalties in professional football has made the sport less exciting than it used to be.

The introduction to an effect paper will naturally reverse the procedure of a cause paper. It will briefly describe or discuss the *cause*—the health insurance program, the cotton gin, and so on—and the rest of the paper will then be devoted to the effects.

As you plan your paper, try to remember a few logical requirements:

Do not oversimplify causes. Most subjects worth writing about have more than one cause. Sometimes particular combinations of causes have to be present at the same time and in certain proportions in order to bring about a particular result. Attributing a young man's juvenile delinquency solely to the poverty of his family oversimplifies what everyone knows about life. Poverty may have been a contributing cause, but there had to be others;

plenty of poor children do not become juvenile delinquents, and plenty of rich ones do.

Beware especially of the *post hoc ergo propter hoc* fallacy: "after this, therefore because of this." After Herbert Hoover was elected president, America had a depression; therefore, America had a depression because Herbert Hoover was elected. An argument like this depends purely on an accident of time; the writer must point out, if possible, actual policies of the Hoover administration that brought about the depression. Otherwise, the argument has no more logical validity than "I lost my job after a black cat crossed my path; therefore, I lost my job because a black cat crossed my path."

Do not oversimplify effects. Uncontrolled enthusiasm is probably the biggest danger here. A writer may be able to present a strong case that an ill-conceived national health insurance program might have adverse effects on medical care; if the writer predicts that millions of people will die of neglect in waiting lines in the doctor's office, however, the writer's case—and common sense—is sure to be viewed skeptically. The school board's pamphlet said that a new high school would be an additional selling point to attract industry; if it had said that dozens of corporations would demand to set up shop in town, it would have oversimplified the effects in an irresponsible and hysterical fashion.

Distinguish when necessary between direct and indirect causes and effects. Don't treat all causes and effects equally. Some are more remote than others, and the distinctions need to be made clear. Political and military conflicts in the Middle East were direct causes of rising oil prices. The invention of the automobile around the turn of this century was an indirect cause. Though indirect causes and effects can sometimes be important, you need to set limits on how many of them you can deal with, or nearly every cause-and-effect paper will turn into a history of the world.

Distinguish when necessary between major and minor causes and effects. The Confederacy's firing on Fort Sumter was a direct cause of the Civil War, but not nearly as important as the issues of secession and slavery. Although acknowledging minor causes and effects, a paper should naturally spend most of its time on major ones.

Do not omit links in a chain of causes and effects. As previously noted, you may not always be faced with a set of separate causes for a particular effect or separate effects from a particular cause. One cause leads to another, the second to a third, and so on—and only then is the given effect brought about. Unless you carefully discuss each part of the sequence, your reader may get lost. One effect of television, for example, may be a growing number of discipline problems in elementary and high school classrooms, but before you can persuade your reader of that point, you will have to examine many intermediate effects.

Play fair. Give some attention, where appropriate, to causes and effects that opponents of your thesis may point to. You may justifiably want to pin the rioting at the rock concert on the police, but your case will be strengthened, not weakened, if you concede that the promoters' selling of more tickets than there were seats and the attempt of a few fans to rush the stage and tear the clothes off the performers' backs also contributed to the disaster. You don't need to make a lavish production of these arguments on the other side; just show that you're aware of them and have given them serious consideration.

WRITING SUGGESTIONS FOR CAUSE-AND-EFFECT PAPERS

Any of the listed subjects offers good opportunities for a cause-and-effect, cause only, or effect only paper. Explore each cause and effect thoroughly; don't just write a list.

1. A personal, unreasonable fear (your own or someone else's).
2. A personal, unreasonable irritation (your own or someone else's).
3. A personal habit or mannerism (your own or someone else's).
4. Outlawing of prayers in public schools.
5. Violence on children's television programs.
6. A personal experience with racial or religious discrimination.
7. Your first romantic attachment.
8. The quality of food at the school cafeteria.
9. The popularity or decline in popularity of a hair style or clothing style.
10. High school graduates who still can't read.
11. Your like or dislike of a particular book or writer, movie, painter, musician, television program.
12. Children's lack of respect for parents.
13. Acceptance of "the pill."
14. A minor invention (Scotch tape, electric toothbrushes, pay toilets, parking meters).
15. Your interest or lack of interest in a sport.
16. Your passionate like or dislike of a food.

What Good Does a Funeral Do . . . Really?

In 1963 Jessica Mitford's best-selling book, *The American Way of Death*, attacked and ridiculed American funeral practices and expenses and in many instances questioned the integrity of the funeral "industry." The debate stimulated by her book is still going on, as this advertisement demonstrates.

What good does a funeral do...really?

Today, there are those who find themselves asking this question.

Certainly the funeral can do nothing for the person whose life has ended beyond providing the dignity of a proper burial. **But no matter where, when, or under what circumstances death may occur, there are needs that must be met**—for the bereaved family; their friends; their close circle in the community.

The funeral helps meet those needs. It helps those who grieve accept the reality of death. They know it happened. But a part of their mind rejects it, runs away from it.

The funeral takes them gently by the shoulders and turns them to face it. And having faced it, having viewed it, things are easier.

Things continue to be easier (though it may not seem so at the time) as arrangements have them talking with sympathetic friends, reflecting upon moments shared, giving testimony to the life that was lived on earth.

Another thing the funeral does—whether the choice is made for a traditional, a contemporary or a humanist service—is to reaffirm the faith, the creed, or philosophy by which one's life was guided.

As the poet John Donne said: "No man is an island . . ." His death touches his world. A funeral considers the feelings of all those who shared his life. It is a moment when grief shared is grief diminished.

It is truly a unique moment of sharing . . . for the family . . . for friends . . . for society.

We will be glad to furnish you with a free copy of Clark's informative, 32-page booklet, "My Duty." It answers many questions, tells you "what to do" when you are asked to take charge. You may also receive a copy without cost by writing to The Clark Grave Vault Company, Dept. N-73, Columbus, Ohio 43201.

©1973 The finest tribute . . . the most trusted protection

WHAT DID THE WRITER SAY, AND WHAT DID YOU THINK?

1. This advertisement appeared in *Woman's Day,* a mass-circulation magazine distributed in supermarkets. Explain the advertiser's choice of this magazine. What other magazines might be logical choices?
2. What is the Clark Company's product? Where is it mentioned?
3. Are the virtues of the product discussed anywhere?
4. What sense does it make for Clark to advertise? Do people ask for the product by brand name? Moreover, most readers won't have occasion to buy the product for many years to come—this makes the ad unique—and are unlikely to remember the brand name. What's the point? What are the practical purposes of this ad?
5. To what audience is the advertisement addressed?

HOW DID THE WRITER SAY IT?

1. What is the effect of the word *really* in the question that begins the advertisement?
2. What is the connotation of "a proper burial" in paragraph 2?
3. In paragraph 2, the ad mentions an effect that funerals do *not* have. Why?
4. How many major effects are mentioned? To which effect is the most attention given?
5. Written on a subject that makes many feel uncomfortable, the ad attempts to achieve a tone of quiet dignity, good taste, and restraint. Does it succeed?

WHAT ABOUT <u>YOUR</u> WRITING?

Things. It's a handy word—too handy, in fact. It's overused. It's a *catch-all word,* so vague in meaning that it can fit in almost anywhere and tempt us away from looking for a more precise word that expresses our intended meaning more accurately. There aren't any laws against *things* (or *thing*); it's not offensive in the advertisement; readers of this book won't have any difficulty finding it here and there in the author's own writing. Sometimes a particular thought may be nearly inexpressible without it. Nobody objects to it in conversation ("How are things?"). Still, in writing, it's too easy, too abstract, too flabby. Try to find a more exact substitute.

Now add these words to your growing list of catch-all words: *aspects, facets,* and *factors.* Avoid them wherever possible. Even when you can't come up with a more specific word, at least settle for a catch-all word that isn't used quite so often.

ORIGINAL	SUGGESTED IMPROVEMENT
And having faced it, having viewed it, things are easier.	And having faced it, having viewed it, people can deal with their own lives more easily.
Things continue to be easier . . .	Facing the reality of death continues to be easier . . .
Another thing the funeral does . . .	Another benefit of the funeral . . .
Freedom of the press has many aspects.	Freedom of the press is a complicated subject.
Ambition is the strongest facet of his personality.	Ambition is his strongest character trait.
One factor contributing to inflation is fixed government expenses like social security and veterans' benefits.	One cause of inflation is fixed government expenses like social security and veterans' benefits.

Who Killed Benny Paret?

NORMAN COUSINS

Norman Cousins, for many years editor of the *Saturday Review*, is now chairman of its editorial board. Active in support of such movements as world government and nuclear disarmament, Cousins has written and edited a number of books, among them *In Place of Folly* (1961) and *Present Tense* (1967).

Note the attention the writer devotes to suggested alternate causes before presenting his own view of the true cause.

Sometime about 1935 or 1936 I had an interview with Mike Jacobs, the prize-fight promoter. I was a fledgling reporter at that time; my beat was education but during the vacation season I found myself on varied assignments, all the way from ship news to sports reporting. In this way I found myself sitting opposite the most powerful figure in the boxing world.

There was nothing spectacular in Mr. Jacobs' manner or appearance; but when he spoke about prize fights, he was no longer a bland little man but a colossus who sounded the way Napoleon must have sounded when he reviewed a battle. You knew you were listening to Number One. His saying something made it true.

We discussed what to him was the only important element in successful promoting—how to please the crowd. So far as he was concerned, there was no mystery to it. You put killers in the ring and the people filled your arena. You hire boxing artists—men who are adroit at feinting, parrying, weaving, jabbing, and dancing, but who don't pack dynamite in their fists— and you wind up counting your empty seats. So you searched for the killers and sluggers and maulers—fellows who could hit with the force of a baseball bat.

I asked Mr. Jacobs if he was speaking literally when he said people came out to see the killer.

"They don't come out to see a tea party," he said evenly. "They come out to see the knockout. They come out to see a man hurt. If they think anything else, they're kidding themselves."

Recently, a young man by the name of Benny Paret[1] was killed in the ring. The killing was seen by millions; it was on television. In the twelfth round, he was hit hard in the head several times, went down, was counted out, and never came out of the coma.

The Paret fight produced a flurry of investigations. Governor Rockefeller was shocked by what happened and appointed a committee to assess the responsibility. The New York State Boxing Commission decided to find out what was wrong. The District Attorney's office expressed its concern. One question that was solemnly studied in all three probes concerned the action of the referee. Did he act in time to stop the fight? Another question had

Published in *Saturday Review*, May 5, 1962, and reprinted by permission of *Saturday Review*.

[1] Benny "Kid" Paret won the welterweight championship on May 27, 1960, in a fifteen-round decision over Don Jordan. He lost the title on April 1, 1961, when knocked out by Emile Griffith in the thirteenth round. In a return match of fifteen rounds on September 30, 1961, Paret gained a decision over Griffith. In Paret's last fight, March 24, 1962, Griffith knocked him out in the twelfth round.

The Paret-Griffith fight, March 24, 1962. Paret slumps to the canvas as the referee stops the fight. (Wide World Photos)

to do with the role of the examining doctors who certified the physical
fitness of the fighters before the bout. Still another question involved Mr.
Paret's manager; did he rush his boy into the fight without adequate time
to recuperate from the previous one?

In short, the investigators looked into every possible cause except the
real one. Benny Paret was killed because the human fist delivers enough
impact, when directed against the head, to produce a massive hemorrhage
in the brain. The human brain is the most delicate and complex mechanism
in all creation. It has a lacework of millions of highly fragile nerve connec-
tions. Nature attempts to protect this exquisitely intricate machinery by
encasing it in a hard shell. Fortunately, the shell is thick enough to withstand
a great deal of pounding. Nature, however, can protect man against everything except man himself. Not every blow to the head will kill a man—but
there is always the risk of concussion and damage to the brain. A prize
fighter may be able to survive even repeated brain concussions and go on
fighting, but the damage to his brain may be permanent.

In any event, it is futile to investigate the referee's role and seek to
determine whether he should have intervened to stop the fight earlier. That
is not where the primary responsibility lies. The primary responsibility lies
with the people who pay to see a man hurt. The referee who stops a fight
too soon from the crowd's viewpoint can expect to be booed. The crowd
wants the knockout; it wants to see a man stretched out on the canvas. This
is the supreme moment in boxing. It is nonsense to talk about prize fighting
as a test of boxing skills. No crowd was ever brought to its feet screaming
and cheering at the sight of two men beautifully dodging and weaving out
of each other's jabs. The time the crowd comes alive is when a man is hit
hard over the heart or the head, when his mouthpiece flies out, when the
blood squirts out of his nose or eyes, when he wobbles under the attack and
his pursuer continues to smash at him with pole-axe impact.

Don't blame it on the referee. Don't even blame it on the fight managers.
Put the blame where it belongs—on the prevailing mores that regard prize
fighting as a perfectly proper enterprise and vehicle of entertainment. No
one doubts that many people enjoy prize fighting and will miss it if it should
be thrown out. And that is precisely the point.

WHAT DID THE WRITER SAY, AND WHAT DID YOU THINK?

1. The article has a declared thesis: identifying the killers of Benny Paret. Within that
   thesis is an implied thesis about boxing in general. What is it?
2. The author dismisses actions of the referee, manager, and doctors as causes: they
   are not "the real one." Would it have been more logical to make a distinction between
   primary causes and secondary causes? Does the author, in fact, begin to contradict
   himself in paragraph 9 when he refers to "the *primary* responsibility"?
3. Do you agree that "it is nonsense to talk about prize fighting as a test of boxing skills"?
4. Explain the meaning of the last sentence: "And that is precisely the point."

HOW DID THE WRITER SAY IT?

1. What is the purpose of the long introductory anecdote about Mike Jacobs? What does the author stress most about Jacobs?
2. How does the description of the human brain in paragraph 8 differ from an objective, scientific description? How does that difference fit in with the author's purposes?
3. Comment on the connotations of *boy* in paragraph 7.
4. Where does the author most directly attempt to arouse the reader's emotions?
5. Vocabulary: *fledgling, bland, colossus, adroit, parrying, mores.*

WHAT ABOUT YOUR WRITING?

"Never begin a sentence with *and.*" The only real problem with that rule is that it shouldn't be a rule at all. It's good enough *advice,* as far as it goes. When readers see *and* at the start of a sentence, their first thought is likely to be that the word introduces a tacked-on idea that logically should be part of the previous sentence. More often than not, they are right.

Still, there's no rule. Precisely because most sentences don't and shouldn't begin with *and,* many good writers sometimes use the word to single out a sentence for special notice and dramatic emphasis. Norman Cousins does it in the last sentence of "Who Killed Benny Paret?" Abraham Lincoln does it in his "Second Inaugural Address":

> Both parties deprecated war; but one of them would *make* war rather than let the nation survive; and the other would *accept* war rather than let it perish. And the war came.

In the powerful last paragraph of Edgar Allan Poe's "The Masque of the Red Death," we find a virtual festival of *ands,* here used not only for dramatic force, but to suggest the eloquence of the King James version of the Bible—many sentences of which also begin with *and.*

> And now was acknowledged the presence of the Red Death. He had come like a thief in the night. And one by one dropped the revellers in the blood-bedewed halls of their revel, and died each in the despairing posture of his fall. And the life of the ebony clock went out with that of the last of the gay. And the flames of the tripods expired. And Darkness and Decay and the Red Death held illimitable dominion over all.

The moral is simple: sentences shouldn't begin with *and* except in special circumstances. In special circumstances, *and* can be effective. When it is effective—clearly effective—go ahead and use it. There's no rule.

Letter to the Pulitzer Prize Committee

SINCLAIR LEWIS

Sinclair Lewis (1885–1951) first attracted popular attention with the publication in 1920 of the best-selling *Main Street,* an attack on small-town provinciality, mingled with strong traces of affection that few reviewers noticed or acknowledged. An outspoken public figure, Lewis wrote a number of controversial, satirical novels directed against the complacency, conformity, and narrow-mindedness that he saw in middle-class American life. Among his novels are *Babbitt* (1922), *Arrowsmith* (1925), *Elmer Gantry* (1927), *Dodsworth* (1929), and *It Can't Happen Here* (1935).

Few of Lewis's activities aroused such debate as his refusal of the Pulitzer Prize in 1926. The prize, still prestigious today, was endowed by Joseph Pulitzer, owner and publisher of the St. Louis *Post-Dispatch* and New York *World.* The first prizes were awarded in 1917. Prizes are given for fiction, drama, history, biography, poetry, music, and several branches of journalism.

When awarded the Nobel Prize in 1930, Lewis accepted.

SIRS:—I wish to acknowledge your choice of my novel *Arrowsmith* for the Pulitzer Prize. That prize I must refuse, and my refusal would be meaningless unless I explained the reasons. 1

All prizes, like all titles, are dangerous. The seekers for prizes tend to labor not for inherent excellence but for alien rewards: they tend to write this, or timorously to avoid writing that, in order to tickle the prejudices of a haphazard committee. And the Pultizer Prize for novels is peculiarly objectionable because the terms of it have been constantly and grievously misrepresented. 2

Those terms are that the prize shall be given "for the American novel published during the year which shall best present the wholesome atmosphere of American life, and the highest standard of American manners and manhood." This phrase, if it means anything whatever, would appear to mean that the appraisal of the novels shall be made not according to their actual literary merit but in obedience to whatever code of Good Form may chance to be popular at the moment. 3

That there is such a limitation of the award is little understood. Because of the condensed manner in which the announcement is usually reported, and because certain publishers have trumpeted that any novel which has received the Pulitzer Prize has thus been established without qualification as *the best* novel, the public has come to believe that the prize is the highest honor which an American novelist can receive. 4

The Pulitzer Prize for novels signifies, already, much more than a convenient thousand dollars to be accepted even by such writers as smile secretly at the actual wording of the terms. It is tending to become a sanctified tradition. There is a general belief that the administrators of the prize are 5

From *The Man from Main Street: A Sinclair Lewis Reader,* edited by Melville H. Cane and Harry E. Maule. Copyright 1953 by the Estate of Sinclair Lewis. Reprinted by permission of Random House, Inc.

a pontifical body with the discernment and power to grant the prize as the ultimate proof of merit. It is believed that they are always guided by a committee of responsible critics, though in the case both of this and other Pulitzer Prizes, the administrators can, and sometimes do, quite arbitrarily reject the recommendations of their supposed advisers.

6   If already the Pulitzer Prize is so important, it is not absurd to suggest that in another generation it may, with the actual terms of the award ignored, become the one thing for which any ambitious novelist will strive; and the administrators of the prize may become a supreme court, a college of cardinals, so rooted and so sacred that to challenge them will be to commit blasphemy. Such is the French Academy,[1] and we have had the spectacle of even an Anatole France[2] intriguing for election.

7   Only by regularly refusing the Pulitzer Prize can novelists keep such a power from being permanently set up over them.

8   Between the Pulitzer Prizes, the American Academy of Arts and Letters and its training-school, the National Institute of Arts and Letters,[3] amateur boards of censorship, and the inquisition of earnest literary ladies, every compulsion is put upon writers to become safe, polite, obedient, and sterile. In protest, I declined election to the National Institute of Arts and Letters some years ago, and now I must decline the Pulitzer Prize.

9   I invite other writers to consider the fact that by accepting the prizes and approval of these vague institutions we are admitting their authority, publicly confirming them as the final judges of literary excellence, and I inquire whether any prize is worth that subservience.

I am, Sirs,
Yours sincerely,
(Signed) SINCLAIR LEWIS

WHAT DID THE WRITER SAY, AND WHAT DID YOU THINK?

1. Express the thesis in one sentence.
2. What does Lewis have against the Pulitzer Prize? Does he support his accusations with specific details?
3. What does he have against all prizes?
4. What purposes does the writer have other than explaining the causes of his refusal?
5. How does the reference to the French Academy and Anatole France fit into the development of the author's point?
6. At the time of Lewis's refusal, a newspaper editorial stated, "He has a perfect right to express his personal aversion to accept the judgment. Not quite so happy is his

[1] Organization, founded 1635, of eminent French literary figures, and others.
[2] French author (1844–1924) of *Penguin Island* (1908) and *The Revolt of the Angels* (1914). He received the Nobel Prize for Literature in 1921.
[3] The National Institute was founded in 1898 as a parallel to the French Academy. The American Academy is an honorary group of fifty members of the National Institute.

assumption that any writer who does accept such a tribute thereby debases his profession and expresses a paltry subservience to arbitrary authority for the sake of gain." Do you agree with the editorial?

7. Does Lewis consider any arguments for the other side? Should he?

HOW DID THE WRITER SAY IT?

1. Is the author's tone polite? Does he want it to be?
2. Does Lewis ever thank the committee for its choice? Should he?
3. Why does Lewis capitalize "Good Form" in paragraph 3?
4. What does Lewis have in mind with the reference to "the inquisitions of earnest literary ladies"?
5. Does the author's language in paragraph 6 oversimplify the probable effects of the prize?
6. Vocabulary: *timorously, haphazard, sanctified, pontifical, discernment, subservience.*

WHAT ABOUT YOUR WRITING?

"That prize I must refuse . . ." Lewis here uses *inversion,* the reversal of normal word order ("I must refuse that prize") to achieve special emphasis. Any departure from the normal will stand out in writing, and that's what Lewis wants for this sentence. Lewis is making a momentous and unprecedented decision. He hopes his decision, moreover, will be an inspiration to other writers. The statement of his decision must, therefore, be made to stand out, and inversion is appropriate.

Inversion need not create glorious drama every time it is used, but it will always create an emphasis lacking in normal word order. Used too much or too crudely, it becomes an awkward and silly affectation: "Utter contempt have I for these proposals" or "Prime minister at last was Winston Churchill." Used discreetly, it's one more tool for a good writer.

NORMAL ORDER	INVERSION
We trust in God.	In God we trust.
The color of my true love's hair is black.	Black is the color of my true love's hair.
He lived foolishly, and he died foolishly.	Foolishly he lived, and foolishly he died.
William Butler Yeats ranks first among twentieth-century poets.	Ranking first among twentieth-century poets is William Butler Yeats.
The hard part comes now.	Now comes the hard part.

Why People Don't Help in a Crisis
JOHN M. DARLEY AND BIBB LATANÉ

John M. Darley and Bibb Latané are university psychologists. The reading selection is a popularization of their prize-winning 1968 study, ''The Unresponsive Bystander: Why Doesn't He Help?'' As you read, notice how the causes, though discussed separately, are also treated as links in a chain (see p. 103).

1   Kitty Genovese is set upon by a maniac as she returns home from work at 3 A.M. Thirty-eight of her neighbors in Kew Gardens, N.Y., come to their windows when she cries out in terror; not one comes to her assistance, even though her assailant takes half an hour to murder her. No one so much as calls the police. She dies.

2   Andrew Mormille is stabbed in the head and neck as he rides in a New York City subway train. Eleven other riders flee to another car as the 17-year-old boy bleeds to death; not one comes to his assistance, even though his attackers have left the car. He dies.

3   Eleanor Bradley trips and breaks her leg while shopping on New York City's Fifth Avenue. Dazed and in shock, she calls for help, but the hurrying stream of people simply parts and flows past. Finally, after 40 minutes, a taxi driver stops and helps her to a doctor.

4   How can so many people watch another human being in distress and do nothing? Why don't they help?

5   Since we started research on bystander responses to emergencies, we have heard many explanations for the lack of intervention in such cases. ''The megalopolis in which we live makes closeness difficult and leads to the alienation of the individual from the group,'' says the psychoanalyst. ''This sort of disaster,'' says the sociologist, ''shakes the sense of safety and sureness of the individuals involved and causes psychological withdrawal.'' ''Apathy,'' say others. ''Indifference.''

6   All of these analyses share one characteristic: they set the indifferent witness apart from the rest of us. Certainly not one of us who reads about these incidents in horror is apathetic, alienated or depersonalized. Certainly these terrifying cases have no personal implications for us. We needn't feel guilty, or re-examine ourselves, or anything like that. Or should we?

7   If we look closely at the behavior of witnesses to these incidents, the people involved begin to seem a little less inhuman and a lot more like the rest of us. They were not indifferent. The 38 witnesses of Kitty Genovese's murder, for example, did not merely look at the scene once and then ignore it. They continued to stare out of their windows, caught, fascinated, distressed, unwilling to act but unable to turn away.

8   Why, then, didn't they act?

9   There are three things the bystander must do if he is to intervene in an

emergency: *notice* that something is happening; *interpret* that event as an emergency; and decide that he has *personal responsibility* for intervention. As we shall show, the presence of other bystanders may at each stage inhibit his action.

The Unseeing Eye

Suppose that a man has a heart attack. He clutches his chest, staggers to   10
the nearest building and slumps sitting to the sidewalk. Will a passerby come to his assistance? First, the bystander has to notice that something is happening. He must tear himself away from his private thoughts and pay attention. But Americans consider it bad manners to look closely at other people in public. We are taught to respect the privacy of others, and when among strangers we close our ears and avoid staring. In a crowd, then, each person is less likely to notice a potential emergency than when alone.

Experimental evidence corroborates this. We asked college students to   11
an interview about their reactions to urban living. As the students waited to see the interviewer, either by themselves or with two other students, they filled out a questionnaire. Solitary students often glanced idly about while filling out their questionnaires; those in groups kept their eyes on their own papers.

As part of the study, we staged an emergency: smoke was released into   12
the waiting room through a vent. Two thirds of the subjects who were alone noticed the smoke immediately, but only 25 percent of those waiting in groups saw it as quickly. Although eventually all the subjects did become aware of the smoke—when the atmosphere grew so smoky as to make them cough and rub their eyes—this study indicates that the more people present, the slower an individual may be to perceive an emergency and the more likely he is not to see it at all.

Seeing Is Not Necessarily Believing

Once an event is noticed, an onlooker must decide if it is truly an   13
emergency. Emergencies are not always clearly labeled as such; "smoke" pouring into a waiting room may be caused by fire, or it may merely indicate a leak in a steam pipe. Screams in the street may signal an assault or a family quarrel. A man lying in a doorway may be having a coronary—or he may simply be sleeping off a drunk.

A person trying to interpret a situation often looks at those around him   14
to see how he should react. If everyone else is calm and indifferent, he will tend to remain so; if everyone else is reacting strongly, he is likely to become aroused. This tendency is not merely slavish conformity; ordinarily we derive much valuable information about new situations from how others around us behave. It's a rare traveler who, in picking a roadside restaurant, chooses to stop at one where no other cars appear in the parking lot.

15   But occasionally the reactions of others provide false information. The studied nonchalance of patients in a dentist's waiting room is a poor indication of their inner anxiety. It is considered embarrassing to "lose your cool" in public. In a potentially acute situation, then, everyone present will appear more unconcerned than he is in fact. A crowd can thus force inaction on its members by implying, through its passivity, that an event is not an emergency. Any individual in such a crowd fears that he may appear a fool if he behaves as though it were.

16   To determine how the presence of other people affects a person's interpretation of an emergency, Latané and Judith Rodin set up another experiment. Subjects were paid $2 to participate in a survey of game and puzzle preferences conducted at Columbia University by the Consumer Testing Bureau. An attractive young market researcher met them at the door and took them to the testing room, where they were given questionnaires to fill out. Before leaving, she told them that she would be working next door in her office, which was separated from the room by a folding room-divider. She then entered her office, where she shuffled papers, opened drawers and made enough noise to remind the subjects of her presence. After four minutes she turned on a high-fidelity tape recorder.

17   On it, the subjects heard the researcher climb up on a chair, perhaps to reach for a stack of papers on the bookcase. They heard a loud crash and a scream as the chair collapsed and she fell, and they heard her moan, "Oh, my foot . . . I . . . I . . . can't move it. Oh, I . . . can't get this . . . thing . . . off me." Her cries gradually got more subdued and controlled.

18   Twenty-six people were alone in the waiting room when the "accident" occurred. Seventy percent of them offered to help the victim. Many pushed back the divider to offer their assistance; others called out to offer their help.

19   Among those waiting in pairs, only 20 percent—8 out of 40—offered to help. The other 32 remained unresponsive. In defining the situation as a nonemergency, they explained to themselves why the other member of the pair did not leave the room; they also removed any reason for action themselves. Whatever had happened, it was believed to be not serious. "A mild sprain," some said. "I didn't want to embarrass her." In a "real" emergency, they assured us, they would be among the first to help.

The Lonely Crowd

20   Even if a person defines an event as an emergency, the presence of other bystanders may still make him less likely to intervene. He feels that his responsibility is diffused and diluted. Thus, if your car breaks down on a busy highway, hundreds of drivers whiz by without anyone's stopping to help—but if you are stuck on a nearly deserted country road, whoever passes you first is likely to stop.

21   To test this diffusion-of-responsibility theory, we simulated an emergency

in which people overheard a victim calling for help. Some thought they were the only person to hear the cries; the rest believed that others heard them, too. As with the witnesses to Kitty Genovese's murder, the subjects could not *see* one another or know what others were doing. The kind of direct group inhibition found in the other two studies could not operate.

For the simulation, we recruited 72 students at New York University to participate in what was referred to as a "group discussion" of personal problems in an urban university. Each student was put in an individual room equipped with a set of headphones and a microphone. It was explained that this precaution had been taken because participants might feel embarrassed about discussing their problems publicly. Also, the experimenter said that he would not listen to the initial discussion, but would only ask for reactions later. Each person was to talk in turn.   22

The first to talk reported that he found it difficult to adjust to New York and his studies. Then, hesitantly and with obvious embarrassment, he mentioned that he was prone to nervous seizures when he was under stress. Other students then talked about their own problems in turn. The number of people in the "discussion" varied. But whatever the apparent size of the group—two, three or six people—only the subject was actually present; the others, as well as the instructions and the speeches of the victim-to-be, were present only on a pre-recorded tape.   23

When it was the first person's turn to talk again, he launched into the following performance, becoming louder and having increasing speech difficulties: "I can see a lot of er of er how other people's problems are similar to mine because er I mean er they're not er e-easy to handle sometimes and er I er um I think I I need er if if could er er somebody er er er give me give me a little er give me a little help here because er I er *uh* I've got a one of the er seiz-er er things coming *on* and and er uh uh (choking sounds) . . ."   24

Eighty-five percent of the people who believed themselves to be alone with the victim came out of their room to help. Sixty-two percent of the people who believed there was *one* other bystander did so. Of those who believed there were four other bystanders, only 31 percent reported the fit. The responsibility-diluting effect of other people was so strong that single individuals were more than twice as likely to report the emergency as those who thought other people also knew about it.   25

The Lesson Learned

People who failed to report the emergency showed few signs of the apathy and indifference thought to characterize "unresponsive bystanders." When the experimenter entered the room to end the situation, the subject often asked if the victim was "all right." Many of them showed physical signs of nervousness; they often had trembling hands and sweating palms. If anything, they seemed more emotionally aroused than did those who reported   26 the emergency. Their emotional behavior was a sign of their continuing conflict concerning whether to respond or not.

27   Thus, the stereotype of the unconcerned, depersonalized *homo urbanus*,[1] blandly watching the misfortunes of others, proves inaccurate. Instead, we find that a bystander to an emergency is an anguished individual in genuine doubt, wanting to do the right thing but compelled to make complex decisions under pressure of stress and fear. His reactions are shaped by the actions of others—and all too frequently by their inaction.

28   And we are that bystander. Caught up by the apparent indifference of others, we may pass by an emergency without helping or even realizing that help is needed. Once we are aware of the influence of those around us, however, we can resist it. We can choose to see distress and step forward to relieve it.

WHAT DID THE WRITERS SAY, AND WHAT DID YOU THINK?

1. The authors discuss three causes for people's failure to help in a crisis. What is the central thesis that ties all the causes together?
2. What element, discussed in all three causes, determines how readily people will respond?
3. The essay begins with three dramatic examples of crises in which bystanders did not help the victim. Does the rest of the essay adequately explain the behavior of the bystanders in all three cases?
4. Which experiment or experiments strike you as most persuasive in supporting the authors' point? Which strike you as least persuasive?
5. What do you think about the morality of the experiments? Should people, without their consent or awareness, be subjected to mental anguish in order to extend human knowledge?

HOW DID THE WRITERS SAY IT?

1. Where is the thesis first stated? Why so late?
2. Why are detailed descriptions of the experiments necessary?
3. What phrase in paragraph 13 reminds the reader of the point previously made before moving on to the next point? What phrase serves the same purpose in paragraph 20?
4. The conclusion states that once we know the causes of failure to act, we can prepare ourselves to resist them. Is this idea a logical outgrowth of what has come before, or is it a tacked-on ending that introduces a sudden, brand-new thought?

[1] City man.

5. As pointed out in the introductory note, "Why People Don't Help in a Crisis" is a popularization for a general audience of a scientific study. In what important respects would the scientific study be different from this essay?
6. Vocabulary: _megalopolis, inhibit, coronary, nonchalance, acute, diffused, simulated._

WHAT ABOUT <u>YOUR</u> WRITING?

After three short examples, the introduction of "Why People Don't Help in a Crisis" is filled with sentences that ask questions. "How can so many people watch another human being in distress and do nothing?" "Why don't they help?" "Or should we?" "Why, then, didn't they act?" There are dozens of ways of starting a paper, and beginning with a question or series of questions and then providing answers in the remainder of your paper can sometimes be extremely effective. The question-and-answer technique can create in your reader a sense of personal participation in the quest for an answer. It can contribute to a feeling of suspense. Certainly, the question-and-answer technique is one of the most commonly used. It can be applied to any of the patterns discussed in the various chapters of this book.

EXAMPLES

Is the corruption we see in public officials simply the accepted way of getting things done today? I think it is—and a few examples will show why.

PROCESS

Have you ever seen those commercials with ladies in elegant gowns putting down a new floor in the rec room? Have you ever felt you'd like to do the same? Don't. It's a long, complicated process.

COMPARISON AND CONTRAST

What would happen if through some time machine we could get Muhammed Ali in the same ring with Jack Dempsey? Who would win? Would it be the quickest hands and feet of all time or the strongest punch?

Taking the mental and emotional leap of getting the first words down on paper can be a problem for any writer, no matter how experienced. The question-and-answer approach is one device that can help.

How Wealth Accumulates and Men Decay

GEORGE BERNARD SHAW

The genius of George Bernard Shaw (1856–1950) in treating complex ideas on the stage in a clear, witty, and often controversial fashion helped make him probably the most important British playwright since Shakespeare. His numerous plays include *Candida* (1893), *Arms and the Man* (1894), *Caesar and Cleopatra* (1899), *Man and Superman* (1905), *Pygmalion* (1913), and *Saint Joan* (1923). In 1925, he was awarded the Nobel Prize for Literature.

An ardent socialist, Shaw belonged to the Fabian Society, a group committed to socialist triumph through gradual permeation of capitalist institutions rather than through Marxist violent revolution. *The Intelligent Woman's Guide to Socialism and Capitalism,* from which the following selection is taken, was published in 1928.

1   I want to stress this personal helplessness we are all stricken with in the face of a system that has passed beyond our knowledge and control. To bring it nearer home, I propose that we switch off from the big things like empires and their wars to little familiar things. Take pins for example! I do not know why it is that I so seldom use a pin when my wife cannot get on without boxes of them at hand; but it is so; and I will therefore take pins as being for some reason specially important to women.

2   There was a time when pinmakers could buy the material; shape it; make the head and the point; ornament it; and take it to market or to your door and sell it to you. They had to know three trades: buying, making, and selling; and the making required skill in several operations. They not only knew how the thing was done from beginning to end, but could do it. But they could not afford to sell you a paper of pins for a farthing. Pins cost so much that a woman's dress allowance was called pin money.

3   By the end of the eighteenth century Adam Smith[1] boasted that it took eighteen men to make a pin, each man doing a little bit of the job and passing the pin on to the next, and none of them being able to make a whole pin or to buy the materials or to sell it when it was made. The most you could say for them was that at least they had some idea of how it was made, though they could not make it. Now as this meant that they were clearly less capable and knowledgeable men than the old pinmakers, you may ask why Adam Smith boasted of it as a triumph of civilization when its effect was so clearly a degrading effect. The reason was that by setting each man to do just one little bit of the work and nothing but that, over and over again, he became very quick at it. The men, it is said, could turn out nearly five thousand pins a day each; and thus pins became plentiful and cheap. The country was supposed to be richer because it had more pins, though it had turned capable men into mere machines doing their work without intelligence, and being fed by the spare food of the capitalist as an engine is fed

From *The Intelligent Woman's Guide to Socialism and Capitalism*. Reprinted by permission of The Society of Authors on behalf of the Bernard Shaw Estate.

[1] Adam Smith (1723–1790), a champion of unrestricted free enterprise, was author of *The Wealth of Nations* (1776).

with coal and oil. That was why the poet Goldsmith,[2] who was a far-sighted economist as well as a poet, complained that "wealth accumulates, and men decay."

Nowadays Adam Smith's eighteen men are as extinct as the diplodocus.   4
The eighteen flesh-and-blood machines are replaced by machines of steel which spout out pins by the hundred million. Even sticking them into pink papers is done by machinery. The result is that with the exception of a few people who design the machines, nobody knows how to make a pin or how a pin is made: that is to say, the modern worker in pin manufacture need not be one-tenth so intelligent and skillful and accomplished as the old pinmaker; and the only compensation we have for this deterioration is that pins are so cheap that a single pin has no expressible value at all. Even with a big profit stuck on to the cost-price you can buy dozens for a farthing; and pins are so recklessly thrown away and wasted that verses have to be written to persuade children (without success) that it is a sin to steal a pin.

Many serious thinkers, like John Ruskin and William Morris,[3] have been   5
greatly troubled by this, just as Goldsmith was, and have asked whether we really believe that it is an advance in wealth to lose our skill and degrade our workers for the sake of being able to waste pins by the ton. We shall see later on, when we come to consider the Distribution of Leisure, that the cure for this is not to go back to the old ways; for if the saving of time by modern machinery were equally divided among us, it would set us all free for higher work than pinmaking or the like. But in the meantime the fact remains that pins are now made by men and women who cannot make anything by themselves, and could not arrange between themselves to make anything even in little bits. They are ignorant and helpless, and cannot lift their finger to begin their day's work until it has all been arranged for them by their employers, who themselves do not understand the machines they buy, and simply pay other people to set them going by carrying out the machine maker's directions.

The same is true of clothes. Formerly the whole work of making clothes,   6
from the shearing of the sheep to the turning out of the finished and washed garment ready to put on, had to be done in the country by the men and women of the household, especially the women; so that to this day an unmarried woman is called a spinster. Nowadays nothing is left of all this but the sheep-shearing; and even that, like the milking of cows, is being done by machinery, as the sewing is. Give a woman a sheep today and ask her to produce a woolen dress for you; and not only will she be quite unable to do it, but you are as likely as not to find that she is not even aware of any connection between sheep and clothes. When she gets her clothes, which she does by buying them at a shop, she knows that there is a difference between wool and cotton and silk, between flannel and merino, perhaps

[2] Oliver Goldsmith (1728–1774), British poet, essayist, novelist, and playwright. The quotation is from "The Deserted Village," ll. 51–52.

[3] Ruskin (1819–1900), best known as an art critic, and Morris (1834–1896), a poet, printer, painter, and designer of furniture, both wrote extensively in support of social and economic reforms.

even between stockinet and other wefts; but as to how they are made, or what they are made of, or how they came to be in the shop ready for her to buy, she knows hardly anything. And the shop assistant from whom she buys is no wiser. The people engaged in the making of them know even less; for many of them are too poor to have much choice of materials when they buy their own clothes.

7   Thus the capitalist system has produced an almost universal ignorance of how things are made and done, whilst at the same time it has caused them to be made and done on a gigantic scale. We have to buy books and encyclopedias to find out what it is we are doing all day; and as the books are written by people who are not doing it, and who get their information from other books, what they tell us is from twenty to fifty years out of date, and unpractical at that. And of course most of us are too tired of our work when we come home to want to read about it: what we need is a cinema to take our minds off it and feed our imagination.

8   It is a funny place, this world of Capitalism, with its astonishing spread of ignorance and helplessness, boasting all the time of its spread of education and enlightenment. There stand the thousands of property owners and the millions of wage workers, none of them able to make anything, none of them knowing what to do until somebody tells them, none of them having the least notion of how it is that they find people paying them money, and things in the shops to buy with it. And when they travel they are surprised to find that savages and Esquimaux and villagers who have to make everything for themselves are more intelligent and resourceful! The wonder would be if they were anything else. We should die of idiocy through disuse of our mental faculties if we did not fill our heads with romantic nonsense out of illustrated newspapers and novels and plays and films. Such stuff keeps us alive; but it falsifies everything for us so absurdly that it leaves us more or less dangerous lunatics in the real world.

9   Excuse my going on like this; but as I am writer of books and plays myself, I know the folly and peril of it better than you do. And when I see that this moment of our utmost ignorance and helplessness, delusion and folly, has been stumbled on by the blind forces of Capitalism as the moment for giving votes to everybody, so that the few wise women are hopelessly overruled by the thousands whose political minds, as far as they can be said to have any political minds at all, have been formed in the cinema, I realize that I had better stop writing plays for a while to discuss political and social realities in this book with those who are intelligent enough to listen to me.

WHAT DID THE WRITER SAY, AND WHAT DID YOU THINK?

1. What is the thesis? Where is it stated?
2. Why does Shaw not want to go back to the good old days when one man was responsible for "buying, making, and selling"?

3. What fundamental change caused the end of the good old days?
4. What are the bad effects of capitalism?
5. Does the author concede that there were any beneficial effects of capitalism?
6. What does the author feel about women having the right to vote?
7. Do you agree that "savages and Esquimaux" are more "intelligent and resourceful" than industrialized peoples? Does Shaw assume the truth of a debatable proposition (see p. 238 on question begging)?
8. Does the author oversimplify or distort economic reality? Granting the charge, how might Shaw respond?
9. Does Shaw discuss here the ways in which socialism would cure the evils he mentions? How, for example, would Shaw suggest that pins be manufactured in a socialist country? How would socialism solve the problem of ignorance about which the author complains so bitterly? Or do these questions miss the author's point?
10. The little leisure time that people have now, Shaw asserts, is spent on filling their heads with "romantic nonsense." Would additional leisure time be devoted to higher things? Or does Shaw envision a socialist government's passing laws against producing such nonsense?

HOW DID THE WRITER SAY IT?

1. Why does the author say that he will start with a discussion of pins? Are his reasons insulting to his audience?
2. Are the comments about the origins of *pin money* and *spinster* pointless digressions, or do they contribute to the selection as a whole?
3. Does Shaw pay any attention to arguments that defenders of capitalism might present? That enemies of socialism might present?
4. Point out any instances of Shaw's celebrated satirical wit.
5. Comment on the purpose of the last sentence. Is it a harmless joke, an offensive display of arrogance, or what? How about "I know the folly and peril of it better than you do" in paragraph 9?
6. Vocabulary: *farthing, diplodocus, merino, stockinet, wefts.*

WHAT ABOUT YOUR WRITING?

In this selection, Shaw manages to make textbook material on economics, sometimes called "the dismal science," not only clear but entertaining. He does it partly through a conversational, personal, and sometimes even gabby style. He talks about himself and his wife and his career as a dramatist. He addresses the reader directly as *you.* He uses colloquial, half-slangy language: *spout out pins, a big profit stuck on, it is a funny place, such stuff keeps us alive, excuse my going on like this.*

A casual, conversational tone in dealing with potentially dull or difficult subjects can be dangerous, of course. You don't want to appear to talk down to your reader (some people may feel that Shaw doesn't escape this danger). You don't want to seem frivolous about issues that deserve serious attention. You don't want your style to be so casual that it becomes sloppy. You don't want your reader to believe that the subject is too difficult for *you*. Still, as the Shaw selection demonstrates, the rewards of an effective conversational style can be so great that the risks are often worth accepting.

For comments on *jargon*—the stuffy, technical language Shaw so successfully avoids—see p. 32.

Chapter 6

DIVISION
AND
CLASSIFICATION

Some topics are difficult or impossible to attack head on. Such topics are often best approached through *analysis:* studying a complex subject by breaking it down into smaller units. *Analysis* itself calls for analysis and can be broken down into *division* and *classification*.

Division

What are the moving parts of a rotary engine? What are the major characteristics of realism in literature? What are the three major divisions of the federal government? The United States of America is divided into fifty states. Can you name them all? Your own state is divided into counties. How many of them can you name?

In *division* (also known as *partition*) a subject commonly thought of as a single unit is reduced to its separate parts. Potential renters of an apartment rarely begin by thinking of the apartment as a whole. They mentally divide it into living room, bedroom, kitchen, and bathroom. If they think it worthwhile, they may go on to subdivisions of each room: wall, ceiling, floor, for example. At any rate, they study each division separately before reaching any useful conclusion about the entire apartment. Soldiers use division to study a rifle; chemists use division to find out the ingredients of a compound; doctors use division in a physical checkup to examine a patient—heart, lungs, blood, and so forth.

Division is a natural, logical, and necessary form of thought. For writing purposes, however, it often tends to be more cut-and-dried than classification, and most English teachers generally prefer classification assignments. Besides, any students who have written a process paper (see Chapter 3) have already used a form of division to break the process into its separate steps. For these reasons, the rest of this chapter concentrates on classification.

Classification

Are you an introvert or an extrovert? Are you lower class, middle class, or upper class? Are you a Democrat, Republican, or Independent? Are you a Protestant, Catholic, Jew, Moslem, Hindu, Buddhist, Sikh, atheist, agnostic, or "other"? Are you heterosexual or homosexual? Are you left-handed, right-handed, or ambidextrous? Are you a nondrinker, light drinker, normal drinker, heavy drinker, or alcoholic?

No answers are necessary. The questions aren't intended to snoop. They're intended to demonstrate the near universality of classification.

In *classification* we analyze a subject like apartments, not *an* apartment; engines, not an engine. We analyze the subject by arranging it into groups or categories rather than separate parts. We divide an apartment into rooms, but we classify apartments into high rises, garden apartments, tenements, and so on. We classify when we make out a shopping list to deal with the thousands of articles in a supermarket: dairy, meats, produce, paper goods, and other obvious groupings. A business manager classifies: complaints I can ignore, complaints I have to do something about. A college catalog classifies: required courses, elective courses.

Without classification certain kinds of systematic thought would be impossible. Biologists, for example, classify in order to make basic sense of the world, in order to be able to function at all. They classify living things into Plants and Animals. They classify Animals into Vertebrates and Invertebrates. They classify Vertebrates into Mammals, Birds, Reptiles, Amphibians, and Fish. Each class has its distinct characteristics, so when biologists meet some wriggly little item they haven't seen before, they have some way of at least beginning to cope with it. As another example, political leaders in presidential elections undoubtedly classify the states. They classify because no other way exists to handle reality. Which states are Sure for Us? Which states are Sure for Them? Which states are Toss-ups? Classification here is not a parlor game or intellectual exercise. It's the only way of determining where the time and money should go.

Classification can sometimes be a game, however, and it can lead to excellent humorous papers. Members of a bad football team could be classified as Hopeless Bums, Hopeless Mediocrities, and Hopeless Physical Wrecks. Household chores could be classified as Chores I Can Put Off for a Week, Chores I Can Put Off for a Month, and Chores I Can Put Off Forever. A student once classified teachers as Fascist Pigs, Middle-of-the-Road Sheep, and Mad Dog Radicals.

The pattern of a classification—or division—paper is straightforward and pretty much self-evident. Each class or division generally represents a major section of the paper. Each is defined and described, with as many examples as are needed for clarity. Each is carefully differentiated from the others when any possibility of confusion occurs.

In writing a classification paper, keep these elementary principles of logic in mind:

Use only one principle of classification. Different classifications can apply at different times to the same subject, depending on one's interests and insights. The essential requirement is that only one basis of classification be used at a time. Cars, for instance, can be classified by size. They can also be classified by manufacturer, price, body style, country of origin, and so on. Choose the principle of classification suitable to your purpose. Something is obviously cockeyed in this arrangement of cars: subcompact, compact, intermediate, Fords, full-size.

EXERCISE

What are the errors in the following classification outlines?

SCHOOLS
  I. Elementary schools
  II. Junior high schools
  III. Parochial schools
  IV. High schools
  V. Colleges and universities

STUDENTS
  I. Bright
  II. Average
  III. Hardworking
  IV. Dull

TEACHERS
  I. Hard graders
  II. Friendly
  III. Easy graders

CIGARETTES
  I. Filtered
  II. Unfiltered
  III. Mentholated

SECTIONS OF AMERICA
  I. East
  II. South
  III. Midwest
  IV. Slums
  V. Far West

POLITICIANS
  I. Good
  II. Bad
  III. Mediocre
  IV. Honest

Be consistent. Once you have determined a principle of classification, stick with it throughout the paper. Mixing principles invariably creates illogical overlapping of classes.

Make the classifications as complete as possible. All individual units within your subject should be able to fit into one of the classes you have devised. Classifying politicians as only good or bad doesn't take care of the many who are neither all one nor all the other; you need another category. In cases when you face the prospect of an endless number of classes, it's generally better to revise the subject a bit than to add a catch-all class like

''Miscellaneous'' or ''Others.'' A paper classifying religions, for example, could go on forever, whereas a paper classifying ''Major Religions in America'' would have a much simpler task.

EXERCISE

Point out incompleteness in the following classification outlines.

ACADEMIC DEGREES
  I. B.A.
 II. B.S.
III. M.A.
IV. Ph.D

CAREER OPPORTUNITIES
  I. Business
 II. Government

TELEVISION PROGRAMS
  I. Comedies
 II. Dramas
III. Sports
IV. Quiz shows

WHERE TO LIVE IN AMERICA
  I. Cities
 II. Suburbs

Acknowledge any complications. Classification is logical and essential, but it's also arbitrary and artificial. It pins labels on materials that weren't born with them. It may be helpful at times to classify people as introverts or extroverts, but a good paper points out that introverts can sometimes be outgoing among close friends and extroverts can sometimes be shy in unfamiliar or threatening circumstances. Similarly, labels like liberal and conservative can be valuable, but a good paper will mention that few people are entirely liberal or conservative about everything.

Follow the persuasive principle. Finally, what of the persuasive principle? A classification paper classifies. What does it have to persuade anyone about?

In a fussy, technical sense, every classification paper has a thesis whether the writer wants one or not. The writer asserts that there are three classes of teachers, or four classes of mental illness, or five classes of surgeons. By the end of the paper, sure enough, there are the three, four, or five classes, logically consistent and complete.

And there, sure enough, if that's all the writer does, is a distortion of the persuasive principle.

A good classification paper can utilize the persuasive principle in far more effective ways. To the logic and order of classification it can add the power and bite of a forceful point of view. In some papers, the naming of classes in itself can express the writer's attitude. An introductory paragraph stating that the three kinds of teachers are Fascist Pigs, Middle-of-the-Road Sheep, and Mad Dog Radicals probably doesn't need an explicit thesis statement that all three classes are obnoxious. A paper with less dramatic labels can declare a thesis by expressing a strong preference for one class over the others. It can express scorn for all classes. It can ridicule traditional classifications. Almost all the subjects for classification brought up in this chapter invite a thesis:

Each different kind of American car has overwhelming drawbacks.

Good politicians in this country are vastly outnumbered by the bad and mediocre.

Every major religion in America has a similar concept of God.

The distinctions among normal drinkers, heavy drinkers, and alcoholics are dangerously vague.

Only one kind of television program makes any appeal to the viewer's intelligence.

It's not hard to see the extra interest such approaches can give a paper. Don't just classify, then. Convince.

WRITING SUGGESTIONS FOR CLASSIFICATION THEMES

Use classification to analyze one of the following subjects. Narrow down any of the subjects as necessary, and remember the importance of working a thesis into your paper. With slight changes, some topics may also lend themselves to analysis by division.

1. Television detectives
2. Snobbishness
3. Drug users
4. People at a concert or sporting event
5. Methods of making excuses
6. Cashiers in supermarkets
7. Clothing
8. Parents
9. Love
10. Hate
11. Laziness
12. News programs or commentators
13. Freshman English students
14. Managers or coaches of athletic teams
15. Ambition
16. Summer jobs
17. Pessimists or optimists
18. Attitudes toward Christmas
19. Attitudes toward money
20. Attitudes toward sex

Ride with English Dignity, German Precision, Italian Flair, and American Practicality

Audi is a middle-priced German-made car distributed in this country by Volkswagen. As you read, try to speculate on what kinds of people the writers of the ad see as the most likely potential customers.

The ad is organized by division rather than classification.

Ride with English dignity, German precision, Italian flair, and American practicality.

When you ride in an Audi 100LS you'll be impressed with the following:

An aura of dignity because the car has just about the same headroom and legroom as England's Rolls-Royce Silver Shadow.

An uncanny feeling of precision because it has the same type of reliable ignition system as Germany's Porsche 911. And the same kind of efficient heating and ventilation system as her Mercedes-Benz 280SE.

A flair for handling because it has the same type of steering system as Italy's racing Ferrari.

And astonishing practicality because it has the same trunk space as America's Lincoln Continental Mark IV. And front-wheel drive like her Cadillac Eldorado.

When you ride in an Audi you get the best England, Germany, Italy and America have to offer.

The Audi 100LS.
It's a lot of cars for the money.

WHAT DID THE WRITER SAY, AND WHAT DID YOU THINK?

1. The description of the Audi is in four parts, each naming an outstanding virtue. What is the principle of division? Could other divisions have been added?
2. Which one sentence contains the thesis?
3. What do the cars the Audi is compared to have in common?

HOW DID THE WRITER SAY IT?

1. What accounts for the unusual mixture of typography at the start of the ad?
2. In paragraph 1, is the phase "you'll be impressed with the following" too formal? If it is appropriate, why is a comparatively formal tone desired?
3. Some people have suggested that some foreign car buyers are motivated by the desire for prestige, status, and so forth. Does this ad appeal at all to such motivations? If so, do ads for domestic cars do the same?
4. Both America and Germany are referred to as "her." Is this conventional usage? Does it serve any special purpose in the advertisement?
5. Until recently, most advertisers avoided direct mention of any competitors, believing that mention of them would give the competitors free advertising. Is the principle a valid one? Does this ad violate it? If so, why?
6. Vocabulary: *aura, uncanny.*

WHAT ABOUT YOUR WRITING?

"It's a lot of cars for the money." This slogan, a pun or play on words, takes a standard expression—*a lot of car, a lot of man*—and reworks it to make a special point, to fit in with a particular purpose. Opinions may differ, of course, on how successful this slogan is. Some people, too, probably still accept unthinkingly the tired old cliché that puns and word plays are the lowest form of literature. In fact, however, writers as diverse as Shakespeare and Thoreau have been entranced by the exciting stylistic possibilities of word plays.

E. E. Cummings, the American poet, once wrote that poetry should do to you what the old burlesque gag does:

Question: Would you hit a woman with a baby?
Answer: No, I'd hit her with a brick.

Cummings' view is that poetry should fool around with words, should try to astonish and delight the reader by revealing previously unnoticed possibilities of language. Although prose is ordinarily more sedate than poetry, it too can profit from the touch of originality, the fresh slant, the new twist that fooling around with words can sometimes contribute.

Most frequently, of course, word plays provide a welcome note of humor. "The orchestra played Beethoven last night. Beethoven lost." A *Time* magazine movie review once described a wagon train surrounded by Indians as being "in the Siouxp."

Word plays lend themselves to satire, too. In Shakespeare's *Henry IV, Part I*, Glendower, a braggart with mystical inclinations, is talking to Hotspur, an honest, downright soldier:

> GLENDOWER: I can call spirits from the vasty deep.
>
> HOTSPUR: Why, so can I . . .
>   But will they come when you do call for them?

Other word plays can be entirely serious. In *Walden,* Thoreau simply treats a common figurative expression with unexpected literalness:

> If you have built castles in the air, your work need not be lost; that is where they should be. Now put the foundations under them.

There's no compulsion to experiment with word plays. They're risky. Unsuccessful word plays are always damaging because they call attention to themselves. They should generally be used in moderation; the writer wants to give an impression of being clever, but not of being a show-off. If you have neither the temperament nor the knack for word plays, you should avoid them completely. With all these cautions, however, a distinctive style helps capture your reader's attention, and skillful fooling around with words can help create a distinctive style.

How Fit Are You?

KENNETH H. COOPER

> Kenneth Cooper's book *Aerobics,* based on his experience as a doctor in the U.S. Air Force, presents a physical fitness program designed to increase the oxygen capacity of the body through exercises like swimming, jogging, walking, and cycling. The reading selection is an excerpt from the second chapter of the book.

1   I was visiting a colleague who was testing volunteers for a special project that would require men in the best possible condition. I passed three of the volunteers in the hall. Two had normal builds, but the third was definitely muscular.

2   "Which of the three do you think will get our recommendation?" my friend asked, tossing their medical records across the desk. I skimmed over the physiological data until I came to the slot where it asked, "Regular exercise?"

3   One wrote, candidly, "None."

4   The second, "Nothing regular. Just ride my bike to the base and back every day. About three miles one way."

5   The third, "Isometrics and weight lifting, one hour a day, five days a week." The muscular one!

From *Aerobics* by Kenneth H. Cooper, M.D., M.P.H. Copyright © 1968 by Kenneth H. Cooper and Kevin Brown. Reprinted by permission of the publisher, M. Evans and Company, Inc., New York, N.Y.

I glanced back over each of the records. All pilots, all in their early 30s, none with any history of illness.   6

"Well?" asked my friend.   7

"I'd bet on the cyclist."   8

"Not the weight lifter?"   9

"Not if that's all he does."   10

My friend smiled. "I think you're right."   11

Next day he proved it. The three came back for their treadmill tests and the nonexerciser and the weight lifter were completely fatigued within the first five minutes. The cyclist was still going strong 10 minutes later, running uphill at a 6½ mph clip. He was recommended for the project. The other two weren't.   12

This story, when I use it in my lectures, always surprises people. The nonexerciser they can believe. The cyclist, maybe. But the weight lifter, or anyone who does strictly isometrics or calisthenics, they all *look* in such good condition!   13

In my business, looks are deceitful. Some exceptionally physically fit men tested in our laboratory were middle-aged types with slight builds, including an occasional one with a paunch. Some of the most unfit we've ever seen were husky young men with cardiac conditions.   14

If this shatters any illusions about slim waistlines and large biceps being the key to good health, I'm sorry. They're not a deterrent, but they're no guarantee either. They're mostly a byproduct. The real key is elsewhere.   15

Take those three volunteers. By ordinary standards, all three should have been accepted. None of them had any physical defects, or ever had any. Why the discrimination?   16

For special projects, the military services can afford to be discriminate. They can afford to classify the physically fit into their three classic categories and choose only the most fit.   17

The nonexerciser represents passive fitness. There's nothing wrong with him—not yet anyway—but there's nothing really right with him either. If he's lucky, he can coast like that for years. But, without any activity, his body is essentially deteriorating.   18

The weight lifter, or those who emphasize isometrics or calisthenics, represent muscular fitness. These types, who have the right motives but the wrong approach, are stuck with the myth that muscular strength or agility means physical fitness. This is one of the great misconceptions in the field of exercise. The muscles that show—the skeletal muscles—are just one system in the body, and by no means the most important. If your exercise program is directed only at the skeletal muscles, you'll never achieve real physical fitness.   19

The cyclist, whether he knew it or not, had found one of the most basic means to overall fitness. . . . By riding three miles to work, six miles round trip, he was earning more than enough points to answer the question, "How much exercise?"[1] and he proved it on the treadmill.   20

---

[1] Cooper had devised a point system for measuring physical fitness.

21   The cyclist represents the third, and best, kind of fitness, overall fitness. We call it endurance fitness, or working capacity, the ability to do prolonged work without undue fatigue. It assumes the absence of any ailment, and it has little to do with pure muscular strength or agility. It has very much to do with the body's *overall* health, the health of the heart, the lungs, the entire cardiovascular system and the other organs, *as well as* the muscles.

WHAT DID THE WRITER SAY, AND WHAT DID YOU THINK?

1. What group does Cooper classify?
2. Is there a thesis? If so, what is it?
3. What is the main advantage of cycling over weight lifting and calisthenics?
4. Does the writer maintain that anything is wrong with weight lifting and calisthenics in themselves?

HOW DOES THE WRITER SAY IT?

1. What purposes are served by beginning with a story rather than starting right out with the system of classification?
2. Does the writer merely describe each class, or does he also provide convenient labels for each?
3. Does the writer recognize the possibility that the second and third classes can overlap?
4. Vocabulary: *physiological, candidly, isometrics, treadmill, calisthenics, skeletal, cardiovascular.*

WHAT ABOUT <u>YOUR</u> WRITING?

"The cyclist, maybe." Isn't that a sentence fragment? "Why the discrimination?" Isn't that another sentence fragment? Aren't sentence fragments illegal? The answers to these questions are *yes, yes,* and *sort of.*

Look at it this way: there's a sensible speed limit on the road. One night you're driving well over the limit. A police officer who is worth anything would stop you to give you a ticket. This night an officer stops you and finds that you're speeding in order to get a pregnant woman to the hospital on time or a badly beaten man to the emergency ward. If the officer is worth anything now, you get a siren escort that enables you to break the law more safely and efficiently.

Your instructor, in some respects, is the police officer. By and large, sentence fragments are not standard written English, and your instructor rightly gives you a ticket for them. Every once in a while, a situation turns up when a fragment can be justified. You want a special dramatic effect, a sudden note of breeziness or informality, perhaps, that a grammatically complete sentence could not achieve as well. In that case, your instructor usually tries to be cooperative.

You don't speed to the emergency ward often, however, and sentence fragments, too, should be saved for special occasions. The burden of proof is on you: the officer wants to see the pregnant woman or beaten man, and the instructor wants to be convinced that the sentence fragment was justified by the demands of your paper. Finally, just as the officer wants assurance that you knew you were speeding and were in constant control, the instructor wants assurance that your sentence fragment was a deliberate stylistic device, not a simple grammatical error.

If I'm So Smart,
How Come I Flunk All the Time?

CHARLES W. SLACK

Charles W. Slack, a psychologist, has written the controversial *Timothy Leary, the Madness of the Sixties, and Me* (1974).

Slack's article employs a popular style and so does not provide much of the statistical data on which the scientific findings are based. Personal experience, therefore, may be your best guide in evaluating the article. To what extent does it correspond with what you already know or fear?

Can twenty flunking students of varying intelligence raise their math and English a full year's level in only thirty working days? 1

Dr. Lloyd Homme, chief of a special educational "fix-it" laboratory in Albuquerque, New Mexico, said Yes and put teams of behavioral scientists together with the flunking students to work on the problem. Any available technology could be used—teaching machines, programmed instruction, computer-assisted methods—to cram a year's knowledge into the boys. 2

Were the experiments a success? The scientists said Yes but the students said No. When grades were measured using standardized tests under strict laboratory conditions, marks went up more than one year on the average. Meanwhile, back at the school, the students were still barely passing, at best. "The experiment was fine for the scientists. They proved their theory on paper and made a name for themselves, but most of us were still flunking in class," remarked one seventeen-year-old. 3

The only clue to the mystery was this common remark: "The teachers ignore us—they've got it in for us." 4

At first the scientists on the team thought the complaint was just sour grapes and told the boys to work harder. When grades still failed to rise, the scientists felt there might be some truth in what the young team members were saying. Not that teachers were to blame, necessarily, but there still might be some negative bias. "You should see what goes on in class!" said the boys. 5

6   "The only thing to do was to take them up on it, go into the classroom with them and see what was holding back their grades," said Dr. Homme.

7   Hence, bearded behavioral scientists ended up in the back row of math and English classes and made observations about the behavior of students and teachers. Homme was surprised to discover that two simple actions made the difference.

8   "With few exceptions, our students acted like dummies," said Dr. Homme, "even though we knew they were ahead of the rest in knowledge. They were so used to playing the class idiot that they didn't know how to show what they knew. Their eyes wandered, they appeared absent-minded or even belligerent. One or two read magazines hidden under their desks, thinking, most likely, that they already knew the classwork. They rarely volunteered and often had to have questions repeated because they weren't listening. Teachers, on the other hand, did not trust our laboratory results. Nobody was going to tell them that 'miracles' could work on Sammy and José."

9   In the eyes of teachers, students seemed to fall into three groups. We'll call them *bright-eyes, scaredy-cats* and *dummies*.

Bright-eyes had perfected the trick of:
1. "eyeballing" the instructor at all times, even from the minute he entered the room.
2. never ducking their eyes away when the instructor glanced at *them*.
3. getting the instructor to call on them when they wanted *without* raising their hands.
4. even making the instructor go out of his way to call on someone else to "give others a chance" (especially useful when bright-eyes themselves are uncertain of the answer).
5. readily admitting ignorance so as not to bluff—but in such a way that it sounds as though ignorance is rare.
6. asking many questions.

Scaredy-cats (the middle group)
1. looked toward the instructor but were afraid to let him "catch their eyes."
2. asked few questions and gave the impression of being "under achievers."
3. appeared uninvolved and had to be "drawn out," so they were likely to be criticized for "inadequate participation."

Dummies (no matter how much they really knew)
1. never looked at the instructor.
2. never asked questions.
3. were stubborn about volunteering information in class.

10   To make matters worse, the tests in school were not standardized and not given nearly as frequently as those given in the laboratory. School test-scores were open to teacher bias. Classroom behavior of students counted a lot toward their class grades. There was no doubt that teachers were

biased against the dummies. The scientists concluded that no matter how much knowledge a dummy gained on his own, his grades in school were unlikely to improve unless he could somehow change his image into a bright-eyes. This would mean . . .

1. Look the teacher in the eye.
2. Ask questions and volunteer answers (even if uncertain).

"Teachers get teacher-training in how to play their roles. Why shouldn't students get student-training in how to play bright-eyes?" asked Homme. 11

Special training sessions were held at the laboratory. Dummies were drilled in eyeballing and hand-raising, which, simple as they sound, weren't easy to do. "I felt so square I could hardly stand it," complained one of the dummies. "That was at first. Later, when I saw others eyeballing and hand-raising and really learning more, I even moved my seat to the front. It flipped the teacher out of her skull. She couldn't get over it." 12

Those who found eyeballing especially difficult were taught to look at the instructor's mouth or the bridge of his nose. "Less threatening to the student," explained Homme. "It seems less aggressive to them." 13

Unfortunately, not all of the dummies were able to pick up new habits during the limited training period. Some learned in the laboratory but couldn't do it in the classroom. These became scaredy-cats—at least a step up. But for the majority, grades improved steadily once they got the hang of their new techniques. The students encouraged and helped each other to hand-raise and eyeball. 14

Teachers' comments reflected the improvement. "There is no doubt that student involvement was increased by the program and as a result grades went up." 15.

By way of advice to others wishing to improve their own eyeballing and hand-raising, student José Martinez suggests: "Don't try to do it all at once. You'll shock the teacher and make it tough for yourself. Begin slowly. Work with a friend and help each other. Do it like a game. Like exercising with weights—it takes practice but it's worth it." 16

Homme agrees. "In fact, results are guaranteed for life," he says. 17

WHAT DID THE WRITER SAY, AND WHAT DID YOU THINK?

1. What is the answer to the question in the title? Is the answer also the thesis of the article?
2. How can test scores on a math test be "open to teacher bias"? Is that what the author said or meant to say?
3. According to the author, teachers grade students to some extent for reasons unconnected to the students' knowledge of the subject. Why does the author not seem terribly upset by this disclosure?
4. The author also seems undisturbed by students' being trained to change their classroom behavior in order to gratify their teachers' tastes. Are the students being trained to be hypocrites and sneaks, or can the training be viewed more positively?

5. Why did it adversely affect students' performances that class tests were given less frequently than in the laboratory?
6. Does the author state what year of school the students were in? Does it matter?

HOW DID THE WRITER SAY IT?

1. What writing pattern or patterns are used in this article besides classification?
2. Are all six characteristics of *bright-eyes* really "tricks," as alleged by the author?
3. Find as many examples of slang as you can.
4. There's nothing to complain about in using slang in a direct quotation. A student might really have said, "It flipped the teacher out of her skull." Is the author's own use of slang—the labels of each classification, for example—appropriate in an article of this kind?
5. Does the writer of this generally informal article ever fall into using educational or scientific jargon (see p. 32)?

WHAT ABOUT <u>YOUR</u> WRITING?

One of the fundamental ingredients of English style is *parallelism:* using the same ("parallel") grammatical forms to express elements of approximately the same ("parallel") importance. This definition may seem more formidable than it really is. Parallelism is so fundamental that we use it all the time.

> Three parallel adjectives:
> The man was *tall, dark,* and *handsome.*
> Four parallel nouns:
> We have to buy a *rug,* a *sofa,* two *chairs,* and a *lamp.*
> Three parallel prepositional phrases:
> . . . *of the people, by the people, for the people.*
> Three parallel independent clauses:
> *I want you. I need you. I love you.*
> Two parallel imperatives:
> *Sit down* and *relax.*
> Four parallel infinitives:
> "*To strive, to seek, to find,* and not *to yield.*"

The parallel grammatical forms point to and reinforce the parallels in thought and importance. Moreover, parallelism is what readers normally expect; it's the normal way that words are put together. Notice how a breakdown in expected parallelism adversely affects these sentences:

> The man was tall, dark, and an athlete.
> . . . of the people, by the people, and serving the people.
> To strive, to seek, to find, and we must not yield.

In his article, Charles W. Slack uses parallelism effectively—sometimes. At other times, he gets careless. Slack divides students into three categories; the categories are labeled by parallel nouns: *bright-eyes, scaredy-cats, dummies.* So far so good. In listing the six characteristics of *bright-eyes,* the author preserves parallel form: each characteristic begins with a present participle (*-ing* endings). So far so good. Each characteristic of *scaredy-cats,* however, is introduced by a *past* participle (*-ed* endings). There's no valid reason for the sudden switch, though the author could argue that at least the past participles are parallel within this one category. Parallelism breaks down beyond dispute in the last category of *dummies.* Characteristics 1 and 2 begin with past participles ("never looked," "never asked") and there is no reason why characteristic 3 should not do the same. Slack's phrase, "were stubborn about volunteering information in class," could easily have been written "stubbornly refused to volunteer information in class."

Bear three points in mind for your own writing:

1. Parallelism isn't just a matter of sterile correctness. It can contribute to genuine stylistic distinction. Some of the most memorable phrases in the language draw much of their strength from parallelism:

Friends, Romans, countrymen . . .

I have nothing to offer but blood, sweat, toil, and tears.

. . . life, liberty, and the pursuit of happiness.

I came, I saw, I conquered.

. . . with malice toward none, with charity for all.

2. Occasional modifying words do not break the basic parallelism and can sometimes help avoid the danger of monotony. These sentences still show parallelism:

He was tall, dark, and astonishingly handsome.

We have to buy a rug, a sofa, two chairs, and most of all a fancy new lamp.

3. Parallelism works only when each member of the parallel series is roughly equivalent in importance. It leads to absurdity in the following cases:

My teacher has knowledge, enthusiasm, concern, and sinus trouble.

We must protect society from murderers, perverts, kidnappers, and litterbugs.

Weasel Words

CARL P. WRIGHTER

"Weasel Words" comes from the book *I Can Sell You Anything* (1972), in which Carl P. Wrighter, an experienced advertising man, shares with his audience an insider's knowledge of the tricks of the trade. The author uses classification to help make sense of the great number of weasel words and to keep the reading selection from turning into a string of unrelated insights and examples.

Advertising has power, all right. And advertising works, all right. And what it really boils down to is that advertising works because you believe   1 it. You're the one who believes Josephine the Plumber really knows about stains. You're the one who believes Winston tastes good like a cigarette should. You're the one who believes Plymouth is coming through. The real question is, why do you believe all these things? And the answer is, because you don't yet understand how advertising makes you believe. You don't understand what to believe, or even how to believe advertising. Well, if you're ready to learn how to separate the wheat from the chaff, if you're ready to learn how to make advertising work *for* you, if you're ready to learn how to stop being a sucker, then you're ready to go to work.

Weasel Words: God's Little Helpers

2   First of all, you know what a weasel is, right? It's a small, slimy animal that eats small birds and other animals, and is especially fond of devouring vermin. Now, consider for a moment the kind of winning personality he must have. I mean, what kind of a guy would get his jollies eating rats and mice? Would you invite him to a party? Take him home to meet your mother? This is one of the slyest and most cunning of all creatures; sneaky, slippery, and thoroughly obnoxious. And so it is with great and warm personal regard for these attributes that we humbly award this King of All Devious the honor of bestowing his name upon our golden sword: the weasel word.

3   A weasel word is "a word used in order to evade or retreat from a direct or forthright statement or position" (Webster). In other words, if we can't say it, we'll weasel it. And, in fact, a weasel word has become more than just an evasion or retreat. We've trained our weasels. They can do anything. They can make you hear things that aren't being said, accept as truths things that have only been implied, and believe things that have only been suggested. Come to think of it, not only do we have our weasels trained, but they, in turn, have got you trained. When *you* hear a weasel word, you automatically hear the implication. Not the real meaning, but the meaning *it* wants *you* to hear. So if you're ready for a little re-education, let's take a good look under a strong light at the two kinds of weasel words.

1. Words That Mean Things They Really Don't Mean

Help

4   That's it. "Help." It means "aid" or "assist." Nothing more. Yet, "help" is the one single word which, in all the annals of advertising, has done the most to say something that couldn't be said. Because "help" is the great qualifier; once you say it, you can say almost anything after it. In short, "help" has helped help us the most.

> Helps keep you young
> Helps prevent cavities
> Helps keep your house germ-free

"Help" qualifies everything. You've never heard anyone say, "This   5
product will keep you young," or "This toothpaste will positively prevent
cavities for all time." Obviously, we can't say anything like that, because
there aren't any products like that made. But by adding that one little word,
"help," in front, we can use the strongest language possible afterward. And
the most fascinating part of it is, you are immune to the word. You literally
don't hear the word "help." You only hear what comes after it. And why
not? That's strong language, and likely to be much more important to you
than the silly little word at the front end.

I would guess that 75 percent of all advertising uses the word "help."   6
Think, for a minute, about how many times each day you hear these
phrases:

Helps stop . . .
Helps prevent . . .
Helps fight . . .
Helps overcome . . .
Helps you feel . . .
Helps you look . . .

I could go on and on, but so could you. Just as a simple exercise, call it
homework if you wish, tonight when you plop down in front of the boob
tube for your customary three and a half hours of violence and/or situation
comedies, take a pad and pencil, and keep score. See if you can count how
many times the word "help" comes up during the commercials. Instead of
going to the bathroom during the pause before Marcus Welby operates, or
raiding the refrigerator prior to witnessing the Mod Squad wipe out a nest
of dope pushers, stick with it. Count the "helps," and discover just how
dirty a four-letter word can be.

Like

Coming in second, but only losing out by a nose, is the word "like," used   7
in comparison. Watch:

It's like getting one bar free
Cleans like a white tornado
It's like taking a trip to Portugal

Okay. "Like" is a qualifier, and is used in much the same way as "help."   8
But "like" is also a comparative element, with a very specific purpose; we
use "like" to get you to stop thinking about the product per se, and to get
you thinking about something that is bigger or better or different from the
product we're selling. In other words, we can make you believe that the
product is more than it is by likening it to something else.

Take a look at that first phrase, straight out of recent Ivory Soap adver-   9
tising. On the surface of it, they tell you that four bars of Ivory cost about
the same as three bars of most other soaps. So, if you're going to spend a
certain amount of money on soap, you can buy four bars instead of three.
Therefore, it's like getting one bar free. Now, the question you have to ask

yourself is, "Why the weasel? Why do they say 'like'? Why don't they just come out and say, 'You get one bar free'?" The answer is, of course, that for one reason or another, you really don't. Here are two possible reasons. One: sure, you get four bars, but in terms of the actual amount of soap that you get, it may very well be the same as in three bars of another brand. Remember, Ivory has a lot of air in it—that's what makes it float. And air takes up room. Room that could otherwise be occupied by more soap. So, in terms of pure product, the amount of actual soap in four bars of Ivory may be only as much as the actual amount of soap in three bars of most others. That's why we can't—or won't—come out with a straightforward declaration such as, "You get 25 percent more soap," or "Buy three bars, and get the fourth one free."

10   Reason number two: the actual cost and value of the product. Did it ever occur to you that Ivory may simply be a cheaper soap to make and, therefore, a cheaper soap to sell? After all, it doesn't have any perfume, or hexachlorophene, or other additives than can raise the cost of manufacturing. It's plain, simple, cheap soap, and so it can be sold for less money while still maintaining a profit margin as great as more expensive soaps. By way of illustrating this, suppose you were trying to decide whether to buy a Mercedes-Benz or a Ford. Let's say the Mercedes cost $7,000, and the Ford $3,500. Now the Ford salesman comes up to you with this deal: as long as you're considering spending $7,000 on a car, buy my Ford for $7,000 and I'll give you a second Ford, free! Well, the same principle can apply to Ivory: as long as you're considering spending 35 cents on soap, buy my cheaper soap, and I'll give you more of it.

11   I'm sure there are other reasons why Ivory uses the weasel "like." Perhaps you've thought of one or two yourself. That's good. You're starting to think.

12   Now, what about that wonderful white tornado? Ajax pulled that one out of the hat some eight years ago and you're still buying it. It's a classic example of the use of the word "like" in which we can force you to think, not about the product itself, but about something bigger, more exciting, certainly more powerful than a bottle of fancy ammonia. The word "like" is used here as a transfer word, which gets you away from the obvious— the odious job of getting down on your hands and knees and scrubbing your kitchen floor—and into the world of fantasy, where we can imply that this little bottle of miracles will supply all the elbow grease you need. Isn't that the name of the game? The whirlwind activity of the tornado replacing the whirlwind motion of your arm? Think about the swirling of the tornado, and all the work it will save you. Think about the power of that devastating windstorm; able to lift houses, overturn cars, and now, pick the dirt up off your floor. And we get the license to do it simply by using the word "like."

13   It's a copywriter's dream, because we don't have to substantiate anything. When we compare our product to "another leading brand," we'd better be able to prove what we say. But how can you compare ammonia to a windstorm? It's ludicrous. It can't be done. The whole statement is so ridiculous it couldn't be challenged by the government or the networks. So

it went on the air, and it worked. Because the little word "like" let us take
you out of the world of reality, and into your own fantasies. . . .

"Like" is a virus that kills. You'd better get immune to it.   14

Other Weasels   15

"Help" and "like" are the two weasels so powerful that they can stand
on their own. There are countless other words, not quite so potent, but
equally effective when used in conjunction with our two basic weasels, or
with each other. Let me show you a few.

Virtual *or* **virtually**

How many times have you responded to an ad that said: 16

Virtually trouble-free . . .
Virtually foolproof . . .
Virtually never needs service . . .

Ever remember what "virtual" means? It means "in essence or effect, but
not in fact." Important—"but not in fact." Yet today the word "virtually"
is interpreted by you as meaning "almost or just about the same as. . . ."
Well, gang, it just isn't true. "Not," in fact, means not, in fact. I was
scanning, rather longingly I must confess, through the brochure Chevrolet
publishes for its Corvette, and I came to this phrase: "The seats in the
. . . Corvette are virtually handmade." They had me, for a minute. I almost
took the bait of that lovely little weasel. I almost decided that those seats
were just about completely handmade. And then I remembered. Those seats
were not, *in fact,* handmade. Remember, "virtually" means "not, in fact,"
or you will, in fact, get sold down the river.

Acts *or* **works**

These two action words are rarely used alone, and are generally accom-   17
panied by "like." They need help to work, mostly because they are verbs,
but their implied meaning is deadly, nonetheless. Here are the key phrases:

Acts like . . .
Acts against . . .
Works like . . .
Works against . . .
Works to prevent (or help prevent) . . .

You see what happens? "Acts" or "works" brings an action to the product
that might not otherwise be there. When we say that a certain cough syrup
"acts on the cough control center," the implication is that the syrup goes
to this mysterious organ and immediately makes it better. But the implication here far exceeds what the truthful promise should be. An act is simply
a deed. So the claim "acts on" simply means it performs a deed on. What
that deed is, we may never know.

The rule of thumb is this: if we can't say "cures" or "fixes" or use any   18
other positive word, we'll nail you with "acts like" or "works against,"
and get you thinking about something else. Don't. . . .

Can be

19   This is for comparison, and what we do is to find an announcer who can really make it sound positive. But keep your ears open. "Crest can be of significant value when used in . . . ," etc., is indicative of an ideal situation, and most of us don't live in ideal situations.

Up to

20   Here's another way of expressing an ideal situation. Remember the cigarette that said it was aged, or "cured for up to eight long, lazy weeks"? Well, that could, and should, be interpreted as meaning that the tobaccos used were cured anywhere from one hour to eight weeks. We like to glamorize the ideal situation; it's up to you to bring it back to reality.

As much as

21   More of the same. "As much as 20 percent greater mileage" with our gasoline again promises the ideal, but qualifies it. . . .

Feel *or* the feel of

22   This is the first of our subjective weasels. When we deal with a subjective word, it is simply a matter of opinion. In our opinion, Naugahyde has the feel of real leather. So we can say it. And, indeed, if you were to touch leather, and then touch Naugahyde, you may very well agree with us. But that doesn't mean it is real leather, only that it feels the same. The best way to handle subjective weasels is to complete the thought yourself, by simply saying, "But it isn't." At least that way you can remain grounded in reality.

The look of *or* looks like

23   "Look" is the same as "feel," our subjective opinion. Did you ever walk into a Woolworth's and see those $29.95 masterpieces hanging in their "Art Gallery"? "The look of a real oil painting," it will say. "But it isn't," you will now reply. And probably be $29.95 richer for it.

2. Words That Have No Specific Meaning

24   If you have kids, then you have all kinds of breakfast cereals in the house. When I was a kid, it was Rice Krispies, the breakfast cereal that went snap, crackle, and pop. (One hell of a claim for a product that is supposed to offer nutritional benefits.) Or Wheaties, the breakfast of champions, whatever that means. Nowadays, we're forced to a confrontation with Quisp, Quake, Lucky Stars, Cocoa-Puffs, Clunkers, Blooies, Snarkles and Razzmatazz. And they all have one thing in common: they're all "fortified." Some are simply "fortified with vitamins," while others are specifically "fortified with vitamin D," or some other letter. But what does it all mean?

25   "Fortified" means "added on to." But "fortified," like so many other weasel words of indefinite meaning, simply doesn't tell us enough. If, for instance, a cereal were to contain one unit of vitamin D, and the manufacturers added some chemical which would produce two units of vitamin D,

they could then claim that the cereal was "fortified with twice as much vitamin D." So what? It would still be about as nutritional as sawdust.

The point is, weasel words with no specific meaning don't tell us enough, but we have come to accept them as factual statements closely associated with something good that has been done to the product. Here's another example.

Flavor *and* taste

These are two totally subjective words that allow us to claim marvelous things about products that are edible. Every cigarette in the world has claimed the best taste. Every supermarket has advertised the most flavorful meat. And let's not forget "aroma," a subdivision of this category. Wouldn't you like to have a nickel for every time a room freshener (a weasel in itself) told you it would make your home "smell fresh as all outdoors"? Well, they can say it, because smell, like taste and flavor, is a subjective thing. And, incidentally, there are no less than three weasels in that phrase. "Smell" is the first. Then, there's "as" (a substitute for the ever-popular "like"), and, finally, "fresh," which, in context, is a subjective comparison, rather than the primary definition of "new."

Now we can use an unlimited number of combinations of these weasels for added impact. "Fresher-smelling clothes." "Fresher-tasting tobacco." "Tastes like grandma used to make." Unfortunately, there's no sure way of bringing these weasels down to size, simply because you can't define them accurately. Trying to ascertain the meaning of "taste" in any context is like trying to push a rope up a hill. All you can do is be aware that these words are subjective, and represent only one opinion—usually that of the manufacturer.

Style *and* good looks

Anyone for buying a new car? Okay, which is the one with the good looks? The smart new styling? What's that you say? All of them? Well, you're right. Because this is another group of subjective opinions. And it is the subjective and collective opinion of both Detroit and Madison Avenue that the following cars have "bold new styling": Buick Riviera, Plymouth Satellite, Dodge Monaco, Mercury Brougham, and you can fill in the spaces for the rest. Subjectively, you have to decide on which bold new styling is, indeed, bold new styling. Then, you might spend a minute or two trying to determine what's going on under that styling. The rest I leave to Ralph Nader.

Different, special, *and* exclusive

To be different, you have to be not the same as. Here, you must rely on your own good judgment and common sense. Exclusive formulas and special combinations of ingredients are coming at you every day, in every way. You must constantly assure yourself that, basically, all products in any given category are the same. So when you hear "special," "exclusive," or "different," you have to establish two things: on what basis are they dif-

26

27

28

29

30

ferent, and is that difference an important one? Let me give you a hypothetical example.

31   All so-called "permanent" antifreeze is basically the same. It is made
from a liquid known as ethylene glycol, which has two amazing properties:
It has a lower freezing point than water, and a higher boiling point than
water. It does not break down (lose its properties), nor will it boil away.
And every permanent antifreeze starts with it as a base. Also, just about
every antifreeze has now got antileak ingredients, as well as antirust and
anticorrosion ingredients. Now, let's suppose that, in formulating the product, one of the companies comes up with a solution that is pink in color, as
opposed to all the others, which are blue. Presto—an exclusivity claim.
"Nothing else looks like it, nothing else performs like it." Or, how about,
"Look at ours, and look at anyone else's. You can see the difference our
exclusive formula makes." Granted, I'm exaggerating. But did I prove a
point?

Summary

32   A weasel word is a word that's used to imply a meaning that cannot be
truthfully stated. Some weasels imply meanings that are not the same as
their actual definition, such as "help," "like," or "fortified." They can act
as qualifiers and/or comparatives. Other weasels, such as "taste" and
"flavor," have no definite meanings, and are simply subjective opinions
offered by the manufacturer. A weasel of omission is one that implies a
claim so strongly that it forces you to supply the bogus fact. Adjectives are
weasels used to convey feelings and emotions to a greater extent than the
product itself can.

33   In dealing with weasels, you must strip away the innuendos and try to
ascertain the facts, if any. To do this, you need to ask questions such as:
How? Why? How many? How much? Stick to basic definitions of words.
Look them up if you have to. Then, apply the strict definition to the text
of the advertisement or commercial. "Like" means similar to, but not the
same as. "Virtually" means the same in essence, but not in fact.

34   Above all, never underestimate the devious qualities of a weasel. Weasels
twist and turn and hide in dark shadows. You must come to grips with them,
or advertising will rule you forever.

35   My advice to you is: Beware of weasels. They are nasty and untrainable,
and they attack pocketbooks.

WHAT DID THE WRITER SAY, AND WHAT DID YOU THINK?

1. What are the two classes of weasel words? Are they clearly distinguished from one
   another?
2. What is the thesis?
3. Does the author believe that weasel words are used consciously to deceive? Do
   weasel words actually tell lies?

4. What is the consumer's best defense against weasel words?
5. Are weasel words limited to advertising, or can they be found as well in areas like government, education, and the like?
6. Why do almost all people consider themselves so sophisticated and cynical about and invulnerable to the appeals of advertising?
7. Does the author strike you as being opposed to all advertising? If not, what kind of advertising would he approve of—and would it sell the product?

HOW DID THE WRITER SAY IT?

1. How angry is the writer? Does the tone of the reading selection reveal an element—possibly unconscious—of joy or pride in the skill of advertisers at outsmarting consumers? Does the tone reveal an element of contempt for the gullibility of consumers?
2. Do you think the author ever goes too far in trying for an informal, conversational style? In trying for humor?
3. Can you come up with a more interesting label than "Other Weasels" for the heading above paragraph 15?
4. Is the selection too long? If so, what could have been eliminated?
5. Is the concluding summary a helpful reminder of the author's main points, or is it only stale repetition?
6. Vocabulary: *elicit, negligible, chaff, vermin, annals, per se, odious, indicative, subjective, hypothetical, innuendos, ascertain.*

WHAT ABOUT YOUR WRITING?

Countless thousands of students have been told never to write *you*. They were misinformed. *You* is a tricky word, and it's easy enough to understand how some teachers, distraught at seeing the word so frequently mismanaged, might invent a rule that outlaws it—but no such rule exists in Standard English.

The tricky part is that *you* is both a pronoun of direct address, aimed at a specific person or group, and an indefinite pronoun meaning something like *people* or *one* or *everybody.* When it's used in writing aimed at a general audience—like most Freshman English writing—it can be taken in both ways and can often turn out to be unintentionally confusing, insulting, or funny. Imagine a casual reader coming across sentences like

When you catch syphilis you must consult your doctor immediately.

Your paranoid concern with what others think of you makes you a likely candidate for suicide.

The new night school program should give you fresh hope for overcoming your illiteracy.

Those sentences demand immediate revision:

Victims of syphilis must consult their doctors immediately.

Paranoid concern with what others think increases the likelihood of suicide.

The new night school program should give fresh hope for overcoming illiteracy.

Most notably in the first paragraph, but in fact all through Wrighter's "Weasel Words," the reader may be entitled to wonder about the effectiveness of the author's use of *you*. "Advertising works because you believe it. You're the one who believes Josephine the Plumber really knows about stains." "You don't understand what to believe, or even how to believe advertising." "You're ready to learn how to stop being a sucker." The reader may respond with an indignant "Who me?" Wrighter wants a powerful paragraph. He wants to provoke, to challenge, to make his subject and point of view compelling and immediate. He may have succeeded. He may also have succeeded in insulting and antagonizing at least some readers and in making them willing to accuse him of arrogance and overstatement.

To be fair to the inventors of imaginary rules, then, it's wise in most classroom writing to be extremely conservative with *you* as an indefinite pronoun. The assumed audience is a general one of mixed ages, sexes, backgrounds, and interests; using *you* for this audience is nearly always asking for trouble.

There's nothing wrong with *you*, however, in writing that does address itself to a specific audience: the purchaser of a bike who now has to put it together, the new employee who wants information on the pension plan and hospitalization program. This book addresses itself to college freshmen taking a course in English Composition, each of whom receives similar reading and writing assignments every day. An audience can't get much more specific than that, and therefore this book feels free to make frequent use of *you*. You must have noticed.

See p. 242 for comments on the use of *I*.

How to Lie with Statistics

DARRELL HUFF

Darrell Huff is a free-lance writer and former magazine editor. He has written a number of articles as well as the books *How to Lie with Statistics* (1954) and *How to Take a Chance* (1959).

The title of the Huff selection seems to indicate process writing (see pp. 45–49), and some sections do indeed provide how-to-do-it instructions. The selection as a whole, however, uses classification as its basic organizing principle: the large general group, statistical lies, is arranged into specific categories of lies.

1   "The average Yaleman, Class of '24," *Time* magazine noted once, commenting on something in the New York *Sun*, "makes $25,111 a year."

2   Well, good for him!

3   But wait a minute. What does this improbably precise and salubrious figure mean? Is it, as it appears to be, evidence that if you send your boy to Yale you won't have to work in your old age and neither will he? Is this average a mean or is it a median? What kind of sample is it based on? You

could lump one Texas oilman with two hundred hungry free-lance writers and report *their* average income as $25,000-odd a year. The arithmetic is impeccable, the figure is convincingly precise, and the amount of meaning there is in it you could put in your eye.

In just such ways is the secret language of statistics, so appealing in a fact-minded culture, being used to sensationalize, inflate, confuse, and oversimplify. Statistical terms are necessary in reporting the mass data of social and economic trends, business conditions, "opinion" polls, this year's census. But without writers who use the words with honesty and understanding and readers who know what they mean, the result can only be semantic nonsense.   4

In popular writing on scientific research, the abused statistic is almost crowding out the picture of the white-jacketed hero laboring overtime without time-and-a-half in an ill-lit laboratory. Like the "little dash of powder, little pot of paint," statistics are making many an important fact "look like what she ain't." Here are some of the ways it is done.   5

The sample with the built-in bias. Our Yalemen, as they say in the Time-Life building, belong to this flourishing group. The exaggerated estimate of their income is not based on all members of the class nor on a random or representative sample of them. At least two interesting categories of 1924-model Yale men have been excluded.   6

First there are those whose present addresses are unknown to their class-mates. Wouldn't you bet that these lost sheep are earning less than the boys from prominent families and the others who can be handily reached from a Wall Street office?   7

There are those who chucked the questionnaire into the nearest waste-basket. Maybe they didn't answer because they were not making enough money to brag about. Like the fellow who found a note clipped to his first paycheck suggesting that he consider the amount of his salary confidential: "Don't worry," he told the boss. "I'm just as ashamed of it as you are."   8

Omitted from our sample then are just two groups most likely to depress the average. The $25,111 figure is beginning to account for itself. It may indeed be a true figure for those of the Class of '24 whose addresses are known and who are willing to stand up and tell how much they earn. But even that requires a possibly dangerous assumption that the gentlemen are telling the truth.   9

To be dependable to any useful degree at all, a sampling study must use a representative sample (which can lead to trouble too) or a truly random one. If *all* the Class of '24 is included, that's all right. If every tenth name on a complete list is used, that is all right too, and so is drawing an adequate number of names out of a hat. The test is this: Does every name in the group have an equal chance to be in the sample?   10

You'll recall that ignoring this requirement was what produced the *Literary Digest's* famed fiasco.[1] When names for polling were taken only from   11

---

[1] The *Literary Digest* predicted that Alfred Landon would defeat Franklin Roosevelt in the presidential election of 1936. Landon carried only two states.

telephone books and subscription lists, people who did not have telephones or *Literary Digest* subscriptions had no chance to be in the sample. They possibly did not mind this underprivilege a bit, but their absence was in the end very hard on the magazine that relied on the figures.

12   This leads to a moral: You can prove about anything you want to by letting your sample bias itself. As a consumer of statistical data—a reader, for example, of a news magazine—remember that no statistical conclusion can rise above the quality of the sample it is based upon. In the absence of information about the procedures behind it, you are not warranted in giving any credence at all to the result.

13   **The truncated, or gee-whiz, graph.** If you want to show some statistical information quickly and clearly, draw a picture of it. Graphic presentation is the thing today. If you don't mind misleading the hasty looker, or if you quite clearly *want* to deceive him, you can save some space by chopping the bottom off many kinds of graphs.

14   Suppose you are showing the upward trend of national income month by month for a year. The total rise, as in one recent year, is 10 percent. It looks like this:

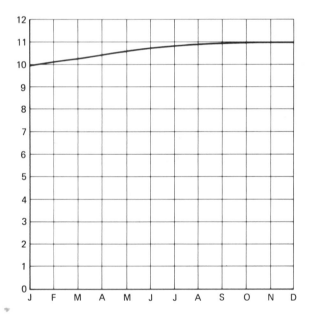

That is clear enough. Anybody can see that the trend is slightly upward. You are showing a 10 percent increase and that is exactly what it looks like.

15   But it lacks schmaltz. So you chop off the bottom, this way:

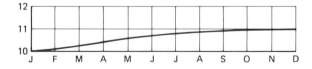

The figures are the same and so is the curve. It is the same graph. Nothing has been falsified—except the impression that it gives. But what the hasty reader sees now is a national-income line that has climbed halfway up the paper in twelve months, all because most of the chart isn't there any more. Like the missing parts of speech in sentences that you met in grammar classes, it is "understood." Of course, the eye doesn't "understand" what isn't there, and a small rise has become, visually, a big one.

The souped-up graph. Sometimes truncating is not enough. The trifling   16
rise in something or other still looks almost as insignificant as it is. You can make that 10 percent look livelier than 100 percent ordinarily does. Simply change the proportion between the ordinate and the abscissa. There's no rule against it, and it does give your graph a prettier shape. All you have to do is let each mark up the side stand for only one-tenth as many dollars as before.

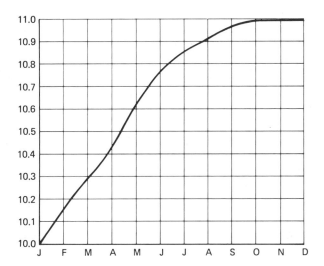

That *is* impressive, isn't it? Anyone looking at it can just feel prosperity throbbing in the arteries of the country. It is a subtler equivalent of editing "National income rose 10 percent" into " . . . climbed a whopping 10 percent." It is vastly more effective, however, because it contains no adjectives or adverbs to spoil the illusion of objectivity. There's nothing anyone can pin on you.

The well-chosen average. I live near a country neighborhood for which I   17
can report an average income of $15,000. I could also report it as $3,500.

If I should want to sell real estate hereabouts to people having a high   18
snobbery content, the first figure would be handy. The second figure, however, is the one to use in an argument against raising taxes, or the local bus fare.

Both are legitimate averages, legally arrived at. Yet it is obvious that at   19
least one of them must be as misleading as an out-and-out lie. The $15,000

figure is a mean, the arithmetic average of the incomes of all the families in the community. The smaller figure is a median; it might be called the income of the average family in the group. It indicates that half the families have less than $3,500 a year and half have more.

20   Here is where some of the confusion about averages comes from. Many human characteristics have the grace to fall into what is called the "normal" distribution. If you draw a picture of it, you get a curve that is shaped like a bell. Mean and median fall at about the same point, so it doesn't make very much difference which you use.

21   But some things refuse to follow this neat curve. Income is one of them. Incomes for most large areas will range from under $1,000 a year to upward of $50,000. Almost everybody will be under $10,000, way over on the left-hand side of that curve.

22   One of the things that made the income figure for the "average Yaleman" meaningless is that we are not told whether it is a mean or a median. It is not that one type of average is invariably better than the other; it depends upon what you are talking about. But neither gives you any real informa-tion—and either may be highly misleading—unless you know which of those kinds of average it is.

23   In the country neighborhood I mentioned, almost everyone has less than the average—the mean, that is—of $15,000. These people are all small farm-ers, except for a trio of millionaire weekenders who bring up the mean enormously.

24   You can be pretty sure that when an income average is given in the form of a mean nearly everybody has less than that.

25   **The insignificant difference or the elusive error.** Your two children Peter and Linda (we might as well give them modish names while we're about it) take intelligence tests. Peter's I.Q., you learn, is 98 and Linda's is 101. Aha! Linda is your brighter child.

26   Is she? An intelligence test is, or purports to be, a sampling of intellect. An I.Q., like other products of sampling, is a figure with a statistical error, which expresses the precision or reliability of the figure. The size of this probable error can be calculated. For their test the makers of the much-used Revised Stanford-Binet have found it to be about 3 percent. So Peter's indicated I.Q. of 98 really means only that there is an even chance that it falls between 95 and 101. There is an equal probability that it falls some-where else—below 95 or above 101. Similarly, Linda's has no better than a fifty-fifty chance of being within the fairly sizeable range of 98 to 104.

27   You can work out some comparisons from that. One is that there is rather better than one chance in four that Peter, with his lower I.Q. rating, is really at least three points smarter than Linda. A statistician doesn't like to con-sider a difference significant unless you can hand him odds a lot longer than that.

28   Ignoring the error in a sampling study leads to all kinds of silly conclu-sions. There are magazine editors to whom readership surveys are gospel;

with a 40 percent readership reported for one article and a 35 percent for another, they demand more like the first. I've seen even smaller differences given tremendous weight, because statistics are a mystery and numbers are impressive. The same thing goes for market surveys and so-called public opinion polls. The rule is that you cannot make a valid comparison between two such figures unless you know the deviations. And unless the difference between the figures is many times greater than the probable error of each, you have only a guess that the one appearing greater really is.

Otherwise you are like the man choosing a camp site from a report of   29
mean temperature alone. One place in California with a mean annual temperature of 61 is San Nicolas Island on the south coast, where it always stays in the comfortable range between 47 and 87. Another with a mean of 61 is in the inland desert, where the thermometer hops around from 15 to 104. The deviation from the mean marks the difference, and you can freeze or roast if you ignore it.

The one-dimensional picture. Suppose you have just two or three figures   30
to compare—say the average weekly wage of carpenters in the United States and another country. The sums might be $60 and $30. An ordinary bar chart makes the difference graphic. That is an honest picture. It looks good for American carpenters, but perhaps it does not have quite the oomph you are after. Can't you make that difference appear overwhelming and at the same time give it what I am afraid is known as eye appeal? Of course you can. Following tradition, you represent these sums by pictures of money bags. If the $30 bag is one inch high, you draw the $60 bag two inches high. That's in proportion, isn't it?

31 The catch is, of course, that the American's money bag, being twice as tall as that of the $30 man, covers an area on your page four times as great. And since your two-dimensional picture represents an object that would in fact have three dimensions, the money bags actually would differ much more than that. The volumes of any two similar solids vary as the cubes of their heights. If the unfortunate foreigner's bag holds $30 worth of dimes, the American's would hold not $60 but a neat $240.

32 You didn't say that, though, did you? And you can't be blamed; you're only doing it the way practically everybody else does.

33 **The ever-impressive decimal.** For a spurious air of precision that will lend all kinds of weight to the most disreputable statistics, consider the decimal.

34 Ask a hundred citizens how many hours they slept last night. Come out with a total of, say, 7.813. Your data are far from precise to begin with. Most people will miss their guess by fifteen minutes or more and some will recall five sleepless minutes as half a night of tossing insomnia.

35 But go ahead, do your arithmetic, announce that people sleep an average of 7.813 hours a night. You will sound as if you knew precisely what you are talking about. If you were foolish enough to say 7.8 (or "almost 8") hours it would sound like what it was—an approximation.

36 **The semiattached figure.** If you can't prove what you want to prove, demonstrate something else and pretend that they are the same thing. In the daze that follows the collision of statistics with the human mind, hardly anybody will notice that difference. The semiattached figure is a durable device guaranteed to stand you in good stead. It always has.

37 If you can't prove that your nostrum cures colds, publish a sworn laboratory report that the stuff killed 31,108 germs in a test tube in eleven seconds. There may be no connection at all between assorted germs in a test tube and the whatever-it-is that produces colds, but people aren't going to reason that sharply, especially while sniffling.

Maybe that one is too obvious and people are beginning to catch on. Here   38
is a trickier version.

Let us say that in a period when race prejudice is growing it is to your   39
advantage to "prove" otherwise. You will not find it a difficult assignment.

Ask that usual cross section of the population if they think Negroes have   40
as good a chance as white people to get jobs. Ask again a few months later.
As Princeton's Office of Public Opinion Research has found out, people
who are most unsympathetic to Negroes are the ones most likely to answer
yes to this question.

As prejudice increases in a country, the percentage of affirmative answers   41
you will get to this question will become larger. What looks on the face of
it like growing opportunity for Negroes actually is mounting prejudice and
nothing else. You have achieved something rather remarkable: the worse
things get, the better your survey makes them look.

The unwarranted assumption, or *post hoc*[2] rides again. The interrelation   42
of cause and effect, so often obscure anyway, can be most neatly hidden in
statistical data.

Somebody once went to a good deal of trouble to find out if cigarette   43
smokers make lower college grades than nonsmokers. They did. This naturally pleased many people, and they made much of it.

The unwarranted assumption, of course, was that smoking had produced   44
dull minds. It seemed vaguely reasonable on the face of it, so it was quite
widely accepted. But it really proved nothing of the sort, any more than it
proved that poor grades drive students to the solace of tobacco. Maybe the
relationship worked in one direction, maybe in the other. And maybe all
this is only an indication that the sociable sort of fellow who is likely to take
his books less than seriously is also likely to sit around and smoke many
cigarettes.

Permitting statistical treatment to befog causal relationships is little better   45
than superstition. It is like the conviction among the people of the Hebrides
that body lice produce good health. Observation over the centuries had
taught them that people in good health had lice and sick people often did
not. *Ergo,* lice made a man healthy. Everybody should have them.

Scantier evidence, treated statistically at the expense of common sense,   46
has made many a medical fortune and many a medical article in magazines,
including professional ones. More sophisticated observers finally got things
straightened out in the Hebrides. As it turned out, almost everybody in
those circles has lice most of the time. But when a man took a fever (quite
possibly carried to him by those same lice) and his body became hot, the
lice left.

Here you have cause and effect not only reversed but intermingled.   47

There you have a primer in some ways to use statistics to deceive. A   48
well-wrapped statistic is better than Hitler's "big lie": it misleads, yet it
can't be pinned onto you.

[2] A kind of logical fallacy. See p. 237.

49   Is this little list altogether too much like a manual for swindlers? Perhaps
I can justify it in the manner of the retired burglar whose published remi-
niscences amounted to a graduate course in how to pick a lock and muffle
a footfall: The crooks already know these tricks. Honest men must learn
them in self-defense.

WHAT DID THE WRITER SAY, AND WHAT DID YOU THINK?

1. What is the difference between a *mean* and a *median*?
2. In paragraph 5, the author quotes part of a poem. To what activity does the poem
   refer?
3. Are the classifications meant to be complete?
4. In paragraph 30, why does the author object to the term *eye appeal*?
5. One of the author's points seems to be that statistical lies aren't lies in the usual
   sense. What might be a more accurate word?
6. Are there enough examples for each kind of lie? Are the examples clear?
7. Why are statistical lies more dangerous than other kinds?
8. Does the author give the impression that he is opposed to all use of statistics?
9. Summarize the thesis in one sentence.
10. In what way can statistical lies and weasel words (see pp. 139–146) be considered
    members of the same family?

HOW DID THE WRITER SAY IT?

1. Are the drawings mainly decorative, or are they essential to the meaning?
2. Why so much humor? Is the author himself amused by what he describes?
3. The author uses slang in the titles of some of the classes: *gee whiz, souped-up*. Is
   the slang merely another device for humor, or does it serve additional purposes?
4. "Simply change the proportion between the ordinate and the abscissa." Is the language here offensively technical? Why does a writer who is clearly skillful at informal
   writing choose to employ language of this sort?
5. Vocabulary: *salubrious, impeccable, semantic, credence, truncated, schmaltz, ordinate, abscissa, spurious, solace, causal*.

WHAT ABOUT <u>YOUR</u> WRITING?

Huff uses contractions frequently: *won't, wouldn't, didn't, that's, you'll*, to list only a few.
Are contractions good English?

The best reply to that question is that the question needs to be rethought. It's like
asking if a tuxedo is good dress. It's good dress for formal dances, but it's bad dress for
mowing the lawn. Shorts and a T-shirt are good dress for mowing the lawn, but bad dress
for a formal dance. There's no one kind of good dress. A good dresser is someone who
knows what kind of clothes to wear for different occasions.

There's no one kind of good English, either. It varies. It's what's appropriate to the subject, situation, and audience. As these elements change, the nature of what's appropriate will change. Tuxedo English is appropriate for ceremonial occasions, serious studies of specialized subjects, and so on. Lincoln's Gettysburg Address is written in formal English. If it had been written in a chatty, conversational style with folksy anecdotes about Lincoln's childhood, it would have been written in bad English and bad taste. On the other hand, shorts-and-T-shirt English is good English for much conversation and the dialogue of certain characters in works of fiction. A quarterback in a huddle says, "Play 32. Left tackle. Let's get the bums"—or something like that. It would be bad English for him to say, "Let us, my teammates, utilize Play 32 to assault the left tackle position of our adversaries."

Most Freshman English papers should probably be written at the sportcoat-and-necktie level. A tuxedo is absurd. Even a business suit might sometimes be a bit stiff for the subject, situation, and audience. But shorts and a T-shirt are also out of place. Grammar still counts. Organization still counts. There aren't as many rules to worry about as in tuxedo English, but there are still plenty of rules.

In "How to Lie with Statistics," Huff is writing sportcoat-and-necktie English. It's informal, but not sloppy. It's casual, but not careless. When slang or contractions seem to work—when they make a complex subject easier to understand or help to create friendly vibrations between writer and reader—Huff uses them. When big words or unfamiliar words or long sentences seem appropriate, he uses them, too. Sportcoat-and-necktie English is a mixture. It requires care and caution. At its best, however, it manages to combine the virtues of the tuxedo and the T-shirt while maintaining an identity of its own.

Chapter 7
DEFINITION

One of the most frequent impediments to clear communication is the failure to define terms. Some conversations and writings aren't just impeded by that failure; they're made incomprehensible. In isolation, a catch phrase like *power to the people,* for example, can mean anything from revolution to better electric service. Far more often, failure to define or to agree on a definition can lead to hours—and years—of futile controversy, complete with name-calling and shaking fists. Think of UN debates on *aggression.* Think of the storms in American history over terms like *free speech, due process, states' rights,* and *quotas.*

A definition theme often includes a "dictionary definition" but goes far beyond it and is best thought of as providing an *extended definition.* It discusses the meaning of words and phrases to which even the best dictionaries can't do full justice.

Dictionary definitions work in two ways, both of them short, and one of them extremely formal. First, a dictionary can define by giving a direct synonym: *liberty* means *freedom; couch* means *sofa; plate* means *dish; cry* means *weep.* Second, a dictionary can, and for many terms must, use the techniques of a formal definition: a term is placed in the class it belongs to and then is differentiated from all the other members of the same class.

Term	Class	Differentiation
convertible	a car	with a top that can be raised and lowered
widow	a woman	whose husband has died
martini	a cocktail	made with gin or vodka and dry vermouth

Dictionary definitions, to repeat, are often incorporated into an extended definition, but no definition paper will discuss a term for which a dictionary definition alone would be sufficient. Some definition papers, in fact, may have as their central point the inadequacy or impossibility of good dictionary definitions for the term under consideration. (The skilled writer, however, will almost always avoid starting off with such tired phrases as "According to the dictionary," or "Webster says that.")

What terms are promising candidates for definition papers? Here are some suggestions:

Abstract concepts: love, morality, patriotism, apathy

Controversial terms: the sexual revolution, the generation gap, women's liberation, police brutality

Slang: funky, square, swinger, vibes

Common phrases and ideas: a good movie, the ideal vacation, the perfect job

Clearly, a definition paper usually turns out to be an expression of opinion, a "What Such-and-Such Means to Me" paper. A good movie for one person will have to stimulate the mind; for another person it will have to give the mind a rest. The expression of an attitude toward the term is what gives life to a definition paper and makes it more interesting to read than a dictionary. In other words, a definition paper benefits from a thesis:

Being a square is not as bad as people think.

An ideal vacation can mean snoozing in the backyard just as much as seeing new sights.

The generation gap is one of humanity's best hopes for progress.

Love is a severe mental illness curable only by time.

Definition papers follow no set pattern. Most turn out to be combinations of patterns that are studied separately in other chapters of this book. Which pattern or combination of patterns is used depends on which works best, and which works best depends on what's being defined and what the writer has to say about it.

A definition paper can compare and contrast. A term can be made clearer and more interesting by distinguishing it from similar terms: a paper on socialism might distinguish it from communism; a paper on love might distinguish it from infatuation. Discussing opposites sometimes works well, too: a definition paper on a *square* might take the same set of circumstances and contrast a square's behavior to a swinger's. These negative techniques—showing what a term is not—often lead to successful papers.

A definition paper can classify. It may be both convenient and insightful to break some terms into separate classifications. Morality, for example, could be considered in two parts: passive morality—not doing evil; and active morality—doing good.

A definition paper can give examples. A paper defining a good movie would naturally discuss specific examples of good movies that fit the definition. Without the examples the paper would probably be abstract and dull.

A definition paper can trace a process. A writer engaged in defining *schizophrenia* might make the illness more understandable with a step-by-step analysis of its progress from the first signs of mental aberration to its full development.

A definition paper can study cause-and-effect relationships. An advocate of women's liberation, in defining the term, could make the definition fuller and more persuasive by devoting some attention to the decades of polite and impolite discrimination that helped cause the birth, or rebirth, of the women's liberation movement.

A definition paper can use narration. Narration (see pp. 206–208) is the telling of a story. A paper on *competition* could show the good and bad sides of the term in action by telling the story of the author's friendly and unfriendly rivalry with a fellow student during high school days.

WRITING SUGGESTIONS FOR DEFINITION THEMES

Any of the terms below lend themselves to extended definitions. Remember that definition papers are not tied down to any one writing pattern. Use whatever approach works best. (See p. 159 for other subject possibilities.)

1. Soul food	13. The heartbreak of psoriasis
2. A ham actor	14. Conscience
3. Good sportsmanship	15. "The real thing" (as used in Coca-Cola ads)
4. Conflict of interest	16. A good salesperson
5. A good teacher	17. Friendship
6. Fad	18. Santa Claus
7. Atheism	19. Jealousy
8. An intellectual	20. Obscenity ✓
9. Courtesy	21. Humanity's best friend
10. Acid rock or punk rock	22. Humanity's worst enemy
11. Worship	23. Fear
12. A good marriage	24. Road hypnosis

Polar Words

CITICORP

Citicorp is a financial holding company that includes the First National City Bank of New York. "Polar Words" first appeared in *Citiviews,* a quarterly commentary distributed to shareholders, and was reprinted as an advertisement about four months after the 1976 presidential election. As you read, notice how the definition of polar words is clarified by the use of examples.

There are certain peculiar words that by themselves have no meaning. 1
They can be used only in relation to their opposites. The word "up" has no meaning apart from the word "down," nor the term "fast" apart from the term "slow." Such words are responsible for much of the confusion, and most of the heat, in human discourse.

An Assistant U.S. Attorney General, the late Thurman Arnold, used to 2
call them *polar* words and warned against many of the traps they set for us. As commonly used, he observed, words like "justice" and "injustice" are typical polar terms:

A reformer who wants to abolish injustice and create a world in which nothing but justice prevails is like a man who wants to make everything "up." Such a man might feel that if he took the lowest in the world and carried it up to the highest point and kept on doing this, everything would eventually become "up." This would certainly move a great many objects and create an enormous amount of activity. It might or might not be useful, according to the standards which we apply. However, it would never result in the abolishment of "down."

In so stating, the author placed himself in peril of being found insensitive 3
to the cause of justice—"insensitive," of course, being still another common entry in the polar sweepstakes. So, for that matter, is the term "efficiency," which is a common ideal of business but has no meaning unless there exists something called "inefficiency." One does not become an advocate of inefficiency merely by pointing this out, although, remarkably enough, there are those who may vaguely suspect as much.

For many people, even to discuss certain words in these terms arouses 4
a dim sense of misgiving. The reason for this reaction is that polar words are our battle ensigns, and it is our instinct to defend the flag under which we march. The words are not guides to rational decision making, nor even to winning debates. They never succeed in persuading the other side, but are primarily morale boosters for the side on which they are used. "The trick," as Arnold observed, "is to find a pair of polar words in which the nice word justifies your own position and the bad word is applied to the other fellow."

Yet most of us choose our own favorite words with no intention of being 5
tricky or deceptive. We genuinely believe in the rightness of our cause— and therefore that only the "nice" words apply to it.

6   In the continuing debate over crime, for example, those who believe that the courts have become too lenient are heard to say: "We must show more concern for the victim and less for the criminal." To which another group retorts that "the criminal himself is a victim of the social conditions that breed crime." No one expects such an argument to result in a revised, rational code of criminal justice. It does help each disputant to feel that he is on the side of the victim, which is, of course, the "right" side. Unfortunately, it is no help to the judge.

7   Judges are not alone. Hardly anyone in government, business or the professions escapes being regularly trapped in the cross fire of polarized debate. We all have our own checklists.

8   A shift in the economy may abruptly transform "investors" into "speculators," and "skinflint bankers" into "reckless lenders" of other people's money. An approaching election usually turns our "statesmen" into "politicians," and afterwards the winners must begin the slow process of rehabilitation—until next time. A widely publicized and unpopular court decision converts the lawyers' "due process" to "legal technicalities." And a "dedicated civil servant" may be converted to a "government bureaucrat" and back again several times in a single day—especially at tax time.

9   In an American election year, the polar words normally float on the horizon like the aurora borealis. They then subside, but never vanish. Nor should we want them to. Such words do, after all, have power to inspire. They provide focal points around which like-minded citizens can rally. They motivate change and social progress.

10   We would do well to remember, however, that polar words are never guides to reasonable solutions or rational goals. They can make us want to move, but never tell us where we ought to go. For this, we need a different kind of dialogue.

11   "Like three impressions of the same seal, the word ought to produce the idea, and the idea ought to be a picture of the fact." So wrote Antoine Lavoisier in the late eighteenth century. Applying this precept to his own field, he sat down and compiled the dictionary that revolutionized the science of chemistry and earned him immortality as the Father of Modern Chemistry. The event is often cited as proof of what clear and careful definition can accomplish. It is unfortunate for the cause of clarity (as it was for him) that a few years later, when Lavoisier applied himself to politics, they cut off his head.

12   The only safety for which the objective observer can hope, perhaps, is to be reminded occasionally that words can be extremely dangerous—and expecially the ones that come in pairs.

13   Lying between these polar battle lines is a vast and dimly lighted no-man's-land where one may occasionally encounter a fragment of fact or a particle of truth. This usually occurs, however, only when the searchers are willing to leave the magic words and rallying cries shimmering awhile in the distance, awaiting some future call to arms. The months immediately fol-

lowing a national election are often good times for such missions. In fact, they may be the *only* times.

It would be a shame to waste them.   14

WHAT DID THE WRITER SAY, AND WHAT DID YOU THINK?

1. Give a one-sentence definition of *polar words*.
2. What harm is done by polar words?
3. What can be said in favor of polar words? How much attention does the advertisement devote to the good side of polar words? Does this attention weaken the attack on them?
4. The advertisement ends with a call for action. Express in your own words what action it recommends.
5. To show your understanding of the definition, find a half dozen additional examples of polar words.

HOW DID THE WRITER SAY IT?

1. What meaning of *polar* is involved in the phrase *polar words*?
2. What is the meaning of *no-man's-land* (par. 13)? Where did the expression originate? What other language in the paragraph shows awareness of the origin?
3. At the end of paragraph 11, in the phrase *they cut off his head,* the pronoun *they* has no antecedent, no noun to which it refers. Should this normally serious writing error be a cause for complaint here?
4. Show how the advertisement tries to establish its fair-mindedness by balancing examples that will appeal to liberals and conservatives.
5. Where does the advertisement most directly add emotional language to its generally quiet and rational approach?
6. Vocabulary: *discourse, aurora borealis.*

WHAT ABOUT <u>YOUR</u> WRITING?

One way of backing up a thesis is by *citation of authority*. A writer reinforces a point by quoting or referring to sources whose views the reader must take seriously. A writer on religion quotes the Bible. A writer on psychoanalysis quotes Freud. A writer on the meaning of words quotes Lavoisier, the compiler of a great scientific dictionary. A writer on the misuse of terms like *justice* and *injustice* quotes Thurman Arnold, a famous legal figure. "The Bible agrees with me," or "Freud agrees with me," or "Lavoisier and Arnold agree with me," says the writer, no longer an isolated voice, but a voice with authority. In addition, the writer conveys the valuable impression of having done a certain amount of serious research before arriving at an opinion.

The citation of authority must be combined with taste and judgment. An authority on one special field, removed from that field, is no longer an authority. Freud's endorsement of an after-shave lotion would be of limited worth. A well-known quarterback's comments about a football coach merit attention, but his feelings about popcorn makers are another matter. Comments of authorities must also be kept in context. Quoting a Supreme Court decision that the Supreme Court itself reversed ten years later is flatly irresponsible. Finally, assuming that even within the proper field and context the authority must always be right is another danger. Most people agree that Thomas Jefferson was a great president, but his decision to make the Louisiana Purchase without consulting Congress was not necessarily correct. Citations of authority can strengthen a point; they can't prove it.

With all these necessary warnings, your own writing can profit from an occasional citation of authority. In Emerson's words, "Next to the originator of a good sentence is the first quoter of it."

The Workaholic

ELLEN GOODMAN

"The Workaholic" comes from Ellen Goodman's syndicated newspaper column. To define a workaholic, Goodman uses the narrative pattern—she tells a story. Are the characters presented as particular individuals, or are they meant to stand for general types?

1   He worked himself to death finally and precisely at 3 A.M. Sunday morning.

2   The obituary didn't say that, of course. It said that he died of a coronary thrombosis—I think that was it—but every one of his friends and acquaintances knew it instantly. He was a perfect Type A, a workaholic, a classic, they said to each other and shook their heads—and thought for five or ten minutes about the way they lived.

3   This man who worked himself to death finally and precisely at 3 A.M. Sunday morning—on his day off—was 51 years old and he was a vice-president. He was, however, one of the six vice-presidents, and one of three who might conceivably—if the president died or retired soon enough—have moved to the top spot. Phil knew that.

4   He worked six days a week, five of them until 8 or 9 at night, during a time when his own company had begun the four-day week for everyone but the executives. He worked like the Important People. He had no outside "extracurricular interests," unless, of course, you think about a monthly golf game that way. To Phil, it was work. He always ate egg-salad sandwiches at his desk. He was, of course, overweight, by 20 or 25 pounds. He thought it was okay though, because he didn't smoke.

5   On Saturdays, Phil wore a sports jacket to the office instead of a suit, because it was the weekend.

He had a lot of people working for him, maybe 60, and most of them   6
liked him most of the time. Three of them will be seriously considered for
his job. The obituary didn't mention that.

But it did list his "survivors" quite accurately. He is survived by his   7
wife, Helen, 48, a good woman of no particular marketable skills, who
worked in an office before marrying and mothering.

She had, according to her daughter, given up trying to compete with his   8
work years ago, when the children were small. A company friend said, "I
know how much you will miss him." And she answered, "I already have."

"Missing him all these years," she must have given up part of herself   9
which had cared too much for the man. She would be "well taken care of."

His eldest of the "dearly beloved" children is a hard-working executive   10
in a manufacturing firm down South. In the day and a half before the funeral,
he went around the neighborhood researching his father, asking the neighbors what he was like. They were embarrassed.

His second child was a girl, who is 24 and newly married. She lives near   11
her mother and they are close, but whenever she was alone with her father,
in a car driving somewhere, they had nothing to say to each other.

The youngest is 20, a boy, a high-school graduate who has spent the last   12
couple of years, like a lot of his friends, doing enough odd jobs to stay in
grass and food. He was the one who tried to grab at his father, and tried to
mean enough to him to keep the man at home.

He was his father's favorite. Over the last two years, Phil stayed up   13
nights worrying about the boy.

The boy once said, "My father and I only board here."   14

At the funeral, the 60-year-old company president told the 48-year-old   15
widow that the 51-year-old deceased had meant much to the company and
would be missed and would be hard to replace. The widow didn't look him
in the eye. She was afraid he would read her bitterness and, after all, she
would need him to straighten out the finances—the stock options and all
that.

Phil was overweight and nervous and worked too hard. If he wasn't at   16
the office, he was worried about it. Phil was a Type A, a heart-attack
natural. You could have picked him out in a minute from a lineup.

So when he finally worked himself to death, at precisely 3 A.M. Sunday   17
morning, no one was really surprised.

By 5 P.M. the afternoon of the funeral, the company president had begun,   18
discreetly of course, with care and taste, to make inquiries about his re-
placement. One of three men. He asked around: "Who's been working the
hardest?"

WHAT DID THE WRITER SAY, AND WHAT DID YOU THINK?

1. Is the thesis directly stated? If not, should it be?
2. Besides driving one to an early grave, what is wrong with being a workaholic? Wasn't
   Phil doing what he wanted, after all?

3. Why are Phil's habits of dress worth mentioning (par. 5)?
4. Does the author express any sympathy for Phil? If not, is the reader expected to feel sympathy, even though unexpressed?
5. Weren't many or most of the people who have achieved greatness actually workaholics? Mozart, Dickens, Edison, and Pasteur are just a few names that come to mind. Einstein once observed, "Well-being and happiness are such trivial goals in life that I can imagine them being entertained only by pigs." Is the alternative to being a workaholic of some kind being a nobody?

HOW DID THE WRITER SAY IT?

1. Quotation marks are sometimes misused for cheap sarcasm or strained cuteness (see pp. 196–197). Are the quotation marks justified around *extracurricular interests* (par. 4), *survivors* (par. 7), *missing him all these years* (par. 9), *well taken care of* (par. 9), and *dearly beloved* (par. 10)?
2. Is there an actual conclusion, or does the article simply end when the story ends?
3. The writer generally tries to give the impression of letting the facts speak for themselves. Where does she editorialize directly?
4. Are the characters given enough individuality to be interesting in themselves, or are they interesting only because of what they represent?

WHAT ABOUT YOUR WRITING?

Effective repetition of words and phrases—sometimes exact repetition, sometimes repetition with a slight twist—is one of a writer's most direct means of driving home a point and achieving a touch of stylistic power. To give dramatic emphasis to the idea that the workaholic's death was a mere formality since he had been inviting death for years, Goodman repeats most of the opening sentence of her article in paragraph 3: "This man who worked himself to death finally and precisely at 3 A.M. Sunday morning . . . " With minor variations, the words recur in the next-to-last paragraph: "So when he finally worked himself to death, at precisely 3 A.M. Sunday morning, no one was really surprised." The repetition here not only intensifies the drama but serves artistically to tie together the beginning and end of the article.

Repetition can be abused, of course. If not handled well, it can become monotonous and irritating. Thus Goodman would not write, "He worked himself to death finally and precisely at 3 A.M. Sunday morning. Yes, worked himself to death. Finally and precisely. Finally. Precisely." Used properly, however, repetition has produced some of the most memorable phrases in the language:

Gentlemen may cry peace, peace—but there is no peace.

We have nothing to fear but fear itself.

It was the best of times, it was the worst of times.

Good bread, good meat, good God, let's eat!

The Fifth Freedom

SEYMOUR ST. JOHN

Seymour St. John was headmaster of the Choate School (now Choate-Rosemary Hall), a private preparatory school in Connecticut.

In "The Fifth Freedom," St. John uses the cause-and-effect pattern to construct his definition.

More than three centuries ago a handful of pioneers crossed the ocean to Jamestown and Plymouth in search of freedoms they were unable to find in their own countries, the freedoms we still cherish today: freedom from want, freedom from fear, freedom of speech, freedom of religion. Today the descendants of the early settlers, and those who have joined them since, are fighting to protect these freedoms at home and throughout the world.

And yet there is a fifth freedom—basic to those four—that we are in danger of losing: *the freedom to be one's best.* St. Exupéry[1] describes a ragged, sensitive-faced Arab child, haunting the streets of a North African town, as a lost Mozart: he would never be trained or developed. Was he free? "No one grasped you by the shoulder while there was still time; and nought will awaken in you the sleeping poet or musician or astronomer that possibly inhabited you from the beginning." The freedom to be one's best is the chance for the development of each person to his highest power.

How is it that we in America have begun to lose this freedom, and how can we regain it for our nation's youth? I believe it has started slipping away from us because of three misunderstandings.

First, the misunderstanding of the meaning of democracy. The principal of a great Philadelphia high school is driven to cry for help in combating the notion that it is undemocratic to run a special program of studies for outstanding boys and girls. Again, when a good independent school in Memphis recently closed, some thoughtful citizens urged that it be taken over by the public-school system and used for boys and girls of high ability, that it have entrance requirements and give an advanced program of studies to superior students who were interested and able to take it. The proposal was rejected because it was undemocratic! Out of this misunderstanding comes the middle-muddle. Courses are geared to the middle of the class. The good student is unchallenged, bored. The loafer receives his passing grade. And the lack of an outstanding course for the outstanding student, the lack of a standard which a boy or girl must meet, passes for democracy.

The second misunderstanding concerns what makes for happiness. The aims of our present-day culture are avowedly ease and material well-being: shorter hours; a shorter week; more return for less accomplishment; more soft-soap excuses and fewer honest, realistic demands. In our schools this is reflected by the vanishing hickory stick and the emerging psychiatrist.

Published in *Saturday Review*, October 10, 1955, and reprinted by permission of *Saturday Review*.

[1] Antoine de Saint Exupéry (1900–1944), French writer and aviator.

The hickory stick had its faults, and the psychiatrist has his strengths. But the trend is clear: *Tout comprendre c'est tout pardonner.*[2] Do we really believe that our softening standards bring happiness? Is it our sound and considered judgment that the tougher subjects of the classics and mathematics should be thrown aside, as suggested by some educators, for doll-playing? Small wonder that Charles Malik, Lebanese delegate at the U.N., writes: "There is in the West"—in the United States—"a general weakening of moral fiber. [Our] leadership does not seem to be adequate to the unprecedented challenges of the age."

6   The last misunderstanding is in the area of values. Here are some of the most influential tenets of teacher education over the past fifty years: there is no eternal truth; there is no absolute moral law; there is no God. Yet all of history has taught us that the denial of these ultimates, the placement of man or state at the core of the universe, results in a paralyzing mass selfishness; and the first signs of it are already frighteningly evident.

7   Arnold Toynbee[3] has said that all progress, all development come from challenge and a consequent response. Without challenge there is no response, no development, no freedom. So first we owe to our children the most demanding, challenging curriculum that is within their capabilities. Michelangelo did not learn to paint by spending his time doodling. Mozart was not an accomplished pianist at the age of eight as the result of spending his days in front of a television set. Like Eve Curie,[4] like Helen Keller,[5] they responded to the challenge of their lives by a disciplined training: and they gained a new freedom.

8   The second opportunity we can give our boys and girls is the right to failure. "Freedom is not only a privilege, it is a test," writes De Nöuy. What kind of a test is it, what kind of freedom where no one can fail? The day is past when the United States can afford to give high school diplomas to all who sit through four years of instruction, regardless of whether any visible results can be discerned. We live in a narrowed world where we must be alert, awake to realism: and realism demands a standard which either must be met or result in failure. These are hard words, but they are brutally true. If we deprive our children of the right to fail we deprive them of their knowledge of the world as it is.

9   Finally, we can expose our children to the best values we have found. By relating our lives to the evidences of the ages, by judging our philosophy in the light of values that history has proven truest, perhaps we shall be able to produce that "ringing message, full of content and truth, satisfying the mind, appealing to the heart, firing the will, a message on which one can stake his whole life." This is the message that could mean joy and strength and leadership—freedom as opposed to serfdom.

[2] "To understand all is to forgive all."
[3] Contemporary British historian.
[4] French author. Daughter of Pierre and Marie Curie, discoverers of radium.
[5] Deaf and blind from the age of two, Helen Keller (1880–1968) became a writer and lecturer.

WHAT DID THE WRITER SAY, AND WHAT DID YOU THINK?

1. What is the fifth freedom? Where is it first defined? Where is it defined again in different words?
2. What is the author's thesis about the fifth freedom?
3. What is the *middle-muddle?*
4. To what does "the vanishing hickory stick" refer?
5. How would the people St. John attacks define *democracy?* How would St. John define it?
6. Does the author give us any reason to treat the comments of Charles Malik, the Lebanese delegate to the UN, with any special respect?
7. Does St. John's insertion of "in the United States" into Malik's comment about "the West" distort Malik's meaning?
8. If we grant the importance of the fifth freedom, what are the practical problems of organizing schools or classes by level of intellectual capacities of the students?

HOW DID THE WRITER SAY IT?

1. The first paragraph discusses material seemingly remote from contemporary American education. What is the purpose of the paragraph?
2. "The middle of the class" in paragraph 4 sounds a good deal like "middle class." Do you think the resemblance is intentional? Why?
3. Paragraph 8 begins, "The second opportunity . . ." What is the first opportunity? Would the writing have been clearer if the author had explicitly labeled it "the first opportunity"?
4. The fifth freedom is endangered, the author states, because of "misunderstandings." Do you think the word is too kind? Is it accurate?
5. Would paragraph 6 have been stronger if it had included specific instances of "paralyzing mass selfishness"?
6. Why is "passes for democracy" in paragraph 4 a better phrase than "is mistaken for democracy" or "is confused with democracy"?
7. Should the source of the quote in paragraph 9 have been identified?
8. Vocabulary: *tenets, serfdom.*

WHAT ABOUT <u>YOUR</u> WRITING?

Don't underestimate the *topic sentence.* Teachers and textbooks sometimes terrorize students into the mistaken belief that topic sentences are synonymous with moral virtue, but topic sentences still demand your attention.

A topic sentence, usually appearing at or near the beginning or end of a paragraph, identifies the subject of the paragraph and frequently indicates the writer's attitude toward the subject. In a well-organized paper, each topic sentence usually expresses a major supporting point for the thesis; then the sentences in the rest of each paragraph directly support that paragraph's own topic sentence. It's often possible to write out the thesis statement and each topic sentence and end with an excellent summary of a whole essay.

St. John in "The Fifth Freedom" begins with a two-paragraph introduction, which presents the thesis:

> There is a fifth freedom . . . that we are in danger of losing: *the freedom to be one's best.*

In a transitional paragraph asking how we began to lose the fifth freedom and what opportunities we have to get it back, St. John says that the loss was caused by three "misunderstandings." Now notice this sequence of topic sentences in consecutive paragraphs:

> First, the misunderstanding of democracy.

> The second misunderstanding concerns what makes for happiness.

> The last misunderstanding is in the area of values.

To restore the fifth freedom, the author continues:

> . . . first we owe to our children the most demanding, challenging curriculum that is within their capabilities.

> The second opportunity we can give our boys and girls is the right to failure.

> Finally, we can expose our children to the best values we have found.

The topic sentences give structure to the essay, and the structure makes it easy for the reader to follow the author's thoughts.

Don't assume from these quoted passages that all well-organized papers must number each of their points. Don't assume that all subjects can be given the tight organization that St. John is able to employ. Don't even assume that every paragraph in every paper needs an explicit topic sentence. Transitional paragraphs like St. John's paragraph 3, for example, link separate sections of a paper, briefly stating the subject just dealt with and looking forward to the next subject. They are rarely more than one or two sentences long and have no topic sentence:

> The writer, then, has involved her characters in an interesting dilemma. How does she get them out of it?

> Having now removed the drumsticks and wings, you are ready for the next step: carving.

Many paragraphs in narration and description may also do without explicit topic sentences. A descriptive paragraph dealing solely with a person's clothing may often have what can be thought of as a topic idea and manage quite well without a topic sentence. A narrative passage about a murderer concealing evidence or a child throwing a temper tantrum may also be sustained by an unstated topic idea. The paragraph you are now reading, in fact, tries to get by without an explicit topic sentence such as "There's nothing sacred about topic sentences."

With all these warnings, the teachers and textbooks are far more right than wrong. Topic sentences are a major aid to organization and clarity. They help your reader, and they help you.

Gobbledygook

STUART CHASE

Stuart Chase worked for many years, starting in 1917, as a consultant to various government agencies. Now over ninety, Mr. Chase has written many books on business-government relationships, among them *Democracy Under Pressure* (1945). His long campaign for clear English is suggested by titles like *The Tyranny of Words* (1938) and *The Power of Words* (1954).

Note how strongly the definition in this reading depends upon examples.

Said Franklin Roosevelt, in one of his early presidential speeches: "I see one-third of a nation ill-housed, ill-clad, ill-nourished." Translated into standard bureaucratic prose his statement would read:

> It is evident that a substantial number of persons within the Continental boundaries of the United States have inadequate financial resources with which to purchase the products of agricultural communities and industrial establishments. It would appear that for a considerable segment of the population, possibly as much as 33.3333[1] percent of the total, there are inadequate housing facilities, and an equally significant proportion is deprived of the proper types of clothing and nutriment.

This rousing satire on gobbledygook—or talk among the bureaucrats—is adapted from a report[2] prepared by the Federal Security Agency in an attempt to break out of the verbal squirrel cage. "Gobbledygook" was coined by an exasperated Congressman, Maury Maverick of Texas, and means using two, or three, or ten words in the place of one, or using a five-syllable word where a single syllable would suffice. Maverick was censuring the forbidding prose of executive departments in Washington, but the term has now spread to windy and pretentious language in general.

"Gobbledygook" itself is a good example of the way a language grows. There was no word for the event before Maverick's invention; one had to say: "You know, that terrible, involved, polysyllabic language those government people use down in Washington." Now one word takes the place of a dozen.

A British member of Parliament, A. P. Herbert, also exasperated with bureaucratic jargon, translated Nelson's[3] immortal phrase, "England expects every man to do his duty":

> England anticipates that, as regards the current emergency, personnel will face up to the issues, and exercise appropriately the functions allocated to their respective occupational groups.

From *The Power of Words*, copyright 1954 by Stuart Chase. Reprinted by permission of Harcourt Brace Jovanovich, Inc.

[1] Not carried beyond four places. [Chase's note]

[2] This and succeeding quotations from F.S.A. report by special permission of the author, Milton Hall. [Chase's note]

[3] Horatio Nelson (1758–1805), English naval hero, victor over the French at Trafalgar.

5   A New Zealand official made the following report after surveying a plot of ground for an athletic field:[4]

It is obvious from the difference in elevation with relation to the short depth of the property that the contour is such as to preclude any reasonable development potential for active recreation.

Seems the plot was too steep.

6   An office manager sent this memo to his chief:

Verbal contact with Mr. Blank regarding the attached notification of promotion has elicited the attached representation intimating that he prefers to decline the assignment.

Seems Mr. Blank didn't want the job.

A doctor testified at an English trial that one of the parties was suffering from "circumorbital haematoma."

Seems the party had a black eye.

In August 1952 the U.S. Department of Agriculture put out a pamphlet entitled: entitled: "Cultural and Pathogenic Variability in Single-Condial and Hyphaltip Isolates of Hemlin-Thosporium Turcicum Pass."

Seems it was about corn leaf disease.

7   On reaching the top of the Finsteraarhorn in 1845, M. Dollfus-Ausset, when he got his breath, exclaimed:

The soul communes in the infinite with those icy peaks which seem to have their roots in the bowels of eternity.

Seems he enjoyed the view.

8   A government department announced:

Voucherable expenditures necessary to provide adequate dental treatment required as adjunct to medical treatment being rendered a pay patient in in-patient status may be incurred as required at the expense of the Public Health Service.

Seems you can charge your dentist bill to the Public Health Service. Or can you? . . .

Reducing the Gobble

9   As government and business offices grow larger, the need for doing something about gobbledygook increases. Fortunately the biggest office in the world is working hard to reduce it. The Federal Security Agency in Washington,[5] with nearly 100 million clients on its books, began analyzing its communication lines some years ago, with gratifying results. Surveys find trouble in three main areas: correspondence with clients about their social security problems, office memos, official reports.

[4] This item and the next two are from the piece on gobbledygook by W. E. Farbstein, New York *Times*, March 29, 1953. [Chase's note]
[5] Now the Department of Health, Education, and Welfare. [Chase's note]

Clarity and brevity, as well as common humanity, are urgently needed in   12
this vast establishment which deals with disability, old age, and unemployment. The surveys found instead many cases of long-windedness, foggy
meanings, clichés, and singsong phrases, and gross neglect of the reader's
point of view. Rather than talking to a real person, the writer was talking
to himself. "We often write like a man walking on stilts."

Here is a typical case of long-windedness: 13

> *Gobbledygook as found:* "We are wondering if sufficient time has passed so
> that you are in a position to indicate whether favorable action may now be taken
> on our recommendation for the reclassification of Mrs. Blank, junior clerk-ste-
> nographer, CAF 2, to assistant clerk-stenographer, CAF 3?"
>
> *Suggested improvement:* "Have you yet been able to act on our recommen-
> dation to reclassify Mrs. Blank?"

Another case:

> Although the Central Efficiency Rating Committee recognizes that there are
> many desirable changes that could be made in the present efficiency rating system
> in order to make it more realistic and more workable than it now is, this committee
> is of the opinion that no further change should be made in the present system
> during the current year. Because of conditions prevailing throughout the country
> and the resultant turnover in personnel, and difficulty in administering the Federal
> programs, further mechanical improvement in the present rating system would
> require staff retraining and other administrative expense which would seem best
> withheld until the official termination of hostilities, and until restoration of regular
> operations.

The F.S.A. invites us to squeeze the gobbledygook out of this statement.   14
Here is my attempt:

> The Central Efficiency Rating Committee recognizes that desirable changes
> could be made in the present system. We believe, however, that no change should
> be attempted until the war is over.

This cuts the statement from 111 to 30 words, about one-quarter of the   15
original, but perhaps the reader can do still better. What of importance have
I left out?

Sometimes in a book which I am reading for information—not for literary   16
pleasure—I run a pencil through the surplus words. Often I can cut a section
to half its length with an improvement in clarity. Magazines like *The
Reader's Digest* have reduced this process to an art. Are long-windedness
and obscurity a cultural lag from the days when writing was reserved for
priests and cloistered scholars? The more words and the deeper the mystery, the greater their prestige and the firmer the hold on their jobs. And
the better the candidate's chance today to have his doctoral thesis accepted.

The F.S.A. surveys found that a great deal of writing was obscure al-   17
though not necessarily prolix. Here is a letter sent to more than 100,000
inquirers, a classic example of murky prose. To clarify it, one needs to *add*
words, not cut them:

In order to be fully insured, an individual must have earned $50 or more in covered employment for as many quarters of the coverage as half the calendar quarters elapsing between 1936 and the quarter in which he reaches age 65 or dies, whichever first occurs.

Probably no one without the technical jargon of the office could translate this; nevertheless, it was sent out to drive clients mad for seven years. One poor fellow wrote back: "I am no longer in covered employment. I have an outside job now."

16   Many words and phrases in officialese seem to come out automatically, as if from lower centers of the brain. In this standardized prose people never *get jobs*, they "secure employment"; *before* and *after* become "prior to" and "subsequent to"; one does not *do*, one "performs"; nobody *knows* a thing, he is "fully cognizant"; one never *says*, he "indicates." A great favorite at present is "implement."

17   Some charming boners occur in this talking-in-one's-sleep. For instance:

The problem of extending coverage to all employees, regardless of size, is not as simple as surface appearances indicate.

Though the proportions of all males and females in ages 16–45 are essentially the same . . .

Dairy cattle, usually and commonly embraced in dairying . . .

18   In its manual to employees, the F.S.A. suggests the following:

Instead of	*Use*
give consideration to	consider
make inquiry regarding	inquire
is of the opinion	believes
comes into conflict with	conflicts
information which is of a confidential nature	confidential information

19   Professional or office gobbledygook often arises from using the passive rather than the active voice. Instead of looking you in the eye, as it were, and writing "This act requires . . . " the office worker looks out of the window and writes: "It is required by this statute that . . . " When the bureau chief says, "We expect Congress to cut your budget," the message is only too clear; but usually he says, "It is expected that the departmental budget estimates will be reduced by Congress."

Gobbled: "All letters prepared for the signature of the Administrator will be single spaced."

Ungobbled: "Single space all letters for the Administrator." (Thus cutting 13 words to 7.)

Only People Can Read

20   The F.S.A. surveys pick up the point . . . that human communication involves a listener as well as a speaker. Only people can read, though a lot of writing seems to be addressed to beings in outer space. To whom are you

talking? The sender of the officialese message often forgets the chap on the other end of the line.

A woman with two small children wrote the F.S.A. asking what she   21
should do about payments, as her husband had lost his memory. "If he never gets able to work," she said, "and stays in an institution would I be able to draw any benefits? . . . I don't know how I am going to live and raise my children since he is disable to work. Please give me some information. . . ."

To this human appeal, she received a shattering blast of gobbledygook,   22
beginning, "State unemployment compensation laws do not provide any benefits for sick or disabled individuals . . . in order to qualify an individual must have a certain number of quarters of coverage . . ." et cetera, et cetera. Certainly if the writer had been thinking about the poor woman he would not have dragged in unessential material about old-age insurance. If he had pictured a mother without means to care for her children, he would have told her where she might get help—from the local office which handles aid to dependent children, for instance.

Gobbledygook of this kind would largely evaporate if we thought of our   23
messages as two way—in the above case, if we pictured ourselves talking on the doorstep of a shabby house to a woman with two children tugging at her skirts, who in her distress does not know which way to turn.

Results of the Survey

The F.S.A. survey showed that office documents could be cut 20 to 50   24
percent, with an improvement in clarity and a great saving to taxpayers in paper and payrolls.

A handbook was prepared and distributed to key officials.[6] They read it,   25
thought about it, and presently began calling section meetings to discuss gobbledygook. More booklets were ordered, and the local output of documents began to improve. A Correspondence Review Section was established as a kind of laboratory to test murky messages. A supervisor could send up samples for analysis and suggestions. The handbook is now used for training new members; and many employees keep it on their desks along with the dictionary. Outside the Bureau some 25,000 copies have been sold (at 20 cents each) to individuals, governments, business firms, all over the world. It is now used officially in the Veterans Administration and in the Department of Agriculture.

The handbook makes clear the enormous amount of gobbledygook which   26
automatically spreads in any large office, together with ways and means to keep it under control. I would guess that at least half of all the words circulating around the bureaus of the world are "irrelevant, incompetent, and immaterial"—to use a favorite legalism; or are just plain "unnecessary"—to ungobble it.

My favorite story of removing the gobble from gobbledygook concerns   27

---

[6] By Milton Hall. [Chase's note]

the Bureau of Standards at Washington. I have told it before but perhaps the reader will forgive the repetition. A New York plumber wrote the Bureau that he had found hydrochloric acid fine for cleaning drains, and was it harmless? Washington replied: "The efficacy of hydrochloric acid is indisputable, but the chlorine residue is incompatible with metallic permanence."

30   The plumber wrote back that he was mighty glad the Bureau agreed with him. The Bureau replied with a note of alarm: "We cannot assume responsibility for the production of toxic and noxious residues with hydrochloric acid, and suggest that you use an alternate procedure." The plumber was happy to learn that the Bureau still agreed with him.

31   Whereupon Washington exploded: "Don't use hydrochloric acid; it eats hell out of the pipes!"

WHAT DID THE WRITER SAY, AND WHAT DID YOU THINK?

1. Summarize the author's thesis about gobbledygook.
2. Does all gobbledygook use too many words?
3. What suggestions does the author make about the causes of gobbledygook?
4. Does Chase give practical advice on how to eliminate gobbledygook?
5. Chase seems fairly optimistic about progress in improving the language. Has his optimism been confirmed?
6. Chase praises *Reader's Digest* condensations. Why do many good writers who dislike gobbledygook as much as Chase does feel there are dangers in such condensations?
7. Can you think of examples of Business Gobbledygook? Military Gobbledygook? Can you find examples of gobbledygook in one of your textbooks?

HOW DID THE WRITER SAY IT?

1. In paragraph 2, what is a "verbal squirrel cage"? Why is the phrase effective?
2. In paragraph 3, what does "event" refer to? Is the reference clear?
3. On p. 172, Chase follows each example of gobbledygook with one-sentence translations. What do all his translations have in common?
4. Are all the examples of gobbledygook in the first part of this selection (paragraphs 1–10) from government bureaucrats? Are they supposed to be?
5. Does the author himself ever unintentionally write gobbledygook?
6. Vocabulary: *jargon, prolix, brevity.*

WHAT ABOUT <u>YOUR</u> WRITING?

The Stuart Chase essay is about writing, and the "What About *Your* Writing?" question can best be answered here with the recommendation that you be on the alert for gobbledygook in your writing and, if you find it, ruthlessly get rid of it.

One marginal comment is necessary. Although Chase is absolutely right when he says that the passive voice frequently contributes to gobbledygook, you shouldn't assume that the passive voice is always automatically wrong.

In a sentence that uses the *active* voice, the subject *does the acting*:

Phillip went to the theater.

The pitcher throws a good curve ball.

I took the final examination.

Most English sentences use the active voice. It sounds natural. It's what readers usually expect.

In a sentence that uses the *passive* voice, the subject stands around "passively" and is *acted upon*.

The theater was gone to by Phillip.

A good curve ball is thrown by the pitcher.

The final examination was taken by me.

Obviously, the passive voice, compared to the active, can be awkward, pompous, wordy, and downright ugly. That's why Chase dislikes it. That's why you should be cautious about it.

For some special situations the passive voice can be altogether acceptable. When the person or thing or group that does the acting is unknown or unimportant, the passive voice often sounds normal and natural—more so than the active voice in some cases—and there's no reason to avoid it. The passive sometimes works well, too, when the writer deliberately wants to sound formal and impersonal.

The flight was canceled because of mechanical difficulties.

I've been called many bad names.

In the Middle Ages, Aristotle was often referred to as "The Philosopher."

Payment must be received within ten days or legal steps will be taken.

Go easy on the passive, then. Most of the time the active works better—much better. But there's no all-encompassing rule against the passive, and there shouldn't be. Notice how often Chase himself uses the passive. In paragraph 27, we find, "A handbook was prepared and distributed," "More booklets were ordered," "A Correspondence Review Section was established," "The handbook is now used."

Chapter 8

DESCRIPTION

Description is nothing new. You've undoubtedly used description in parts of papers you have already written. In an example paper you may have written a description of a litter-filled street to support your thesis that city services have declined. In a process paper you may have written an introductory paragraph describing the beautiful pie you were going to tell the reader how to bake. In a classification paper on bathing suits or hair styles, you had to describe each class. Description is not new, but devoting an entire paper to it is new and demands separate consideration.

Some descriptions can be completely *objective*: they can describe the size and color of measles spots, the size and speed of a missile. Objective descriptions make no judgments about the ugliness of the spots or the scariness of the missile. Ordinarily intended to meet special needs, objective descriptions are not within the province of this chapter.

The *impressionistic* or *interpretive* description paper is our basic concern. The writer of this paper uses description to convey an attitude. Any objective description of measles spots, for instance, is subordinate here to convincing the reader of the ugliness or triviality or seriousness of the spots.

Rules, guidelines, and handy hints are of less practical value than usual in writing the comparatively freewheeling description paper. Only three major points need to be stressed, and none of them is especially restrictive.

First, **description papers tend to rely more than others on a direct appeal to the reader's emotions.** A description of a room will more probably have a thesis like *The room was frightening* than *The room was big*. To make their emotional appeal, description papers also tend to concentrate more than others on using colorful language. Such hard-to-pin-down elements as mood and tone tend to be major concerns in description papers. These are pretty spectacular generalizations, of course; they don't apply to all description papers, and they certainly shouldn't be interpreted as implying that other patterns of writing can't or shouldn't appeal to emotions, use colorful language, and so on. As a whole, though, good description papers do receive praise more for their insight and sensitivity than for their masterful logic.

Nobody can teach you how to make your writing tingle with deep perceptions. Insight and sensitivity come from within. It might help, however, to suggest a few approaches that can give your writing a push in the right direction toward attaining the lively emotional appeal of good description.

1. *Try a deliberately unconventional thesis.* If a room would strike ninety-nine people out of a hundred as ugly, try pointing out its hidden beauties. If everyone agrees that a young woman is painfully shy, try showing that she really has a superiority complex. Don't lie, and don't attempt to support a thesis you believe is idiotic; do see if you can make a case for an unconventional idea.

2. *Show your powers of observation by stressing specific details.* Virtually all good writing uses specifics, lots of them. A description paper absolutely depends on them. Try to take a seemingly trivial detail and show its surprising relevancy. Demonstrate that you had the ability to notice the detail in the first place and then to have its significance register on your mind. If you write a paper attempting to show that a certain man pays no attention to his appearance, don't stop at saying that he looks messy; bring up the bread crumbs in his moustache and the toe protruding through the hole in his tennis sneakers. Too trivial? Not at all. As long as the details support the thesis, they add life to the paper.

3. *Use specific language.* Another principle of most good writing is of particular importance in description. The effect of a specific detail can be weakened if the language used to present the detail is not itself specific. *A toe protruded through a hole in his tennis sneakers* shows observation of specific details. *A toe had fought its way through a hole in his tennis sneakers to the relatively clean air outside* shows observation of specific details dramatized by specific language.

4. *Stress the psychological impact of what you describe.* A good description will be accurate, but it will be exciting, too. Your description of a dusty old room won't convey a sense of immediacy by itemizing the locations of all the clumps of dust; your reader should have not only a picture of what the room looks like, but also a strong sense of how depressed or indignant or philosophical the room made you feel.

So much for emotional appeal.

Second, **choose an appropriate organizing principle, and stick to it.** Some authorities suggest that in describing the appearance of a person, the writer might start with the head and go down to the toes (or vice versa, of course). In describing a landscape, the writer might start with objects farthest away and progress to the closest objects. Many writers should be able to do better. The authorities want to achieve order but sometimes seem to invite rigidity.

Still, they have a case, and cautious agreement with them is the only reasonable course. Nobody wants rigidity, but chaos is even worse. Certainly, a writer needs enough of a predetermined organizing principle to decide which descriptive details come first and which come last. It's easy to understand hesitation about the cut-and-dried mathematics of top-to-bottom or far-to-near, but not all the formulas need to be that definite. Some description papers may be organized on a looser principle like attractive features—unattractive features, first impressions—second impressions, impact on senses like sight, touch, and hearing. Structure of some kind is necessary. In addition, even the top-to-bottom and far-to-near principles seldom turn out to be as dreary as they sound. A good writer, after all, doesn't ordinarily make formal announcements like, "moving down from the forehead, I shall now discuss the nose," or "The next closest object is . . ." Don't adopt an organizing principle, then, that makes a prisoner of you and your reader, but do adopt a principle. There's freedom of choice, but you have to make a choice.

Third, **the description paper must commit itself to the discipline of the persuasive principle.** With all this material on freedom and emotional appeal, this last point is particularly important. It's precisely because of the relatively free-form nature of much descriptive writing that the persuasive principle has to be insisted on so strongly. Freedom and sloppiness are not the same. Thesis and support of thesis in many respects are the main ingredients for holding the description paper together. Without a thesis, a process paper can still trace a process. Without a thesis, a description paper goes off in all directions and disintegrates into a shapeless mass. It doesn't describe; it simply takes inventory. Without a thesis, a description paper has no backbone—and, like a body without a backbone, has no freedom to do, or be, anything.

There's not much this book can say about the general nature of the persuasive principle that it hasn't already said. Throughout much of Chapter 1, the book showed how a paper on education was narrowed down to a description of Professor X with the thesis "Professor X is an incompetent teacher." On pages 8–9, a sample first paragraph showed how such a paper might begin. A description paper doesn't merely benefit from a thesis. It needs one in order to exist.

WRITING SUGGESTIONS FOR DESCRIPTION THEMES

Some of the suggested topics here are more specific than usual. Don't feel hemmed in. Use them only as starting points for your own ideas. Notice that many topics can be treated in two different ways. You can write a description of a general or composite type of airline flight attendant or lifeguard or hospital waiting room, having no one specific person, place, or thing in mind; you can also write a description of an *individual* person, place, or thing: flight attendant Susan Early, lifeguard John Braun, the waiting room at St. Luke's.

1. Beggars
2. Know-it-all car mechanics
3. Traffic jams
4. Lifeguards
5. Spoiled children
6. Haunted houses
7. People eating lobster or corn on the cob
8. Thunderstorms
9. Dentists
10. Animals in the zoo
11. Bus drivers
12. Airline flight attendants
13. Pinball machine fanatics
14. Normally busy places, now deserted
15. Stutterers
16. Retarded children
17. Drunks
18. Hospital waiting rooms
19. The contents of a pocketbook
20. Overcommercialized tourist attractions
21. Housing developments
22. Amusement parks
23. Vans or campers
24. Sports stadiums

Dinty Moore's Restaurant

SHANA ALEXANDER

Shana Alexander has been editor-in-chief of *McCall's* magazine and is now a contributing editor for *Newsweek*. She writes frequently on current issues, and a collection of her columns, *The Feminine Eye*, was published in 1970. Her most recent book is *Talking Woman* (1976).

As you read, notice how this description of an old restaurant and its owner leads to meditations about our own times.

The fascinations of Watergate have been its sudden strokes and surprises.   1
My personal stunner came the day somebody said J. Edgar Hoover and Daniel Ellsberg's[1] father-in-law used to eat together 30 years ago in Dinty Moore's restaurant. At that, Watergate faded and Dinty Moore's came floating up out of my past, all its lights ablaze, polished brass and mirrors

From *Newsweek*, August 20, 1973. Reprinted by permission of Shana Alexander.

[1] Hoover (1895–1972) was the director of the F.B.I. Ellsberg, a former government employee, leaked to the press the "Pentagon Papers," a classified record of policy discussions on Vietnam.

gleaming—a gala, ghostly cruise ship bearing my childhood back to me.

2   Moore's was the best restaurant in New York City, and I grew up there, dining out once a week or so with my parents from the time I was old enough to hold a fork. Although I often saw J. Edgar Hoover and other famous figures tucking away the corned beef and cabbage, the "nose-warmers" of oxtail soup, the rice pudding nonpareil—politicians ate better in those days, and so did crooks—it was not the celebrities who impressed me but the ionized, charged-up atmosphere of the place. Anything might happen in this closed, immaculate world of delicious food and fierce emotions where once a customer was tossed out the door for ordering a hamburger *without* onions; where out on the sidewalk enraged rabbis in black hats and beards picketed because the menu listed "kosher calf's liver and Irish bacon."

A Piece of Ireland

3   Moore's was a self-contained, white-tie universe, so Irish that years later when I landed in Dublin, I felt utterly at home. Ireland seemed a larger, much-diluted, open-air Moore's. The white-tiled kitchen in the rear was wide open to public view, and my sister and I had cooking lessons there after school. While our classmates were wearing white gloves and learning the right way to fox-trot, we wore big white tablecloths tied around us, waiter-style, and learned the right way to cook carrots and peas (rapidly, with a pinch of sugar) and potatoes (unpeeled, with a handful of salt).

4   Our teacher was the old man himself. Everyone called him "the old man," including his family. To his face he was "Mr. Moore," or "Jim." Nobody ever called him "Dinty," not even the cartoonist George McManus, who immortalized him in his abrasive comic strip "Bringing Up Father."

5   McManus was right about the long-smoldering warfare of the Irish household. In the Moore family nobody talked to anybody else if he could help it. Mr. Moore and his wife occupied separate floors above the restaurant and had not spoken in decades; the children rarely spoke either, except to borrow some money, or to plot against one parent or the other.

6   The old man believed there was only one right way to do everything. All food must be young and all ingredients perfectly fresh. The only acceptable canned food is applesauce. The only cooking sherry is Harvey's Bristol Cream. Hamburgers can only be made from prime rib. Female lobsters are sweeter. Cooking is concentration. "Watch everything on the stove," he told us, "the way you watch a piece of toast."

Postcard Cookery

7   When the old man went to Palm Beach in winter he sent back daily postcards: "Caught a tuna today; crust on pot pie should not be too thick." "Weather beautiful; put enough barley in soup." Each vacation at least 25 postcards arrived, every one a reminder to prepare the food exactly as it had been prepared for a quarter century.

Mr. Moore had rigid standards. Leaving your mother and gambling were 8
unforgivable; larceny was lower down the scale. When my mother protested
that Jim should not waste his time and energy making up elaborate food
hampers to send to my sister and me at camp, he told her he had to do the
monthly baskets anyway "for the boys up the river."

In hot weather, you had to avoid iced drinks; sip warm soup instead. 9
When my sister visited Jim in Florida and got a bad sunburn, he knew what
to do: "Soak a large linen handkerchief in ice cubes in a silver bowl. Wring
out in Gordon's gin . . . must be Gordon's . . . and apply to affected parts."
She swore it worked like a charm.

In memory, the old man is a wobble of chins, an aroma of bay rum, a 10
shirt front of creamy pongee, a fine London suit with a cuff of long under-
wear peeking out, a pink, just-barbered face and a few long strands of hair
plastered on gleaming scalp. From him I learned inflexible rules about
everything that is most important in life—food, sex, death and deportment.
The sex lecture occurred when I was 12 or 13. One wintry night he glanced
at me sharply, then bellowed, "Moran: Bring me a plate of oysters. Don't
open 'em." Years before the waiter had got a $500 tip for placing a $5,000
bet on the Dempsey-Firpo fight, and surprises after that were anticlimax.
Moran presented the bivalves without comment, and Mr. Moore deftly
opened one with the tiny gold penknife on his watch chain. He thrust the
mucid, cold object under my nose, rapped his big knuckles hard on the table
to rivet my attention and said sternly, "Listen here, girlie! An oyster has
everything *you* have. So don't leave your mother when her hair turns gray."
So much for the facts of life. I was a woman now.

Jim Moore died in his restaurant in his 84th year. They laid him out in 11
the parlor upstairs, and the next afternoon I saw for the first time in my life
the small, rouged face of death. But he had already beat death long ago. He
was an Irish Catholic of the most barnacled kind, yet his belief in God had
not been unduly calcified by organized religion. When I say he beat death
I am not being fanciful; he smacked it in the face with a mackerel.

Old Cronies

As he aged, the old man badly missed his departed cronies, and one quiet 12
afternoon the absurdity of their absence grew intolerable. He fixed up two
packages wrapped in parchment paper and tied in butcher string, climbed
into the open, cream-colored, wicker-sided Packard that always stood in
front of the door, and instructed his chauffeur to drive to the Hebrew cem-
etery. At the grave of his friend Sam Harris, the theatrical producer, the
old man placed a beautiful hunk of his own corned beef and reminded him
aloud how inconsiderate he had been to die young. By the time Jim had
driven on to Mount Calvary and the grave of George M. Cohan,[2] he was
steaming mad. The other parcel was a fish, which he beat against the head-

[2] American composer (1878–1942) who wrote "Give My Regards to Broadway," "Over
There," and other well-known songs.

stone. "Cohan!" he shouted. "In case you don't know, today's Friday, and I just want you to see what you're missing!"

13   Our world very much misses men like Jim Moore. He was more than a man with absolute standards; he was a man who lived up to those standards—publicly; like his kitchen, his life and his foibles were totally exposed. His cards were always on the table along with the food. Like his old customer, J. Edgar Hoover, the old man had a bottom line below which he would not go. Unlike the Watergate pragmatists, bent on reelection of the President at all costs, Jim could never believe the ends justified the means. He was too smart. His whole life was a testament that bad means, like bad raw ingredients, positively *guarantee* a bad end.

WHAT DID THE WRITER SAY, AND WHAT DID YOU THINK?

1. What is the author's thesis about Moore?
2. How does the author use Moore to shed light on the Watergate scandal?
3. Moore's philosophizing about the oysters will strike most readers as less than profound. Is the author respectful, amused, or what?
4. Does the mention of so much silliness and bossiness in Moore weaken the thesis?
5. What is the meaning of "the ends justify the means"?
6. Find some examples of your own to support or attack the author's assertion that bad means guarantee bad ends.

HOW DID THE WRITER SAY IT?

1. Is the article well organized? Does it, for example, start out as a description of a restaurant and then drift into a description of a man?
2. Are Moore's religious attitudes connected to the thesis?
3. Are Moore's family difficulties connected to the thesis?
4. The author writes that Moore "beat death"—referring to the scene at George M. Cohan's grave. Does she attempt to show that Moore also "beat death" in the more usual sense?
5. The author maintains that the most important things in life are "food, sex, death, and deportment." Is this comment intended to amuse or to be taken seriously?
6. Vocabulary: *nonpareil, ionized, abrasive, pongee, deftly, mucid, barnacled, calcified, cronies, foibles, pragmatists.*

WHAT ABOUT <u>YOUR</u> WRITING?

In paragraph 10, after quoting Moore's ordering the waiter to bring him "oysters," the author writes that the waiter "presented the bivalves." It's possible that the author felt _bivalves_ suggested a squishy blob better than _oysters._ It's at least as possible, however, that she fell victim to _elegant variation._

Too many writers worry about repeating a word in the same sentence or in sentences close to each other. This worry sometimes leads them into using synonyms—often "elegant" ones—that can be more distracting than any repetition.

As mother brought the turkey to the table, I thought of how often that fowl had added to the joys of Thanksgiving.

In planning your wedding, remember that nuptial ceremonies are largely a matter of individual choice.

A previous "What About _Your_ Writing?" section, while warning against monotony, has discussed how repetition can often be an effective stylistic device (see p. 166). But even when the issue is direct communication of meaning rather than a distinguished style, straightforward repetition is preferable to elegant variation.

As mother brought the turkey to the table, I thought of how often turkey had added to the joys of Thanksgiving.

In planning your wedding, remember that weddings are largely a matter of individual choice.

The quest for elegant variation is what sometimes leads people to misuse the thesaurus. Fearful of repetition, they consult the thesaurus for a synonym, assuming that all words in the same group have the same meaning. They don't. _Handsome_ and _pretty,_ for example, are likely to be in the same group; they belong within a certain related family of meanings, but they don't mean the same, and they are not interchangeable. The thesaurus is generally most helpful when writers already know the word they want but can't quite recall it. Used improperly, the thesaurus leads writers to create sentences like _Defenestration has had serious pecuniary ramifications for schools_ instead of _Broken windows have added to schools' financial problems._

Aside from common sense concern about monotony, the only serious danger in repetition is when the same word in the same sentence or in sentences close to each other _changes in meaning._ (This warning includes different forms of the same word: _Convention-conventional,_ for example.) Do, at all costs, avoid confusing repetition like

The heart of our medical research project is heart failure.

The one bright spot in his report card was his brightness in math.

I can't bear the thought of the polar bear's becoming extinct.

The plain truth is that Deborah is very plain-looking.

The two little shavers love to watch their daddy shave.

Our Enemy, the Cat

ALAN DEVOE

Alan Devoe (1909–1955) held editorial positions on a number of magazines. His many articles and books on nature include *Phudd Hill* (1937), *Down to Earth* (1940), *Lives Around Us* (1942), *Speaking of Animals* (1947), and *This Fascinating Animal World* (1951).

Devoe uses a good many words that may be unfamiliar to you, but the selection is remarkably easy to read. Meaning is almost always clear from context—the word or words surrounding the unfamiliar word. Don't refer to the dictionary until you've completed the reading.

1

1   We tie bright ribbons around their necks, and occasionally little tinkling bells, and we affect to think that they are as sweet and vapid as the coy name "kitty" by which we call them would imply. It is a curious illusion. For, purring beside our fireplaces and pattering along our back fences, we have got a wild beast as uncowed and uncorrupted as any under heaven.

2   It is five millenniums since we snared the wild horse and broke his spirit to our whim, and for centuries beyond counting we have been able to persuade the once-free dog to fawn and cringe and lick our hands. But a man must be singularly blind with vanity to fancy that in the three—ten?—thousand years during which we have harbored cats beneath our rooftrees, we have succeeded in reducing them to any such insipid estate. It is not a "pet" (that most degraded of creatures) that we have got in our house, whatever we may like to think. It is a wild beast; and there adheres to its sleek fur no smallest hint of the odor of humanity.

3   It would be a salutary thing if those who write our simpering verses and tales about "tabby-sit-by-the-fire" could bring themselves to see her honestly, to look into her life with eyes unblurred by wishful sentiment. It would be a good thing—to start at the beginning—to follow her abroad into the moonlight on one of those raw spring evenings when the first skunk cabbages are thrusting their veined tips through the melting snow and when the loins of catdom are hot with lust.

4   The love-play of domestic creatures is mostly a rather comic thing, and loud are the superior guffaws of rustic humans to see the clumsy, fumbling antics that take place in the kennels and the stockpen. But the man had better not laugh who sees cats in their rut. He is looking upon something very like aboriginal passion, untainted by any of the overlaid refinements, suppressions, and modifications that have been acquired by most of mankind's beasts. The mating of cats has neither the bathetic clumsiness of dogs' nor the lumbering ponderousness of cattle's, but—conducted in a lonely secret place, away from human view—is marked by a quick concentrated intensity of lust that lies not far from the borderline of agony. The

From *The American Mercury*, December 1937. Reprinted by permission of *The American Mercury*, P.O. Box 1306, Torrance, Calif. 90505.

female, in the tense moment of the prelude, tears with her teeth at her mate's throat, and, as the climax of the creatures' frenzy comes, the lean silky-furred flanks quiver vibrantly as a taut wire. Then quietly, in the spring night, the two beasts go their ways.

It will be usually May before the kittens come; and that episode, too, will take place secretly, in its ancient feline fashion, where no maudlin human eye may see. Great is the pique in many a house when "pussy," with dragging belly and distended dugs, disappears one night—scorning the cushioned maternity-bed that has been prepared for her—and creeps on silent feet to the dankest cranny of the cellar, there in decent aloneness to void her blood and babies. She does not care, any more than a lynx does, or a puma, to be pried upon while she licks the birth-hoods from her squirming progeny and cleans away the membrane with her rough pink tongue. 5

A kitten is not a pretty thing at birth. For many days it is a wriggling mite of lumpy flesh and sinew, blind and unaware, making soft sucking noises with its wet, toothless mouth, and smelling of milk. Daily, hourly, the rough tongue of the tabby ministers to it in its helplessness, glossing the baby-fur with viscid spittle, licking away the uncontrolled dung, cleaning away the crumbly pellet of dried blood from its pointed ears. By that tenth or fourteenth day when its eyes wholly unseal, blue and weak in their newness, the infant cat is clean to immaculateness, and an inalienable fastidiousness is deep-lodged in its spirit. 6

It is now—when the kitten makes its first rushes and sallies from its birthplace, and, with extraordinary gymnastics of its chubby body, encounters chair-legs and human feet and other curious phenomena—that it elicits from man those particular expressions of gurgling delight which we reserve for very tiny fluffy creatures who act very comically. But the infant cat has no coy intent to be amusing. If he is comic, it is only because of the incongruity of so demure a look and so wild a heart. For in that furry head of his, grim and ancient urges are already dictating. 7

Hardly larger than a powder-puff, he crouches on the rug and watches a fleck of lint. His little blue eyes are bright, and presently his haunches tense and tremble. The tiny body shivers in an ague of excitement. He pounces, a little clumsily perhaps, and pinions the fleeting lint-fleck with his paws. In the fractional second of that lunge, the ten small needles of his claws have shot from their sheaths of flesh and muscle. It is a good game; but it is not an idle one. It is the kitten's introduction into the ancient ritual of the kill. Those queer little stiff-legged rushings and prancings are the heritage of an old death-dance, and those jerkings of his hind legs, as he rolls on his back, are the preparation for that day when—in desperate conflict with a bigger beast than himself—he will win the fight by the time-old feline technique of disembowelment. Even now, in his early infancy, he is wholly and inalienably a cat. 8

While he is still young he has already formulated his attitude toward the human race into whose midst he has been born. It is an attitude not easily described, but compounded of a great pride, a great reserve, a towering 9 integrity. It is even to be fancied that there is something in it of a sort of bleak contempt. Solemnly the cat watches these great hulking two-legged creatures into whose strange tribe he has unaccountably been born—and who are so clumsy, so noisy, so vexing to his quiet spirit—and in his feline heart is neither love nor gratitude. He learns to take the food which they give him, to relish the warmth and the comfort and the caresses which they can offer, but these profferments do not persuade his wild mistrustful heart to surrender itself. He will not sell himself, as a dog will, for a scrap of meat; he will not enter into an allegiance. He is unchangeably and incorruptibly a cat, and he will accommodate himself to the ways and spirit of mankind no more than the stern necessity of his unnatural environment requires.

2

10   Quietly he dozes by the fire or on a lap, and purrs in his happiness because he loves the heat. But let him choose to move, and if any human hand tries to restrain him for more than a moment he will struggle and unsheath his claws and lash out with a furious hate. Let a whip touch him and he will slink off in a sullen fury, uncowed and outraged and unrepenting. For the things which man gives to him are not so precious or essential that he will trade them for his birth-right, which is the right to be himself—a furred four-footed being of ancient lineage, loving silence and aloneness and the night, and esteeming the smell of rat's blood above any possible human excellence.

11   He may live for perhaps ten years; occasionally even for twenty. Year after year he drinks the daily milk that is put faithfully before him, dozes in laps whose contours please him, accepts with casual pleasure the rubbing of human fingers under his chin—and withdraws, in every significant hour of his life, as far away from human society as he is able. Far from the house, in a meadow or a woods if he can find one, he crouches immobile for hours, his lithe body flattened concealingly in the grass or ferns, and waits for prey.

12   With a single pounce he can break a rabbit's spine as though it were a brittle twig. When he has caught a tawny meadow-mouse or a mole, he has, too, the ancient cat-ecstasy of toying and playing with it, letting it die slowly, in a long agony, for his amusement. Sometimes, in a dim remembrance from the remote past of his race, he may bring home his kill; but mostly he returns to the house as neat and demure as when he left, with his chops licked clean of blood.

13   Immaculate, unobtrusive, deep withdrawn into himself, he passes through the long years of his enforced companionship with humanity. He takes from his masters (how absurd a word it is) however much they may care to give him; of himself he surrenders nothing. However often he be decked with ribbons and cuddled and petted and made much over, his cold pride never grows less, and his grave calm gaze—tinged perhaps with a gentle distaste—is never lighted by adoration. To the end he adores only his own gods, the gods of mating, of hunting, and of the lonely darkness.

One day, often with no forewarning whatever, he is gone from the house   14
and never returns. He has felt the presaging shadow of death, and he goes
to meet it in the old unchanging way of the wild—alone. A cat does not
want to die with the smell of humanity in his nostrils and the noise of
humanity in his delicate peaked ears. Unless death strikes very quickly and
suddenly, he creeps away to where it is proper that a proud wild beast
should die—not on one of man's rugs or cushions, but in a lonely quiet
place, with his muzzle pressed against the cold earth.

WHAT DID THE WRITER SAY, AND WHAT DID YOU THINK?

1. What is the thesis?
2. The title seems clearly inaccurate or inappropriate. Why?
3. Could the author justify the title by arguing that it is true in a deeper sense than we first took it?
4. In trying to support a point, a writer should show awareness of any points the opposition can raise. How does Devoe deal with apparent evidence of a cat's affection for human beings?
5. Why does Devoe express contempt for dogs?

HOW DID THE WRITER SAY IT?

1. How many paragraphs are used for the introduction?
2. How does the description of skunk cabbages in paragraph 3 fit in with the purpose of that paragraph?
3. What principle of organization does Devoe apply to his description? How does he decide what comes first, what comes second, and so on?
4. Different people have different thoughts about wild animals. What words and phrases show that Devoe admires cats?
5. Instead of blandly writing, "The cat is an avid hunter," Devoe writes that the cat loves "the smell of rat's blood." Where else does Devoe's choice of specific words stress the uncivilized, animal nature of the cat?
6. Where does the author use *inversion* (see p. 113)?
7. Vocabulary: *vapid, uncowed, millenniums, whim, fawn, insipid, adheres, salutary, simpering, rustic, aboriginal, bathetic, lumbering, ponderousness, maudlin, pique, distended, dugs, dankest, cranny, void, progeny, sinew, glossing, viscid, dung, fastidiousness, sallies, incongruity, demure, ague, pinions, profferments, lineage, unobtrusive, presaging, muzzle.*

WHAT ABOUT <u>YOUR</u> WRITING?

Inseparable from Devoe's presentation of his own point of view about cats is his attack
on what he considers conventional and repellently sentimental attitudes. His scorn for

those attitudes gives his thesis a dimension that it would not otherwise have had. The scorn runs through the entire article but is especially pronounced in the introduction.

Getting started is a problem for many writers, and Devoe here demonstrates one of the most effective ways of dealing with the problem: *Many people think such and such, but . . .* Instead of opening with a direct and sometimes flat statement of your thesis, let your thesis emerge as a response to some other people's ignorance or superstition or senti- mentality or general wrongheadedness. Your thesis will then exist in a dramatic context, not an intellectual vacuum, and will have built right into it the appeal of a lively argument.

Most people think such and such about cats, says Devoe, *but . . .* With a thesis that spanking small children is often the best method of handling certain difficulties, you might begin with a few satirical references to the belief that three-year-olds appreciate the fine points of logic and that the ideal family is a loosely organized debating society. With a thesis that country music is fun, you might begin by observing that respectable people traditionally are supposed to scorn country music as trivial and commercialized nonsense. Then, perhaps, declare that you guess you're just not respectable, *but . . .*

For another suggestion on getting started, consult the comments on questions, pp. 118–119.

Luxurious Newport: 1907

CLEVELAND MOFFETT

Cleveland Moffett (1863–1926) was a newspaper reporter, editor, novelist, and playwright. He is sometimes associated with the "muckrakers," a group of writers of the 1890s and 1900s who shared an interest in exposing previously overlooked problems: political corruption, business scandals, poor living and working conditions, and the like. "Luxurious Newport" was written in 1907 for *Cosmopolitan* magazine.

In interpreting the many financial facts and figures of "Luxurious Newport," readers should bear in mind, of course, the huge increase in the cost of living since 1907. They should also remember, however, that the federal income tax was not permanently established until 1913.

The great mansions in Newport, Rhode Island, are now mostly public property, preserved as tourist attractions.

1   "Newport is the most expensive city in the world; it's twice as expensive as New York," declares a friend of mine who pays eight thousand dollars a season for the rent of his cottage. To be sure, this "cottage" is a handsome stone house in attractive grounds, perhaps the costliest of those that are rented regularly, but it certainly may be said that a rental varying from three to seven thousand dollars for the three or four months is an ordinary affair in Newport, and occasionally when one of the millionaires' villas is to be let, *then* the price is twelve or fifteen thousand dollars from June to Sep- tember. And people are glad to pay it!

2   As a matter of fact, fifteen thousand dollars is a small enough sum to pay when one considers what the owner has already paid for the land, the house and the grounds. The simple stone wall, for instance, around one of these

"The Breakers": the Vanderbilt summer home, Newport, Rhode Island. (Photo: Wayne Andrews)

million-dollar places cost one hundred thousand dollars; its gates and carv-
ings kept the stone-cutters busy for a year. Significant, is it not, one hundred
thousand dollars for a stone wall!

3   Look at this horse-chestnut. Its branches spread sixty feet, and your
extended arms scarcely compass its girth. Surely, you say, this tree has
stood here for generations. Not at all; it has stood here for two or three
months, and the same is true of those maples down by the driveway and of
that rare old tulip-tree by the hedge and of yonder group of sturdy red
cedars. One year ago the maples were growing twenty miles away, the
horse-chestnut thirty miles away, and the tulip-tree fifty miles away. Then
the order came that these trees must shade and beautify this lawn and frame
a picture of the sea for the piazza people. So two gangs of Italians were sent
forth with picks and shovels, and under each chosen tree they dug two
tunnels, leaving the roots in a great ball of solid earth. Then they skidded
it up on heavy timbers and moved it on rollers and made it fast on a special
truck and hitched on thirty horses, for the weight was thirty tons, and thus
mile after mile they dragged it here and planted it, and the time consumed
was six weeks, and the cost was *nine hundred dollars for that one tree!*

4   One might think that, with extensive greenhouses to draw upon, the mistress of one of these handsome places would have flowers in abundance for
all occasions, but such is not the case. The greenhouses merely supply the
family's daily needs, and a florist is called upon for elaborate dinners, balls,
and fêtes. So that a fashionable family will easily spend a thousand dollars
a month in the season simply on flowers for small dinners such as are given,
say once a week.

5   And this brings us to the lavish fêtes that take place every year in Newport—those famous entertainments that are described and discussed all over
the country. It is easy to exaggerate their cost; but the sober fact seems to
be that ten or twelve thousand dollars is no unusual price to pay for one of
these remarkable affairs. The dinner, say for two hundred guests at the
caterer's charge of ten dollars each, comes to two thousand dollars, without
wine or cigars. Besides this there is a first supper at midnight, after the
special entertainment provided, and a second supper at five or six in the
morning, after the dancing; which easily brings the total for eating and
drinking up to three thousand dollars. Add another thousand dollars for
flowers and music. Add two thousand more for cotillion favors—watches,
fans, and articles of gold and silver. Then add two thousand more for a
theater built especially for the occasion on the lawn and torn down the next
morning, a spacious theater, be it said, and handsomely decorated. Add
several thousand dollars more for a complete vaudeville entertainment with
singers and dancers, acrobats and jugglers, all brought on expressly from
New York, or perhaps (as happened once) the entire company of a New
York theater brought down and the theater closed. When you have counted
all that and various minor things, say five hundred dollars for electric-light-
ing effects on the grounds, you will see clearly enough what becomes of ten
or twelve or even fifteen thousand dollars on such an occasion. And New-

port may have two or three entertainments like this in a single week! . . .

I asked [a dressmaker] what it costs one of these ladies whose duty it is   6
to shine in Newport for her gowns.

"Ten thousand dollars a year," he answered promptly. "We have clients   7
who spend twelve thousand a year, but ten is enough. We have many who
spend seven thousand a year. If a woman spends only five thousand a year,
we do not take her very seriously."

"You mean five thousand for gowns alone?"   8

"Of course."   9

And I was left to imagine what might be the ladies' bills for hats, boots,   10
lingerie, etc., not to forget the sinuous automobiling veils that were fluttering
all about us.

"How many gowns does a smart woman need for the Newport season?"   11
I inquired.

He thought a moment. "Counting everything, about twenty."   12

"And how much will they cost apiece?"   13

"That depends on the number of handsome ones. You can't get a really   14
first-class gown *from us* for less than five hundred dollars." . . .

I have heard that our American women spend less on dress than their   15
rich Russian sisters, but the following summary of items, made after careful
investigation and consultations with several New York dressmakers and
milliners, shows that they are doing fairly well for the daughters of a young
republic. I may add that the dressmakers and milliners in question were the
most prominent and responsible in the city, all on Fifth Avenue, and without
exception they insisted that this summary is *considerably too low*. Indeed,
one of the leading dressmakers declared that sixty thousand dollars would
not be too high a total.

Estimate of the Amount Spent on Dress per Year by Many Rich American Women

Furs and accessories	$5000
Dinner-gowns	5000
Ball- and opera-gowns	8000
Opera-cloaks, evening and carriage-wraps	2500
Afternoon, visiting, and luncheon-toilettes	3000
Morning gowns, shirt-waists, and informal frocks	3000
Automobiling-furs and costumes	2000
Negligées	800
Lingerie	1500
Hats and veils	1200
Riding habits, boots, gloves, etc.	750
Shoes and slippers, $800; hosiery, $500	1300
Fans, laces, small jewels, etc.	2500
Gloves, $450; cleaners' bills, $1000; handkerchiefs, $600	2050
Total	$38,600

What is a smart automobile stable and what does it cost? Here we find   16
wide extremes, for many families have only one or two automobiles, while

some have eight or nine, and John Jacob Astor[1] has had as many as seventeen at one time. I am told that four automobiles are considered a satisfactory number—a gasolene brougham for runs into the country, an electric victoria for the Avenue, a little runabout for errands, and an imported racing-car, the total cost being about thirty thousand dollars. To operate and care for these four machines, two chauffeurs and a helper are required, and with their wages and the garage charges, and the outlay for gasolene, repairs, etc., the running expenses, I am assured by an expert, reach seven hundred dollars a month.

17   This is a trifle, however, compared with what is spent on one of the many steam yachts that gather in Newport harbor every summer. In addition to the original cost of such a yacht, anything from half a million down, the running expenses will vary from three thousand dollars a month for one of moderate size to twenty thousand dollars a month for a big three-hundred-footer like J. Pierpont Morgan's[2] *Corsair* and John Jacob Astor's *Nourmahal*. These are practically ocean steamships with all the luxuries of a Fifth Avenue mansion—delicious cooking, elaborate service, exquisite decorations. . . .

18   A general impression of the cost and complexity of a quiet Newport establishment may be obtained by glancing over the following specimen pay-roll:

	Yearly
Occupation	*Salary*
Special chef from Paris	$5000
Second chef	1200
Private secretary to the lady	3000
Private tutor	2000
Governess	1000
Two nurses	1000
Housekeeper	1000
Five maids	1200
Head coachman	1200
Second and third coachmen	1200
Chauffeur	1000
Butler	900
Second butler	600
Head gardener	1000
Four helpers	2500
Total	$23,800

---

[1] John Jacob Astor III (1864–1912) was manager of the huge Astor family fortune, based on furs and Manhattan real estate (such as the Waldorf-Astoria hotel). He died in the sinking of the *Titanic*.

[2] J. Pierpont Morgan (1837–1913) was, and still is, regarded as a symbol of wealth and power. A famous art and book collector, he was head of the family bank and formed the U.S. Steel Corporation. He was frequently accused of having undue influence on government policies.

Nearly twenty-five thousand dollars a year for help alone, and I am not   19
speaking now of the richest families, whose payrolls would be much larger.
Some famous chef, for instance, like "Joseph," whom the Vanderbilts[3]
brought over, would receive ten thousand dollars a year. And we know
what a steam yacht costs! And a stud-farm! So, summing up the year for
one of our multimillionaires, we may set down the main items thus:

Running expenses of houses in Newport and New York with wages and salaries to, say twenty-five people, with food, wines, etc., but no special entertaining	$30,000
Expenses of entertaining, brilliant balls, dinners, fêtes, flowers, etc.	50,000
Steam-yacht	50,000
Expenses of stable and stud-farm, with wages of, say thirty men	40,000
Grounds, greenhouses, gardens, with wages of, say twenty men	20,000
Expenses of two other places, say at Palm Beach and in the Adirondacks	20,000
Clothes for husband and wife, daughters, and younger children	20,000
Pocket-money for husband and wife, daughters, and younger children..	50,000
Automobiles	10,000
Traveling expenses with private cars, special suites on steamers, at hotels, etc.	10,000
Total	$300,000

Three hundred thousand dollars a year, without counting gifts and char-   20
ities, doctors and trained nurses, new horses and automobiles, new furniture
and jewelry, pet dogs with fur-trimmed coats, talking dolls in lace dresses
at one hundred dollars each, and numberless other things, not to omit various follies, possibly gambling with thousands of dollars risked by the ladies
at bridge and tens of thousands by the men at faro, roulette, and baccarat!

After such a statement, one begins to understand the attitude of a well-   21
known Newport couple, he with an income of fifty thousand dollars and she
with an income of three hundred and twenty thousand dollars, who recently
admitted that they could scarcely make both ends meet on a thousand dollars a day, and were so desperately driven to pay their bills that they actually
issued a statement in the newspapers last summer, to appease the clamoring
shopkeepers.

WHAT DID THE WRITER SAY, AND WHAT DID YOU THINK?

1. Read in isolation, much of this article could pass as objective reporting, but the article
   as a whole has a clear thesis. What is it?
2. Is the thesis ever stated directly? If not, where does the author come closest to revealing his views openly?
3. What instance of lavish spending seems most to upset the author?

[3] The Vanderbilt family fortune was based on railroads and included control of the New
York Central. See p. 191 for a photograph of the Vanderbilt summer home in Newport.

4. "If you've got it, flaunt it," goes a contemporary advertising slogan. What was so wrong about living it up in Newport?

HOW DID THE WRITER SAY IT?

1. The author does not try to write a description of Newport. How has he limited his subject?
2. Although the article is loosely organized, a basic organizing principle is at work. What principle has the author used?
3. Are the columns of financial figures dull? Why or why not? Would it be fair to say that the writer relies mostly on mere lists of numbers to make his point?
4. Explain the implied meaning of the last sentence in paragraph 2: "Significant, is it not, one hundred thousand dollars for a stone wall!"
5. The article was written more than seventy years ago. What words or phrases strike a modern reader as old-fashioned?
6. Vocabulary: *compass, girth, piazza, fêtes, cotillion, sinuous, toilettes, brougham, victoria.*

WHAT ABOUT <u>YOUR</u> WRITING?

Punctuation isn't always a simple matter of rules. Sometimes it can be a matter of taste.

In Moffett's piece on Newport, the first three paragraphs—and four of the first five paragraphs—all end with exclamation points. (In the third paragraph the exclamation point even gets reinforced by italics.) That's pouring it on far too much. Exclamation points have their place in emotional outbursts and commands, of course, but emphasis should come primarily from the selection and arrangement of words. Writers excessively dependent on artificial aids like exclamation points, quotation marks, and italics to create emphasis usually cheapen their effects and betray a lack of confidence in their use of words or their readers' intelligence.

Go easy, then, on pushy, comic-book punctuation—punctuation designed to push the reader's emotions in a certain direction when the words themselves haven't done the job adequately. The only way to fix a lame sentence is to fix the language; tossing in a pushy exclamation point doesn't make the sentence more powerful but only lets the reader know you wish it were more powerful. And two exclamation points are twice as bad, not twice as good. If your intended sarcasm in a sentence hasn't come through effectively with your words, pushy little quotation marks aren't usually going to help.

COMIC-BOOK PUNCTUATION	IMPROVED
I had never seen anyone with such an ego! Never!!	Never had I seen anyone with such an ego.
Art? The movie was *filth!*	The movie was not art. It was filth.
Professor Jones was a teacher (?) in Art History.	Professor Jones was a poor Art History teacher.
My respect for my "father" might increase if he sometimes acted like one.	My respect for my father might increase if he sometimes acted like one.

Don't assume that punctuation has suddenly been banned. All the resources of the language, including punctuation, are at your disposal. When a character in a novel is choking to death, nobody will object to the exclamation point when he says, "Aaargh!" In a textbook, nobody will object to the italics in a sentence like "The first principle of good writing is *the persuasive principle.*" The more spectacular forms of punctuation, however, require caution and moderation. It's a matter of taste.

Here Lies Miss Groby

JAMES THURBER

A celebrated cartoonist as well as a writer, James Thurber (1894–1961) blended whimsy and usually gentle satire to create such humorous classics as "The Secret Life of Walter Mitty," "The Catbird Seat," "The Night the Bed Fell," and "University Days." His books include *Is Sex Necessary?* (written with E. B. White, 1929), *My Life and Hard Times* (1933), *Fables for Our Time* (1940), and a children's tale, *The Thirteen Clocks* (1950).

As you read, note how carefully Thurber has limited his subject. He does not try to describe everything about Miss Groby.

Miss Groby taught me English composition thirty years ago. It wasn't   1
what prose said that interested Miss Groby; it was the way prose said it. The shape of a sentence crucified on a blackboard (parsed, she called it) brought a light to her eye. She hunted for Topic Sentences and Transitional Sentences the way little girls hunt for white violets in springtime. What she loved most of all were Figures of Speech. You remember her. You must have had her, too. Her influence will never die out of the land. A small schoolgirl asked me the other day if I could give her an example of metonymy. (There are several kinds of metonymies, you may recall, but the one that will come to mind most easily, I think, is Container for the Thing Contained.) The vision of Miss Groby came clearly before me when the little girl mentioned the old, familiar word. I saw her sitting at her desk, taking the rubber band off the roll-call cards, running it back upon the fingers of her right hand, and surveying us all separately with quick little henlike turns of her head.

Here lies Miss Groby, not dead, I think, but put away on a shelf with   2
the other T squares and rulers whose edges had lost their certainty. The fierce light that Miss Groby brought to English literature was the light of Identification. Perhaps, at the end, she could no longer retain the dates of the birth and death of one of the Lake poets.[1] That would have sent her to

[1] Term applied to the poets William Wordsworth (1770–1850), Samuel Taylor Coleridge (1772–1834), and Robert Southey (1774–1843), who lived in the Lake District of England and were assumed by some critics to have similar ideas.

the principal of the school with her resignation. Or perhaps she could not remember, finally, exactly how many Cornishmen there were who had sworn that Trelawny should not die,[2] or precisely how many springs were left to Housman's lad in which to go about the woodlands to see the cherry hung with snow.[3]

3   Verse was one of Miss Groby's delights because there was so much in both its form and content that could be counted. I believe she would have got an enormous thrill out of Wordsworth's famous lines about Lucy if they had been written this way:

> A violet by a mossy stone
> Half hidden from the eye,
> Fair as a star when ninety-eight
> Are shining in the sky.[4]

4   It is hard for me to believe that Miss Groby ever saw any famous work of literature from far enough away to know what it meant. She was forever climbing up the margins of books and crawling between their lines, hunting for the little gold of phrase, making marks with a pencil. As Palamides hunted the Questing Beast,[5] she hunted the Figure of Speech. She hunted it through the clangorous halls of Shakespeare and through the green forests of Scott.[6]

5   Night after night, for homework, Miss Groby set us to searching in "Ivanhoe" and "Julius Caesar" for metaphors, similes, metonymies, apostrophes, personifications, and all the rest. It got so that figures of speech jumped out of the pages at you, obscuring the sense and pattern of the novel

---

[2] A reference to lines from "Song of the Western Men" by Robert Stephen Hawker (1803–1875).

> And have they fixed the where and when?
> And shall Trelawny die?
> Here's twenty thousand Cornish men
> Will know the reason why!

[3] A reference to one of the poems in *A Shropshire Lad* by A. E. Housman (1859–1936). The opening line is "Loveliest of trees, the cherry now." The second and third stanzas read

> Now of my threescore years and ten,
> Twenty will not come again,
> And take from seventy springs a score,
> It only leaves me fifty more.

> And since to look at things in bloom,
> Fifty springs are little room
> About the woodlands I will go
> To see the cherry hung with snow.*

* From "Loveliest of trees, the cherry now" from "A Shropshire Lad"—Authorised Edition—from *The Collected Poems of A. E. Housman*. Copyright 1939, 1940, © 1965 by Holt, Rinehart and Winston. Copyright © 1967, 1968 by Robert E. Symons. Reprinted by permission of Holt, Rinehart and Winston, Publishers. Reprinted also by permission of The Society of Authors as the literary representative of the Estate of A. E. Housman; and Jonathan Cape Ltd., publishers of A. E. Housman's *Collected Poems*.

[4] From Wordsworth's "She Dwelt Among Untrodden Ways." The original lines read, "Fair as a star, when only one / Is shining in the sky."

[5] Sir Palamides and the Questing Beast are figures from *Morte d'Arthur* by Sir Thomas Malory (d. 1471).

[6] Sir Walter Scott (1771–1832) was the author of *Ivanhoe* and other historical novels.

or play you were trying to read. "Friends, Romans, countrymen, lend me your ears." Take that, for instance. There is an unusual but perfect example of Container for the Thing Contained. If you read the funeral oration unwarily—that is to say, for its meaning—you might easily miss the C.F.T.T.C. Antony is, of course, not asking for their ears in the sense that he wants them cut off and handed over; he is asking for the function of those ears, for their power to hear, for, in a word, the thing they contain.

At first I began to fear that all the characters in Shakespeare and Scott   6
were crazy. They confused cause with effect, the sign for the thing signified, the thing held for the thing holding it. But after a while I began to suspect that it was I myself who was crazy. I would find myself lying awake at night saying over and over, "The thinger for the thing contained." In a great but probably misguided attempt to keep my mind on its hinges, I would stare at the ceiling and try to think of an example of the Thing Contained for the Container. It struck me as odd that Miss Groby had never thought of that inversion. I finally hit on one, which I still remember. If a woman were to grab up a bottle of Grade A and say to her husband, "Get away from me or I'll hit you with the milk," that would be a Thing Contained for the Container. The next day in class I raised my hand and brought my curious discovery straight out before Miss Groby and my astonished schoolmates. I was eager and serious about it and it never occurred to me that the other children would laugh. They laughed loudly and long. When Miss Groby had quieted them she said to me rather coldly, "That was not really amusing, James." That's the mixed-up kind of thing that happened to me in my teens.

In later years I came across another excellent example of this figure of   7
speech in a joke long since familiar to people who know vaudeville or burlesque (or radio, for that matter). It goes something like this:

A: What's your head all bandaged up for?
B: I got hit with some tomatoes.
A: How could that bruise you up so bad?
B: These tomatoes were in a can.

I wonder what Miss Groby would have thought of that one.   8
I dream of my old English teacher occasionally. It seems that we are   9
always in Sherwood Forest and that from far away I can hear Robin Hood winding his silver horn.

"Drat that man for making such a racket on his cornet!" cries Miss   10
Groby. "He scared away a perfectly darling Container for the Thing Contained, a great big, beautiful one. It leaped right back into its context when that man blew that cornet. It was the most wonderful Container for the Thing Contained I ever saw here in the Forest of Arden."[7]

"This is Sherwood Forest," I say to her.   11
"That doesn't make any difference at all that I can see," she says to me.   12
Then I wake up, tossing and moaning.   13

[7] The Forest of Arden is the setting for Shakespeare's comedy *As You Like It*.

WHAT DID THE WRITER SAY, AND WHAT DID YOU THINK?

1. To what one characteristic of Miss Groby has the author limited his description?
2. What does the author most hold against Miss Groby?
3. Does the author actually object to learning about figures of speech?
4. The author still dreams about Miss Groby. What accounts for the strong effect that she had?
5. What point is demonstrated in the conversation about Sherwood Forest and the Forest of Arden?
6. Did you feel that Miss Groby was a real person or a fictional embodiment of a certain character type?

HOW DID THE WRITER SAY IT?

1. Are all the details related to the main idea?
2. Do the many literary references convey sufficient meaning to readers who may be unfamiliar with them?
3. Check the dictionary. Does Thurber adequately define *metonymy*?
4. What details give the reader a sense of Miss Groby's personality?
5. Why does the author not tell us anything about Miss Groby's physical appearance?
6. Vocabulary: *parsed, apostrophes, unwarily, winding.*

WHAT ABOUT <u>YOUR</u> WRITING?

"The shape of a sentence diagrammed on a blackboard brought a light to her eye." That's what most authors would have settled for. The writing would have been competent, and nobody would have complained.

Now look at what Thurber wrote in the third sentence of "Here Lies Miss Groby." "The shape of a sentence crucified on a blackboard . . . brought a light to her eye." Not *diagrammed. Crucified.* That's the difference between competent and good. Sometimes it's the difference between competent and great.

Crucified suggests, far better than *diagrammed*, what the poor tortured sentence really looked like. It conveys a note of humor as we see a word usually associated with a monumentally important event associated here with a routine classroom activity. It conveys the author's feelings of reverence for words and dismay at seeing them mutilated. It conveys the author's feelings toward Miss Groby: she murders something beautiful and precious, but forgive her, for she knows not what she does.

In your own writing, don't automatically accept the first word that comes to mind. Too often, the word is likely to be abstract, only a vague approximation of what you want to express. *Use specific words.* In particular, *use specific verbs*, for verbs in themselves are action words, and the more specific the verb, the more probable that a sense of action will be communicated.

Don't settle for "He looked at her" when you really mean *stared* or *gawked* or *leered* or *ogled* or *squinted* or *studied* or *glanced.* Don't settle for "He hit him" when you really mean *slapped* or *punched* or *smacked* or *belted* or *jabbed* or *socked* or *poked* or *clubbed*. Don't settle for "She laughed" when you really mean *giggled* or *guffawed* or *tittered* or *roared* or *chuckled*. Using specific words, especially specific verbs, isn't guaranteed to give your writing Thurber's special magic, but it is guaranteed to make your writing more lively and interesting. Certainly, you'll be thinking the way most good writers do.

Thurber didn't settle for *diagrammed*.

The Battle of the Ants

HENRY DAVID THOREAU

The fame of Henry David Thoreau (1817–1862) rests on two achievements. First, during the Mexican War he refused to pay a state poll tax as a symbolic protest against a venture he believed was designed to add new slave states to the Union. For this offense, he spent a night in jail. His essay "Civil Disobedience" (1849), an account of his extralegal experiences and the philosophy that led to them, has helped shape the events of our own century in its impact on Gandhi, Martin Luther King, Jr., and others. Second, he wrote *Walden* (1854), a classic of American literature, relating how he spent two years in a cabin he built himself at Walden Pond near his home town of Concord, Massachusetts, "and earned my living by the labor of my hands only."

The reading selection is an excerpt from the chapter "Brute Neighbors" in *Walden*. It immediately follows a paragraph devoted to the harmless activities of some of the animals at the pond.

I was witness to events of a less peaceful character. One day when I   1
went out to my wood-pile, or rather my pile of stumps, I observed two large ants, the one red, the other much larger, nearly half an inch long, and black, fiercely contending with one another. Having once got hold they never let go, but struggled and wrestled and rolled on the chips incessantly. Looking farther, I was surprised to find that the chips were covered with such combatants, that it was not a *duellum*, but a *bellum*,[1] a war between two races of ants, the red always pitted against the black, and frequently two red ones to one black. The legions of these Myrmidons[2] covered all the hills and vales in my wood-yard, and the ground was already strewn with the dead and dying, both red and black. It was the only battle which I have ever witnessed, the only battle-field I ever trod while the battle was raging; internecine war; the red republicans on the one hand, and the black imperialists on the other. On every side they were engaged in deadly combat, yet without any noise that I could hear, and human soldiers never fought so resolutely. I watched a couple that were fast locked in each other's em-

[1] Not a duel, but a war.

[2] Followers of Achilles in the Trojan War, as described in Homer's *Iliad*. The Greek word for "ant" is *myrmes*, and according to legend the Myrmidons were first created when the god Zeus turned the ants in an old oak tree into people.

braces, in a little sunny valley amid the chips, now at noonday prepared to fight till the sun went down, or life went out. The smaller red champion had fastened himself like a vice to his adversary's front, and through all the tumblings on that field never for an instant ceased to gnaw at one of his feelers near the root, having already caused the other to go by the board; while the stronger black one dashed him from side to side, and, as I saw on looking nearer, had already divested him of several of his members. They fought with more pertinacity than bulldogs. Neither manifested the least disposition to retreat. It was evident that their battle-cry was "Conquer or die." In the meanwhile there came along a single red ant on the hillside of this valley, evidently full of excitement, who either had despatched his foe, or had not yet taken part in the battle; probably the latter, for he had lost none of his limbs; whose mother had charged him to return with his shield or upon it.[3] Or perchance he was some Achilles, who had nourished his wrath apart, and had now come to avenge or rescue his Patroclus.[4] He saw this unequal combat from afar,—for the blacks were nearly twice the size of the red,—he drew near with rapid pace till he stood on his guard within half an inch of the combatants; then, watching his opportunity, he sprang upon the black warrior, and commenced his operations near the root of his right fore leg, leaving the foe to select among his own members; and so there were three united for life, as if a new kind of attraction had been invented which put all other locks and cements to shame. I should not have wondered by this time to find that they had their respective musical bands stationed on some eminent chip, and playing their national airs the while, to excite the slow and cheer the dying combatants. I was myself excited somewhat even as if they had been men. The more you think of it, the less the difference. And certainly there is not the fight recorded in Concord history, at least, if in the history of America, that will bear a moment's comparison with this, whether for the numbers engaged in it, or for the patriotism and heroism displayed. For numbers and for carnage it was an Austerlitz or Dresden.[5] Concord Fight! Two killed on the patriots' side, and Luther Blanchard wounded! Why here every ant was a Buttrick,— "Fire! for God's sake fire!"—and thousands shared the fate of Davis and Hosmer.[6] There was not one hireling there. I have no doubt that it was a principle they fought for, as much as our ancestors, and not to avoid a three-penny tax on their tea;[7] and the results of this battle will be as important and memorable to those whom it concerns as those of the battle of Bunker Hill, at least.

2   I took up the chip on which the three I have particularly described were

[3] Traditional command of ancient Spartan mothers to their soldier sons.
[4] Achilles, who had withdrawn from participation in the Trojan War because of an insult, returned to combat when his friend Patroclus was killed.
[5] Battles won by Napoleon.
[6] John Buttrick commanded the American forces at Concord Bridge during the first pitched battle of the Revolutionary War, April 19, 1775. Isaac Davis and David Hosmer were the "two killed on the patriots' side."
[7] The tax that led to the Boston Tea Party.

struggling, carried it into my house, and placed it under a tumbler on my window-sill, in order to see the issue. Holding a microscope to the first-mentioned red ant, I saw that, though he was assiduously gnawing at the near fore leg of his enemy, having severed his remaining feeler, his own breast was all torn away, exposing what vitals he had there to the jaws of the black warrior, whose breastplate was apparently too thick for him to pierce; and the dark carbuncles of the sufferer's eyes shone with ferocity such as war only could excite. They struggled half an hour longer under the tumbler, and when I looked again the black soldier had severed the heads of his foes from their bodies, and the still living heads were hanging on either side of him like ghastly trophies at his saddle-bow, still apparently as firmly fastened as ever, and he was endeavoring with feeble struggles, being without feelers and with only the remnant of a leg, and I know not how many other wounds, to divest himself of them; which at length, after half an hour more, he accomplished. I raised the glass, and he went off over the window-sill in that crippled state. Whether he finally survived that combat, and spent the remainder of his days in some Hôtel des Invalides,[8] I do not know; but I thought that his industry would not be worth much thereafter. I never learned which party was victorious, nor the cause of the war; but I felt for the rest of that day as if I had had my feelings excited and harrowed by witnessing the struggle, the ferocity and carnage, of a human battle before my door.

Kirby and Spence tell us that the battles of ants have long been celebrated and the date of them recorded, though they say that Huber[9] is the only modern author who appears to have witnessed them. "Æneas Sylvius,"[10] say they, "after giving a very circumstantial account of one contested with great obstinacy by a great and small species on the trunk of a pear tree," adds that " 'this action was fought in the pontificate of Eugenius the Fourth, in the presence of Nicholas Pistoriensis, an eminent lawyer, who related the whole history of the battle with the greatest fidelity.' A similar engagement between great and small ants is recorded by Olaus Magnus,[11] in which the small ones, being victorious, are said to have buried the bodies of their own soldiers, but left those of their giant enemies a prey to the birds. This event happened previous to the expulsion of the tyrant Christiern the Second from Sweden." The battle which I witnessed took place in the Presidency of Polk, five years before the passage of Webster's Fugitive-Slave Bill.[12]

3

[8] A French veterans' hospital.

[9] Kirby, Spence, and Huber were nineteenth-century authorities on insect behavior.

[10] Pen name for Pope Pius II (1405–1464).

[11] Swedish-born priest (1490–1558).

[12] James K. Polk (1795–1849) was Democratic president from 1845 to 1849. Daniel Webster (1782–1852), U.S. senator and cabinet officer, whose opposition to the annexation of Texas and the Mexican War had helped make him a spokesman for Northern liberals and radicals, lost most of his Northern support when he backed the 1850 Compromise. The Compromise included the Fugitive Slave Bill, which strengthened laws making it a federal crime for Northerners to assist slaves to escape and compelled Northerners to help the authorities in apprehending slaves.

WHAT DID THE WRITER SAY, AND WHAT DID YOU THINK?

1. Is "Ant wars are similar to human wars" an acceptable statement of the thesis of this selection?
2. Some readers may object to the suggested thesis in Question 1 because it doesn't satisfactorily express the author's own attitude. What is that attitude? Are ants glorified? Are humans denigrated?
3. What is Thoreau's attitude toward war, as presented in this selection?
4. How is the comment, "I have no doubt it was a principle they fought for" to be interpreted? Can Thoreau have any way of knowing what the ants fought for?
5. What attitude toward nature is implied?

HOW DID THE WRITER SAY IT?

1. Point out all places where similarities between ants and humans are directly or indirectly suggested.
2. In paragraph 1, Thoreau's wood-yard did not have "hills and vales" in any normal sense. What does the phrase mean?
3. Does Thoreau's final comment about Webster and the Fugitive Slave Bill have any relation to the rest of this selection, or is Thoreau just taking a passing swipe at a man and law he despised?
4. What purpose is served by the references to ancient history?
5. Where does Thoreau directly express his personal feelings? Does he do it often?
6. Vocabulary: *vales, strewn, internecine, resolutely, champion, divested, members, pertinacity, hireling, issue, assiduously, carbuncles, harrowed, carnage, pontificate.*

WHAT ABOUT YOUR WRITING?

An *allusion* is a reference, usually brief and often indirect, to a character, event, activity, work of art, and so on, distinct from what is being discussed. In describing the battle of the ants, Thoreau alludes to the Trojan War, ancient Sparta, the Revolutionary War, James Polk, Daniel Webster. Well-managed allusions, employed sparingly—don't use them for mere showing off—can add depth to a writer's style and thought. They can reveal unsuspected resemblances, relate unfamiliar material to material the reader knows, make abstract subjects seem more specific, and help establish confidence in a writer's range of knowledge.

You don't need to be an expert in any particular field to add an occasional allusion to your writing; anyone with ordinary education and some experience of life has a rich fund on which to draw.

Television: My father reminds me of Walter Cronkite. Whenever I see him, he's talking.

History: The teacher gave unannounced quizzes throughout the term. Every week was another Pearl Harbor.

Movies: The stranger had Robert Redford eyes, a Clark Gable moustache, and a Woody Allen physique.

Famous quotes: It's true that nothing is more powerful than an idea whose time has come, but encounter groups are an idea whose time has gone.

Sports: The administration has given up. Its game plan can be summed up in one word: Punt.

Literature: The lawyers indicated at first that we would be entitled to a beautiful tax deduction. Then they told us about Catch-22.

Advertisements: The senator's previously incorruptible image has been severely damaged. His only resemblance nowadays to Mr. Clean is that he's fat and bald.

Chapter 9

NARRATION

"Tell me a story," children say again and again. They're bored or restless, and they know the wonders a good story can perform.

In the New Testament, we can see that Jesus knew of those wonders, too. Time after time, He used parables—short tales directly embodying moral or spiritual lessons—to link general, abstract truths to the immediate experiences of His audience, and so help make the truths clear, memorable, and fresh. The Parable of the Good Samaritan is one among many that have helped to shape our culture.

Narration, then, is the telling of a story, and the shared experience of the human race suggests that a well-told story has few rivals in lasting fascination.

This chapter, of course, is concerned with telling a story as one of the patterns by which a thesis can be supported. That's by no means the only purpose of narration. Although Jesus' parables and Aesop's fables (a fable is a parable in which animals replace human beings and the moral is almost always specifically stated) tell stories to support a point, many modern writers of stories are far more interested in conveying a sense of life than in conveying ideas. "Yes," says the reader of these stories. "That's what a family argument"—or a first kiss or being a soldier or having the air-conditioner break down—"is really like." A thesis, as such, either does not exist or is so subordinate to other concerns that it may as well not exist. This approach to narration has produced plenty of great fiction, but it's not what your narration theme is about.

Chances are that your narration theme, in fact, isn't going to be fiction at all. Nothing is wrong with trying your hand at making up a parable, fable, or other piece of fiction, but most narration themes proceed in far different ways. You'll probably be telling the story of what once really happened to you or to people you know. (Like any good story teller, naturally, you'll emphasize some elements and de-emphasize or ignore others, depending on the point of the story.) All the reading selections in this chapter, aside from the advertisement, deal with authentic events in the lives of real people.

Imagine a scene in which some friends are uttering what strikes you as sentimental foolishness about the glories of camping. You say, "I think camping is horrible. Let me tell you what happened to me." And you tell your story. That's the essence of the narration paper: a point, and a story to back it up.

There are millions of stories and thousands of ways to tell them. **Tell your own story in your own way** is as good a piece of advice as any. As you do so, it's reasonable to remember the various bores you may have listened to or read and try to avoid their mistakes: the bores who worried about what day of the week it was when they were bitten by a snake, who constantly repeated the same phrases (*you know, and then I, you see*), who went on long after the interesting part of their story had been told. Profit from their examples, but tell your own story in your own way.

That advice has a fine ring to it, but it's certainly on the abstract side. "Your own way," for example, will undoubtedly change from one story to another. To get less abstract, in *most* narration papers *most* of the time, you should keep the following suggestions in mind:

Stress the story. The story must have a thesis, but the story itself is what gives life to the paper. **Write a story, not a sermon.** Aesop's fables are remembered because of the charm and wit of the stories, not the grandeur of the morals.

Remember that a good story has conflict. Some critics would be prepared to argue that without conflict it's impossible to have a story at all. In any event, conflict is usually the starting point for reader interest. Three patterns of conflict are the most common. First, *conflict between people:* you went camping with a friend, and while you were swatting mosquitoes and seeing poison ivy everywhere, your friend was driving you crazy with lofty poetic comments about leaving the artificialities of civilization behind. Second, *conflict between people and their environment* (a social custom or prejudice, a religious tradition, a force of nature such as a hurricane, and so on): you knew beforehand that you were allergic to everything green and you remembered a newspaper article about a boy who caught rabies from being bitten by a squirrel, but everyone in your circle was on a nature kick and the social pressure was too great to resist. Third, *conflict within a person:*

all through your shivers and shakes in the woods, one side of you was calling the other side a neurotic coward who didn't appreciate true beauty. Clearly, you do not need to confine your story to only one kind of conflict.

Use lots of convincing realistic details. The good story will give a sense of having actually happened, and convincing realistic details are your best device for transmitting that sense, as well as for preventing the sermon from taking over from the story. Don't just mention insect pests—mention mosquitoes. Don't just mention mosquitoes—mention the huge one with blood lust that got into your tent and summoned up dim memories of a malaria victim in an old *Tarzan* movie.

Play fair. Stories of pure innocence versus pure evil, of totally good guys versus totally bad guys, tend to be unconvincing because they are gross distortions of what everyone knows about the complexities of life. Support your thesis energetically, by all means, but don't neglect to show some awareness of the complexities. The paper on camping, for example, will be a more powerful and persuasive put-down if it grudgingly concedes somewhere that the woods *were* beautiful, after all, and that while hating every minute of your stay, you were able occasionally to notice the beauty.

WRITING SUGGESTIONS FOR NARRATION THEMES

Choose one of the famous quotations or proverbs below, and write a narration that supports it. You will probably draw on personal experience for your basic material, but you should also feel free to decorate or invent whenever convenient. Some of the suggestions might be appropriate for a fable or parable.

1. What a tangled web we weave / When first we practice to deceive.
   —Walter Scott

2. Haste makes waste.

3. Nobody ever went broke underestimating the intelligence of the American public.
   —H. L. Mencken

4. Faith is believing what you know ain't so.
   —Mark Twain

5. Charity begins at home.

6. The way to a man's heart is through his stomach.

7. Few things are harder to put up with than the annoyance of a good example.
   —Mark Twain

8. Patriotism is the last refuge of a scoundrel.
   —Samuel Johnson

9. Genius is one percent inspiration and ninety-nine percent perspiration.
           —Thomas A. Edison

10. Winning isn't the most important thing. It's the only thing.
           —Vince Lombardi

11. Those who do not know history are condemned to repeat it.
           —George Santayana

12. Wickedness is a myth invented by good people to account for the curious attractiveness of others.
           —Oscar Wilde

13. There is an exception to every rule.

14. The mass of men lead lives of quiet desperation.
           —Henry David Thoreau

15. A fool and his money are soon parted.

16. A man who hates dogs and children can't be all bad.
           —W. C. Fields

17. A thing of beauty is a joy forever.
           —John Keats

18. Everything I like is either illegal, immoral, or fattening.

19. In America, nothing fails like success.
           —F. Scott Fitzgerald

20. Luck is the residue of design.
           —Branch Rickey

21. Absence makes the heart grow fonder.

The <u>Modern</u> Little Red Hen

Pennwalt is a diversified manufacturer of chemicals and medical and dental supplies. ''The *Modern* Little Red Hen'' provides an interesting contrast to the George Bernard Shaw selection on pp. 120–122.

The Modern Little Red Hen.

Once upon a time, there was a little red hen who scratched about the barnyard until she uncovered some grains of wheat. She called her neighbors and said, "If we plant this wheat, we shall have bread to eat. Who will help me plant it?"

"Not I," said the cow.

"Not I," said the duck.

"Not I," said the pig.

"Not I," said the goose.

"Then I will," said the little red hen. And she did. The wheat grew tall and ripened into golden grain. "Who will help me reap my wheat?" asked the little red hen.

"Not I," said the duck.

"Out of my classification," said the pig.

"I'd lose my seniority," said the cow.

"I'd lose my unemployment compensation," said the goose.

"Then I will," said the little red hen, and she did.

At last it came time to bake the bread. "Who will help me bake the bread?" asked the little red hen.

"That would be overtime for me," said the cow.

"I'd lose my welfare benefits," said the duck.

"I'm a dropout and never learned how," said the pig.

"If I'm to be the only helper, that's discrimination," said the goose.

"Then I will," said the little red hen.

She baked five loaves and held them up for her neighbors to see.

They all wanted some and, in fact, demanded a share. But the little red hen said, "No, I can eat the five loaves myself."

"Excess profits!" cried the cow.

"Capitalist leech!" screamed the duck.

"I demand equal rights!" yelled the goose.

And the pig just grunted. And they painted "unfair" picket signs and marched round and round the little red hen, shouting obscenities.

When the government agent came, he said to the little red hen, "You must not be greedy."

"But I earned the bread," said the little red hen.

"Exactly," said the agent. "That is the wonderful free enterprise system. Anyone in the barnyard can earn as much as he wants. But under our modern government regulations, the productive workers must divide their product with the idle."

And they lived happily ever after, including the little red hen, who smiled and clucked, "I am grateful. I am grateful."

But her neighbors wondered why she never again baked any more bread.

At the conclusion of the required business of the 1975 Pennwalt Annual Meeting, Chairman and President William P. Drake, commenting on the state of the company in today's economy, read this, his own adaptation of a modern version of the well-known fable of The Little Red Hen.

For 125 years we've been making things people need – including profits.

C O R P O R A T I O N
Three Parkway, Philadelphia, Pa. 19102
Chemicals • Health Products • Specialized Equipment

WHAT DID THE WRITER SAY, AND WHAT DID YOU THINK?

1. What is the *original* story of the little red hen?
2. The moral is not stated directly. Express the moral in your own words.
3. A fable inevitably oversimplifies human existence. Where do the oversimplifications seem most pronounced? What points strike you as most valid or most effective?
4. Putting ethics aside, what is wrong with the treatment of the little red hen by the other barnyard animals and the government agent? What are the bad results?
5. What is illogical about the comments of the government agent?

HOW DID THE WRITER SAY IT?

1. In what ways does the style of this story echo the style of a traditional children's story?
2. Where is repetition used to strengthen the writer's points?
3. Does the picture add to the meaning of the story, or is it intended primarily as a decoration?
4. What do you think is the purpose of Pennwalt's statement at the end of the ad that the company has been making profits for 125 years?
5. Vocabulary: *leech.*

WHAT ABOUT **YOUR** WRITING?

People write about what they know and what means something to them. That's normal and sensible, but when the subject is controversial, readers may worry about ingrained bias. Is the writer a truthful, fair-minded observer, or have the writer's views been warped by special influences and interests?

In the note at the end of "The *Modern* Little Red Hen," for example, we see that the story was written by William P. Drake, chairman and president of a major corporation. Before its appearance as an ad, it was read to officers and stockholders at the corporation's annual meeting. That's why government regulations are a perfectly natural matter of concern. Perhaps that's also why the story argues so energetically against government regulations. True, the story is either well-written or not well-written; true, its argument is either strong or weak. But no readers expect an attack on business from this source, and if they suspect a writer of selfish motives, the writer is in trouble.

The problem is universal. A student paper advocating the elimination of grades pushes the issues of human dignity and human rights, but the reader suspects personal bias: the student is having difficulty in physics and doesn't want to flunk. A doctor presents a closely reasoned argument against national health insurance; solid as the argument may be, the reader hesitates to endorse it, speculating that the doctor may be worried more about personal income than about medicine.

The approach in "The *Modern* Little Red Hen" is probably the best. State right out whatever personal involvement there may be, and state it clearly. (Stating it early is also a good idea; some readers may wish that the note about Drake had appeared at the start of the story.) Get that out of the way, and then present your point of view for all it's worth. After admitting your personal involvement, turn it to your advantage, if you can. Isn't it likely, after all, that few people know more about government regulations than a corporation president? And isn't it a credit to management that despite all those nasty rules the Pennwalt Corporation is still making a profit? The student who wants to eliminate grades might as well acknowledge at the outset any elements of pure self-interest: the danger of a poor grade in physics or the tensions of parental nagging, for example. With these elements out of the way, the student can proceed to present the case against grades and perhaps even suggest that only a student can have an authentic realization of the psychological damage that the grading system can do.

Don't cover up. An honest acknowledgment of personal involvement, if such involvement exists, can only earn an honest reader's respect.

Angels on a Pin
ALEXANDER CALANDRA

An amusing narrative by a university professor, "Angels on a Pin" leads to some serious speculation about student-teacher relationships and the nature of education. *Scholasticism,* referred to in Calandra's last paragraph, was a medieval school of philosophy and theology broadly devoted to creating harmony between reason and faith. The significant achievements of Scholastic philosophers often tend to be forgotten today, and Scholasticism is now associated by many with hairsplitting logical disputation on trivial subjects such as the semilegendary debate about how many angels can stand on the head of a pin.

1   Some time ago, I received a call from a colleague who asked if I would be the referee on the grading of an examination question. He was about to give a student a zero for his answer to a physics question, while the student claimed he should receive a perfect score and would if the system were not set up against the student. The instructor and the student agreed to submit this to an impartial arbiter, and I was selected.

2   I went to my colleague's office and read the examination question: "Show how it is possible to determine the height of a tall building with the aid of a barometer."

3   The student had answered: "Take the barometer to the top of the building, attach a long rope to it, lower the barometer to the street, and then bring it up, measuring the length of the rope. The length of the rope is the height of the building."

4   I pointed out that the student really had a strong case for full credit, since he had answered the question completely and correctly. On the other hand, if full credit were given, it could well contribute to a high grade for the student in his physics course. A high grade is supposed to certify competence in physics, but the answer did not confirm this. I suggested that the student have another try at answering the question. I was not surprised that my colleague agreed, but I was surprised that the student did.

Published in *Saturday Review,* December 21, 1968, and reprinted by permission of *Saturday Review*.

I gave the student six minutes to answer the question, with the warning   5
that his answer should show some knowledge of physics. At the end of five
minutes, he had not written anything. I asked if he wished to give up, but
he said no. He had many answers to this problem; he was just thinking of
the best one. I excused myself for interrupting him, and asked him to please
go on. In the next minute, he dashed off his answer, which read:

"Take the barometer to the top of the building and lean over the edge of   6
the roof. Drop the barometer, timing its fall with a stopwatch. Then, using
the formula $S = \frac{1}{2}at^2$, calculate the height of the building."

At this point, I asked my colleague if *he* would give up. He conceded,   7
and I gave the student almost full credit.

In leaving my colleague's office, I recalled that the student had said he   8
had other answers to the problem, so I asked him what they were. "Oh,
yes," said the student. "There are many ways of getting the height of a tall
building with the aid of a barometer. For example, you could take the
barometer out on a sunny day and measure the height of the barometer, the
length of its shadow, and the length of the shadow of the building, and by
the use of simple proportion, determine the height of the building."

"Fine," I said. "And the others?"   9

"Yes," said the student. "There is a very basic measurement method   10
that you will like. In this method, you take the barometer and begin to walk
up the stairs. As you climb the stairs, you mark off the length of the barometer along the wall. You then count the number of marks, and this will
give you the height of the building in barometer units. A very direct method.

"Of course, if you want a more sophisticated method, you can tie the   11
barometer to the end of a string, swing it as a pendulum, and determine the
value of 'g' at the street level and at the top of the building. From the
difference between the two values of 'g,' the height of the building can, in
principle, be calculated."

Finally, he concluded, there are many other ways of solving the problem.   12
"Probably the best," he said, "is to take the barometer to the basement
and knock on the superintendent's door. When the superintendent answers,
you speak to him as follows: 'Mr. Superintendent, here I have a fine barometer. If you will tell me the height of this building, I will give you this
barometer.' "

At this point, I asked the student if he really did not know the conven-   13
tional answer to this question. He admitted that he did, but said that he was
fed up with high school and college instructors trying to teach him how to
think, to use the "scientific method," and to explore the deep inner logic
of the subject in a pedantic way, as is often done in the new mathematics,
rather than teaching him the structure of the subject. With this in mind, he
decided to revive scholasticism as an academic lark to challenge the Sput-
nik-panicked classrooms of America.[1]

---

[1] The first man-made satellite, Sputnik I, was launched by the Soviet Union on October 4,
1957. The Soviet success helped stimulate a renewed emphasis on science in American education.

WHAT DID THE WRITER SAY, AND WHAT DID YOU THINK?

1. What is the conventional answer to the examination question?
2. Express in your own words what irritated the student and what he was trying to prove.
3. Is the author's opinion the same as the student's?
4. Do you agree with the comments about the new math?
5. Was the student treated fairly?

HOW DID THE WRITER SAY IT?

1. Except for intelligence, the student is individualized very little. Why? Can you find *any* instances where he is given some individuality?
2. Which seemingly trivial details increase the drama and believability of the narration?
3. Most writing patterns present the thesis early. Why is the thesis here not presented until the last paragraph?
4. What elements of an example paper are in this selection?
5. Vocabulary: *arbiter, pedantic.*

WHAT ABOUT YOUR WRITING?

Watch out for *very*. Of all the trouble-making words in the language, *very* has possibly contributed most to sloppy writing. *Very* is an intensifier. You can smack it in front of nearly any adjective and strengthen—intensify—the meaning: *very pretty, very silly,* and so forth. The trouble is that the strengthening tends to be so generalized and imprecise that usually little of any substance is actually added to meaning. Sometimes meaning is even diminished or confused.

"There is a very basic measurement method that you will like," says the student in Calandra's article (paragraph 10). What did the student intend to say? If something is basic in itself, can it be any more basic? To be basic is to be the foundation, the core, the nucleus, the *base*. Did the student, in fact, intend to suggest ultrafine distinctions between measurement methods that are very basic and those that are only a little bit basic, quite basic, and very very basic? It's more likely that he was merely using *very* as most people do—carelessly. When he refers to "a very direct method" later in the paragraph, is he truly comparing it to other methods that are direct, but not *very* direct, just somewhat direct? And if the other methods are only somewhat direct, why bother thinking of them as direct at all? There are better words.

In fairness to the student, he is supposed to be talking, and conversation can never be as precise as writing. No speaker can take a break of a few minutes to ponder a choice of words, as a writer can. This is a book about writing, however, and in writing, the vague intensifier *very* is far more irritating than in speech. Nobody suggests that the word be outlawed, but in your own writing you'd do well to avoid it whenever you can. Start by looking for one-word synonyms: instead of *very pretty*, try *beautiful;* instead of *very silly,* try *ridiculous.*

Really is another overused intensifier, particularly when used as the equivalent of *very*. *Very* may not mean much, but at least it means itself. *Really* doesn't even have that much going for it in the following sentences:

They ate a really fine dinner.

The stairs are really steep.

The new furniture was really expensive.

So watch out for *really,* too. Its only legitimate use comes when the writer has in mind a distinction between what is factual or *real* in opposition to what is false or imaginary. Calandra uses the word correctly when he writes

I pointed out that the student really had a strong case for full credit.

I asked the student if he really did not know the conventional answer to this question.

from The Unkindest Cut

MARCIA MILLMAN

Marcia Millman teaches sociology at the University of California, Santa Cruz. She is co-editor of *Another Voice: Feminist Perspectives on Social Life and Social Science.* As you read, remember that the purpose of the narration is to prove a point, not merely to gain sympathy for an isolated individual.

. . . The stature of a physician in the eyes of his patient is a significant factor in the patient's response to illness and in his willingness to accept a recommendation for a potentially uncomfortable or dangerous procedure. Should the resident or intern disagree with an attending physician's assessment of a problem or suggestion of therapy, this should not be discussed within the patient's hearing. Likewise, the patient's confidence in the physician should not be undermined by innuendo or actual disparagement of the physician's judgment. It is essential to avoid caustic or intemperate comments in the chart, which is today almost a public document . . .

—From a memorandum issued to interns
and residents in ——— Hospital.

One of the basic rules in medical practice is that patients should not be   1
informed of disagreement among doctors concerning their diagnosis and treatment. Even when medical consultants or house officers do not agree with the decisions of the attending doctor, they are expressly forbidden to communicate their doubts to the patient. Asked why differences of opinion are kept hidden from patients, most doctors will argue that patients would be upset were they to know about disagreement about their treatment. Doctors generally agree that all the physicians working on a case should

"maintain a party line" to feed to the patient in consideration of his feelings. However sincere they may be in wanting to spare the patient from worry, it is also clear that doctors serve their own interests when they withhold information from the patient. Indeed, protecting themselves from the discomfort and inconvenience of sharing all the information with the patient frequently takes precedence over protecting the patient's emotional or even physical well-being.

2   There are two kinds of information that doctors routinely withhold from patients: one kind has to do with facts about the patient's illness; the other kind has to do with evaluations of the competence or performance of the other doctors involved in the case, or the wisdom of the treatment that other doctors have recommended. Although doctors rationalize withholding such information (of both sorts) on the grounds of "protecting" the patient from upsetting information, in fact they are more precisely protecting themselves and their colleagues. For the less that patients know about the problems of their treatment and the faults or errors of their doctors, the less able they are to disagree or make trouble for their physicians. . . .

3   The following incident, described in some detail, illustrates such a situation.

4   A thirty-five-year-old female patient, who was a biochemist by occupation, was told over several years by many doctors that her recurrent abdominal pains were merely "functional" (psychological) and that diagnostic x-rays were unnecessary. Even when she appeared on several consecutive nights in the Emergency Room complaining of severe pain she was given a mild tranquilizer and sent home. But when she arrived the following week in her doctor's office, obviously jaundiced, her complaints could no longer be passed off as the fabrications of what the doctor imagined to be a hysterical woman. Nervously, her doctor insisted that she be admitted to the hospital on the spot, insisting that "the buck stops here" (despite the fact that *he* had been the one who had discounted the symptoms all along). Diagnostic x-rays were done to see whether she had gastrointestinal or gall bladder disease. During the gall bladder x-ray, her liver failed to release the visualizing dye as it normally should have, and so it was evident that there was something wrong with her hepato-biliary system. A simple explanation might have been that her liver was temporarily misfunctioning only because of gall bladder disease and an obstructive stone in her bile duct. But because of results which appeared in laboratory studies of her blood, the doctor suspected that she had an intrinsic liver disease, independent of any disorder of the gall bladder. He informed her that a liver biopsy should be done immediately. When she questioned him about the procedure he admitted that it carried a very small risk of serious hemorrhaging, but boasted that she need not worry—he had done hundreds and never lost a single patient.

5   Since her illness had gone unattended for so long, the patient saw no reason to rush into a liver biopsy. She proposed, instead, that a specialist in liver diseases be consulted before proceeding with the test, and she also asked whether they might delay the biopsy for a few days to see if her liver

function tests would return to normal, for such a change would indicate that her liver malfunction was merely temporary and secondary to gall bladder disease. If they could wait a few days, a liver biopsy might therefore be avoided.

Her doctor responded to these suggestions by informing her that *he* was the doctor and *she* the patient, and that he was practically certain that she suffered from chronic active hepatitis, a very serious disease, and that she had better not delay the procedure since only a liver biopsy could confirm the diagnosis. Furthermore, if he were correct, she would have to be put on a regimen of steroids.   6

Yielding to the pressure and having checked around town to make sure that the doctor was well regarded, the patient agreed to the procedure. The biopsy was performed with the customary joking of her physician. She was awake during the procedure; a paper towel was placed over her eyes so she couldn't watch, and the physician inserted a needle into her liver, in order to withdraw a sample of the organ. Since she experienced no pain in the procedure the doctor tried to humor her out of her annoyance with him by complimenting her. As he placed the specimen in a jar he joked that they had done so well he could take her around the country to demonstrate tolerance for liver biopsies. She replied that she had better things to do with her time.   7

After being returned to her room, the patient was visited by two other patients on the floor under the care of the same doctor who were scheduled to have *their* livers biopsied the next day. They had come by to find out what the test was really like, and one remarked: "There's something strange about this. All you hear on this floor is liver biopsy, liver biopsy. All of his patients can't have the same disease." The patient shared the others' suspicion when she learned of the doctor's widespread use of the test, and she wondered whether he was especially interested in discovering diseases of the liver.   8

The night after the procedure, the patient was unable to reach her doctor to hear the results of the test but she managed to persuade an intern assigned to her case (he had just moved to the city and was lonely and she promised to find him some friends) to bring her his medical books so that she could read about the varieties of hepatitis. Looking up chronic active hepatitis, she was stunned to read that the disease had no cure and that it was usually fatal within a few years. When the intern came to collect his books she pointed to the section she had read and asked when she would know the results of the liver biopsy. The intern looked distressed and explained that he had not realized the seriousness of the disease or he would not have let her read about the illness unprepared for the news. But he urged her not to jump to conclusions and asked her not to say anything about it, or he might get into trouble for having shown her his books. As for the results of the biopsy, he told her that he was not allowed as an intern to relay that information to her, and she would have to wait until her own doctor discussed it with her.   9

10   The next day was the start of the July fourth holiday weekend and the patient was told that her doctor could not be reached and would be unavailable for a couple of days. Over the holiday the patient tried to find out the results of the test, indicating that she knew the seriousness of the suspected disease. But the house officers and the associate covering for her physician all apologized and explained that she would have to wait until her own doctor returned. She expressed fright and concern about their evasiveness, but was unable to obtain any further information. During the two-day wait she became increasingly depressed about their reluctance to tell her the results of the test. When her doctor finally returned he was vague about the test results, and claimed that he had not yet had a chance to examine the specimen himself, and had only heard a report over the telephone.

11   Upon looking at her newest blood tests, however, he expressed puzzlement and discomfort, and quietly remarked, "this is certainly a surprise." With seeming embarrassment rather than obvious pleasure he informed the patient that her liver function as measured by her most recent blood tests had now returned to normal, and this indicated that after all (as she had suggested in requesting the delay of the biopsy) her jaundice and liver disorder had only been a temporary problem caused by a stone in the bile duct. She could now be scheduled for surgery the following day. Asked if she had any preference for surgeons, she replied, with obvious mixed relief and annoyance, "A competent one—it's about time this case was handled properly." He joked back: "Oh, I thought I'd get you a surgeon who needs the money."

12   Even after the doctor seemed to change his mind about the illness the patient was still concerned about the mysterious results of the liver biopsy. When her doctor had suspected liver disease only a few days before, he had told her that with such a condition she would be unable to tolerate surgery. Because of all that had happened she had little confidence that the matter had been adequately resolved, and she was reluctant to agree to an operation until she was certain of what the biopsy showed. Since she was to have surgery the next day, she had extracted a promise from her doctor that he would call her and tell her the test results that evening, as soon as he had a chance to examine the specimen. But he assured her that there was no need for her to worry—he was certain that her liver was fine. When the doctor failed to call that evening she tried to reach his answering service every half hour, but was repeatedly told that he was unavailable. Seeing no alternative, and aware of the carelessness that had characterized her treatment thus far, the patient refused to sign the consent form or take the preoperative sleeping medication until she heard the results of the test. At midnight, when she refused to go to bed and threatened to make a scene in the hospital corridor unless her doctor became available, a furious resident finally placed the call and was immediately connected with the physician. Still, her doctor was reluctant to elaborate and all he would say was, "Don't worry, the biopsy didn't show anything wrong with your liver."

After the operation the patient continued to be puzzled about why all the 13
doctors had been so evasive about reporting the test results, when doing so
would seemingly have assured her that she had a curable rather than an
incurable disease and would have saved her from two days of extreme
distress. As the time came to be released from the hospital she asked her
physician if she could read her chart, but even after obtaining his permission
(he boasted that he had nothing to hide—he had never been sued), when
she went to the nurses' station and reached out to take the record, a nurse
stopped her hand and pushed it away. Obviously annoyed with the patient's
assertiveness, the nurse smugly informed her that even though her medical
physician had agreed, when her surgeon had been informed of her request
to see the chart he had left word that she was not to be allowed to look at
it.

She returned to her room, furious and even more determined to see the 14
chart. She knew that it was ultimately within her legal rights to obtain a
copy, and it was just a question of how much trouble and expense they
would put her through. She was curious to see whether the surgeon, who
was making his morning rounds, would mention that he had blocked her
access to the chart, and she decided not to raise the matter at first but to
await his response. He came by moments later, and after silently checking
on her wound, he turned to go, having made no reference to his veto of her
request. She called to him as he was stepping out the door:

"Dr. Williams—I understand you object to my seeing my chart. Would 15
you mind telling me why?"

He looked unperturbed and replied, "It's not that I object. But it's not 16
our policy to show our patients their charts. And our patients don't want
to see their charts."

She raised her eyebrows in mock surprise and answered sweetly, "But 17
I want to see my chart. That's why I asked to see it."

A smile of contempt crossed his face. "Why do you want to see your 18
chart? It's really not very interesting reading."

She replied: "Because I'd like to know all the facts pertinent to my ill- 19
ness."

He began to show signs of impatience and the placid smile looked more 20
like a sneer. "Well, I'm sorry, but it's not a good idea and it wouldn't mean
anything to you anyway. You wouldn't understand anything you were reading and then you'd have a million questions."

He had started to leave, but she felt that she now had an advantage. 21
"Don't worry, Dr. Williams. If I have any questions I promise I won't ask
you for any answers."

Assuming his usual look of icy imperturbability, he turned to go. "Go 22
ahead, read your chart. I don't care."

The patient waited triumphantly in her room for fifteen minutes, thinking 23
that even terrible experiences could have their better moments, and then
she marched out to the nurses' station. She thought it would be more effective to say nothing as she helped herself to her record, but she happily

took in the sight of the glaring nurses who silently watched her. A resident standing nearby remarked: "You know, even when *doctors* are patients they don't see their own charts."

24 She answered cheerfully, feeling that she could afford to be generous now. "That's their problem, not mine."

25 After returning to her room she shut the door behind her and climbed into bed with the chart. (She always kept the door closed for privacy and had insisted that the doctors and nurses knock before entering her room; they had complied but it irritated them.) Hurriedly, she searched through the record for the report on the liver biopsy. She discovered that it was only a single line written on an otherwise blank sheet of paper. It merely read: "No Analysis, Specimen Insufficient for Diagnosis."

26 The evasiveness of the doctors was finally explained to the patient. No one had wanted her to learn that the procedure had been a total waste. The physician, through miscalculation or bad luck, had failed to insert the needle into the proper place and had therefore missed getting a proper sample. Rather than let her know that her doctor had failed to complete the procedure successfully, the house officers and covering physician had instead allowed her to believe for two days that she was dying. And when directly asked about the test results, her own doctor had evasively lied by saying, "The test didn't show anything wrong with your liver," since the test had shown nothing at all.

WHAT DID THE WRITER SAY, AND WHAT DID YOU THINK?

1. The reading selection is an excerpt from a chapter that includes several additional stories. Is the one story here enough to support the thesis or would more have been helpful?
2. If you were a doctor, could you find any way to justify the treatment of the patient? Does the writer give adequate attention to the doctors' side? Is it your impression that the story is based on interviews with the doctors and the patient, or only with the patient?
3. Does the author present this story as typical or unusual?
4. What do you feel is the worst single instance in the narration of malpractice or irresponsibility?
5. Do the doctors ever actually lie to the patient?

HOW DID THE WRITER SAY IT?

1. Why is the patient never given a name, even a fictional one?
2. Does the author narrate the events objectively, or does she directly present her own judgments and opinions?
3. Could the amount of medical terminology have been reduced? Should it have been? Can the nonspecialist follow enough to understand what is going on?

4. Is the character of the patient sufficiently developed to make her interesting as a person, or is it only her situation that is interesting?
5. In the author's own words, the story is "described in some detail." Why are the many details so important?
6. Vocabulary: _innuendo, disparagement, caustic, intemperate, jaundiced, fabrications, hepato-biliary, intrinsic, biopsy, regimen, steroids, pertinent, placid, imperturbability, complied._

WHAT ABOUT <u>YOUR</u> WRITING?

"Don't worry, Dr. Williams. If I have any questions I promise I won't ask _you_ for any answers." At last the frustration and rage are out in the open. We no longer just read comments about the people. We hear the people talking for themselves. We are there.

Good dialogue can help any narration, whether fiction or nonfiction. The author seems to butt out, ceasing to exist in the traditional role of a filter between the reader and the events—interpreting, describing, judging. These are the words the people spoke, and readers are on their own. The author may mention a tone of voice or a gesture—Millman probably tells us more than we need to know about them—or may drop in an occasional _he said_ or _she said_ so that readers can keep track of the speaker, but essentially the author butts out. Good dialogue is immediate, dramatic, persuasive. Apart from anything else, it gives the reader a pleasurable sense of recognition: "This is the way people talk," the reader says. "This is authentic."

Dialogue can also be used profitably in many kinds of writing other than narration. It might, for instance, lead to some original introductions for any of the patterns this book has already discussed.

> "Did you have a good time on your date, dear?"
> "Aw, Mom."
> "Was she a nice girl?"
> "Aw, Mom."
> "What does her father do?"
> "Aw, Mom."
> The generation gap—in my house, at least—is more than a myth.

> "So what should we do about protecting the environment?" my teacher asks.
> If I had the nerve, I'd like to answer, "First of all, let's stop talking about it every single minute. Enough is enough."

Many creative writing teachers are inclined to feel that writing good dialogue is a gift. You have it or you don't. You were born with an ear for dialogue or you weren't. Still, some elementary pointers might be helpful.

Keep your comments simple. Confine yourself to _he said, she said, he asked, she answered,_ and similar phrases. Avoid fancy variations like _he asserted, he expostulated, she queried, she gasped, he hissed._

Don't worry about Standard English. If the person who's talking would swear, say _ain't,_ confuse _who_ and _whom,_ make the person talk that way. Don't, whatever you do, use swear words to show off how tough and courageous and unflinchingly honest you are. Just be accurate.

Change paragraphs with each speaker. You'll find violations of this advice among some of the best writers, but it seems ordinary common sense. Changing paragraphs makes the dialogue easier to follow by giving the reader a direct visual indication that there's been a change of speaker.

The Crazy Lady Double

CYNTHIA OZICK

Cynthia Ozick is author of *The Pagan Rabbi and Other Stories* (1971) and *Bloodshed and Three Novellas* (1976). In addition to her fiction, she has published poetry, numerous articles, and translations.

As you read, ask yourself why the author stresses that the events she writes about happened twenty years earlier. Are the events presented as an interesting account of how dismal life used to be for women in the bad old days, or are they meant to shed light on current conditions?

1   A long, long time ago, in another century—1951, in fact—when you, dear younger readers, were most likely still in your nuclear-family playpen (where, if female, you cuddled a rag-baby to your potential titties, or, if male, let down virile drool over your plastic bulldozer), Lionel Trilling[1] told me never, never to use a parenthesis in the very first sentence. This was in a graduate English seminar at Columbia University. To get into this seminar, you had to submit to a grilling wherein you renounced all former allegiance to the then-current literary religion, New Criticism,[2] which considered that only the text existed, not the world. I passed the interview by lying, cunningly, and against my real convictions. I said that probably the world *did* exist—and walked triumphantly into the seminar room.

2   There were four big tables arranged in a square, with everyone's feet sticking out into the open middle of the square. You could tell who was nervous, and how much, by watching the pairs of feet twist around each other. Professor Trilling presided awesomely from the high bar of the square. His head was a majestic granite-gray, like a centurion in command; he *looked* famous. His clean shoes twitched only slightly, and only when he was angry.

[1] Distinguished scholar, critic, and teacher (1905–1975), author of *Matthew Arnold* (1939), *The Liberal Imagination* (1950), *A Gathering of Fugitives* (1956), *The Experience of Literature* (1967), *Sincerity and Authenticity* (1972), and many other books.

[2] An approach to literature that stresses close reading and analysis of the text, generally disregarding such presumably extraneous issues as the author's biography and the historical period in which the work was written.

It turned out he was angry at me a lot of the time. He was angry because   3
he thought me a disrupter, a rioter, a provocateur, and a fool; also crazy.
And this was twenty years ago, before these things were *de rigueur* in the
universities. Everything was very quiet in those days. There were only the
Cold War and Korea and Joe McCarthy[3] and the Old Old Nixon, and the
only revolutionaries around were in Henry James's *The Princess Casamassima*.[4]

Habit governed the seminar. Where you sat the first day was where you   4
settled forever. So, to avoid the stigmatization of the ghetto, I was careful
not to sit next to the other woman in the class: the Crazy Lady.

At first the Crazy Lady appeared to be remarkably intelligent. She was   5
older than the rest of us, somewhere in her thirties (which was why we
thought of her as a Lady), with wild tan hair, a noticeably breathing bosom,
eccentric gold-rimmed old-pensioner glasses, and a tooth-crowded wild
mouth that seemed to get wilder the more she talked. She talked like a
motorcycle, fast and urgent. Everything she said was almost brilliant, only
not actually on point, and frenetic with hostility. She was tough and negative. She volunteered a lot and she stood up and wobbled with rage, pulling
at her hair and mouth. She fought Trilling point for point, piecemeal and
wholesale, mixing up queerly-angled literary insights with all sorts of private
and public fury. After the first meetings, he was fed up with her. The rest
of us accepted that she probably wasn't all there, but in a room where
everyone was on the make for recognition—you talked to save your life,
and the only way to save your life was to be the smartest one that day—she
was a nuisance, a distraction, a pain in the ass. The class became a bunch
of Good Germans, determinedly indifferent onlookers to a vindictive match
between Trilling and the Crazy Lady, until finally he subdued her by shut-
ting his eyes, and, when that didn't always work, by cutting her dead and
lecturing right across the sound of her strong, strange voice.

All this was before R. D. Laing[5] had invented the superiority of madness,   6
of course, and, cowards all, no one liked the thought of being tarred with
the Crazy Lady's brush. Ignored by the boss, in the middle of everything
she would suddenly begin to mutter to herself. She mentioned certain institutions she'd been in, and said we all belonged there. The people who
sat on either side of her shifted chairs. If the Great Man ostracized the
Crazy Lady, we had to do it too. But one day the Crazy Lady came in late
and sat down in the seat next to mine, and stayed there the rest of the
semester.

Then an odd thing happened. There, right next to me, was the noisy   7
Crazy Lady, tall, with that sticking-out sighing chest of hers, orangey curls
dripping over her nose, snuffling furiously for attention. And there was I,

---

[3] Joseph McCarthy (1908–1957) was U.S. Senator from Wisconsin from 1947 until his death.
He alleged that the government was harboring Communists and Communist agents in important
positions and is associated by many with witch-hunting and irresponsibile accusations.

[4] Novel published in 1886.

[5] Contemporary psychiatrist, critical of arbitrary standards for determining insanity.

a brownish runt, a dozen years younger and flatter and shyer than the Crazy Lady, in no way her twin, physically or psychologically. In those days I was bone-skinny, small, sallow, and myopic, and so scared I could trigger diarrhea at one glance from the Great Man. All this stress on looks is important. The Crazy Lady and I had our separate bodies, our separate brains. We handed in our separate papers.

8   But the Great Man never turned toward me, never at all, and if ambition broke feverishly through shyness so that I dared to push an idea audibly out of me, he shut his eyes when I put up my hand. This went on for a long time. I never got to speak, and I began to have the depressing feeling that Lionel Trilling hated me. It was no small thing to be hated by the man who had written "Wordsworth and the Rabbis" and *Matthew Arnold,* after all. What in hell was going on? I was in trouble, because, like everyone else in that demented contest, I wanted to excel. Then, one slow afternoon, wearily, the Great Man let his eyes fall on me. He called me by name, but it was not my name—it was the Crazy Lady's. The next week the papers came back—and there, right at the top of mine, in the Great Man's own handwriting, was a rebuke to the Crazy Lady for starting an essay with a parenthesis in the first sentence, a habit he took to be a continuing sign of that unruly and unfocused mentality so often exhibited in class. And then a Singular Revelation crept coldly through me. Because the Crazy Lady and I sat side by side, because we were a connected blur of Woman, Lionel Trilling, master of ultimate distinctions, couldn't tell us apart. The Crazy Lady and I! He couldn't tell us apart! It didn't matter that the Crazy Lady was crazy! *He couldn't tell us apart!*

Moral 1: All cats are gray at night,[6] all darkies look alike.

Moral 2: Even among intellectual humanists, every woman has a *Doppelgänger*[7]—every other woman.

WHAT DID THE WRITER SAY, AND WHAT DID YOU THINK?

1. Explain the reference to the "Old, Old Nixon."
2. Explain the meaning of "Good Germans."
3. Do the morals adequately state the thesis? Explain.
4. What would the narration have been like if told from Trilling's point of view?
5. Does the author give sufficient evidence to establish sexist attitudes in her teacher? Does what she describes differ from a teacher's normal confusion of the names of two students who sit next to each other?
6. Does anything in this reading selection suggest that Trilling would have treated a crazy man differently from the way he treated the crazy lady?
7. Is anything wrong with using a parenthesis in the first sentence?
8. How does the author's attitude toward the crazy lady differ from Trilling's?

[6] See Benjamin Franklin's "Advice on Choosing a Mistress" (pp. 242–244).
[7] A ghostly double.

HOW DID THE WRITER SAY IT?

1. Where does the author express her scorn for the view that a parenthesis should not be used in a first sentence?
2. In paragraph 1, the author calls the year 1951 "another century." Why?
3. Explain the unorthodox capitalization of *Crazy Lady, Great Man,* and so on.
4. Where does the author use repetition for emphasis?
5. Is the author's use of normally frowned-upon words like *ass* intended primarily to shock or offend, or does it have more legitimate purposes?
6. Vocabulary: *virile, awesomely, centurion, provocateur, de rigueur, stigmatization, frenetic, vindictive, ostracized, myopic, audibly.*

WHAT ABOUT <u>YOUR</u> WRITING?

To avoid monotony, the good writer varies sentence length. Long and short sentences are neither good nor bad in themselves: variety is the key.

In the Ozick selection, notice how paragraph 4 begins with two short sentences and concludes with a much longer one. Notice how paragraph 5 begins with a short sentence, then goes to a longer one, then goes back to a short one. In the last paragraph, notice the first sentence of forty words followed by a sentence of seven words. Toward the end of the last paragraph, notice the long sentence beginning with "Because the Crazy Lady," followed by four short sentences.

Mathematical formulas are inapplicable, of course. There's no magic number of words at which a sentence ceases to be short and suddenly becomes long. There's no special point, for that matter, at which readers suddenly cease to be interested and become bored. Monotonous sentence length, however, contributes to boredom, and variety can often contribute to interest. So try to vary sentence length.

Shooting an Elephant

GEORGE ORWELL

George Orwell (1903–1950) is known to most American readers for his novels *Animal Farm* (1945) and *Nineteen Eighty-four* (1948). Himself an ardent socialist, Orwell's rugged and sometimes fierce independence is seen in his frequently expressed scorn for Soviet totalitarianism and its apologists. His other books are *Down and Out in Paris and London* (1933), *Burmese Days* (1934), *A Clergyman's Daughter* (1935), *Keep the Aspidistra Flying* (1936), *The Road to Wigan Pier* (1937), *Homage to Catalonia* (1938), and *Coming Up for Air* (1939). Some of his essays like "Shooting an Elephant," "Such, Such Were the Joys," "Marrakech," "England, Your England," "The Art of Donald McGill," "Politics and the English Language," and "Dickens" have helped set standards of excellence in contemporary prose.

From *Shooting an Elephant and Other Essays* by George Orwell; copyright 1945, 1946, 1949, 1950 by Sonia Brownell Orwell. Reprinted by permission of Harcourt Brace Jovanovich, Inc.; Sonia Brownell Orwell; and Martin Secker & Warburg.

The events described in "Shooting an Elephant" took place between 1923 and 1928. The essay itself was written sometime between 1931 and 1936. Note how much more attention Orwell pays to telling the story than to stating the moral.

1   In Moulmein, in Lower Burma, I was hated by large numbers of people— the only time in my life that I have been important enough for this to happen to me. I was sub-divisional police officer of the town, and in an aimless, petty kind of way anti-European feeling was very bitter. No one had the guts to raise a riot, but if a European woman went through the bazaars alone somebody would probably spit betel juice[1] over her dress. As a police officer I was an obvious target and was baited whenever it seemed safe to do so. When a nimble Burman tripped me up on the football field and the referee (another Burman) looked the other way, the crowd yelled with hideous laughter. This happened more than once. In the end the sneering yellow faces of young men that met me everywhere, the insults hooted after me when I was at a safe distance, got badly on my nerves. The young Buddhist priests were the worst of all. There were several thousands of them in the town and none of them seemed to have anything to do except stand on street corners and jeer at Europeans.

2   All this was perplexing and upsetting. For at that time I had already made up my mind that imperialism was an evil thing and the sooner I chucked up my job and got out of it the better. Theoretically—and secretly, of course— I was all for the Burmese and all against their oppressors, the British. As for the job I was doing, I hated it more bitterly than I can perhaps make clear. In a job like that you see the dirty work of Empire at close quarters. The wretched prisoners huddling in the stinking cages of the lock-ups, the grey, cowed faces of the long-term convicts, the scarred buttocks of the men who had been flogged with bamboos—all these oppressed me with an intolerable sense of guilt. But I could get nothing into perspective. I was young and ill-educated and I had had to think out my problems in the utter silence that is imposed on every Englishman in the East. I did not even know that the British Empire is dying, still less did I know that it is a great deal better than the younger empires that are going to supplant it. All I knew was that I was stuck between my hatred of the empire I served and my rage against the evil-spirited little beasts who tried to make my job impossible. With one part of my mind I thought of the British Raj[2] as an unbreakable tyranny, as something clamped down, in *saecula saeculorum*,[3] upon the will of prostrate peoples; with another part I thought that the greatest joy in the world would be to drive a bayonet into a Buddhist priest's guts. Feelings like these are the normal by-products of imperialism; ask any Anglo-Indian official, if you can catch him off duty.

3   One day something happened which in a round-about way was enlight-

---

[1] The betel nut, the seed of a betel palm, is used in parts of the Far East much as Americans use chewing gum.

[2] Rule, reign.

[3] Time out of mind, through the ages.

ening. It was a tiny incident in itself, but it gave me a better glimpse than I had had before of the real nature of imperialism—the real motives for which despotic governments act. Early one morning the sub-inspector at a police station the other end of the town rang me up on the phone and said that an elephant was ravaging the bazaar. Would I please come and do something about it? I did not know what I could do, but I wanted to see what was happening and I got onto a pony and started out. I took my rifle, an old .44 Winchester and much too small to kill an elephant, but I thought the noise might be useful *in terrorem*.[4] Various Burmans stopped me on the way and told me about the elephant's doings. It was not, of course, a wild elephant, but a tame one which had gone "must."[5] It had been chained up, as tame elephants always are when their attack of "must" is due, but on the previous night it had broken its chain and escaped. Its mahout,[6] the only person who could manage it when it was in that state, had set out in pursuit, but had taken the wrong direction and was now twelve hours' journey away, and in the morning the elephant had suddenly reappeared in the town. The Burmese population had no weapons and were quite helpless against it. It had already destroyed somebody's bamboo hut; killed a cow and raided some fruit-stalls and devoured the stock; also it had met the municipal rubbish van, and, when the driver jumped out and took to his heels, had turned the van over and inflicted violences upon it.

The Burmese sub-inspector and some Indian constables were waiting for me in the quarter where the elephant had been seen. It was a very poor quarter, a labyrinth of squalid bamboo huts, thatched with palm-leaf, winding all over a steep hillside. I remember that it was a cloudy, stuffy morning at the beginning of the rains. We began questioning the people as to where the elephant had gone, and, as usual, failed to get any definite information. That is invariably the case in the East; a story always sounds clear enough at a distance, but the nearer you get to the scene of events the vaguer it becomes. Some of the people said that the elephant had gone in one direction, some said that he had gone in another, some professed not even to have heard of an elephant. I had almost made up my mind that the whole story was a pack of lies, when we heard yells a little distance away. There was a loud, scandalized cry of "Go away, child! Go away this instant!" and an old woman with a switch in her hand came round the corner of a hut, violently shooing away a crowd of naked children. Some more women followed, clicking their tongues and exclaiming; evidently there was something that the children ought not to have seen. I rounded the hut and saw a man's dead body sprawling in the mud. He was an Indian, a black Dravidian coolie, almost naked, and he could not have been dead many minutes. The people said that the elephant had come suddenly upon him round the corner of the hut, caught him with its trunk, put its foot on his back and ground him into the earth. This was the rainy season and the ground was

4

---

[4] As a warning.
[5] Period of frenzy in elephants, associated with sexual excitement.
[6] Elephant keeper and driver.

soft, and his face had scored a trench a foot deep and a couple of yards long. He was lying on his belly with arms crucified and head sharply twisted to one side. His face was coated with mud, the eyes wide open, the teeth bared and grinning with an expression of unendurable agony. (Never tell me, by the way, that the dead look peaceful. Most of the corpses I have seen looked devilish.) The friction of the great beast's foot had stripped the skin from his back as neatly as one skins a rabbit. As soon as I saw the dead man I sent an orderly to a friend's house nearby to borrow an elephant rifle. I had already sent back the pony, not wanting it to go mad with fright and throw me if it smelled the elephant.

5   The orderly came back in a few minutes with a rifle and five cartridges, and meanwhile some Burmans had arrived and told us that the elephant was in the paddy fields below, only a few hundred yards away. As I started forward practically the whole population of the quarter flocked out of the houses and followed me. They had seen the rifle and were all shouting excitedly that I was going to shoot the elephant. They had not shown much interest in the elephant when he was merely ravaging their homes, but it was different now that he was going to be shot. It was a bit of fun to them, as it would be to an English crowd; besides, they wanted the meat. It made me vaguely uneasy. I had no intention of shooting the elephant—I had merely sent for the rifle to defend myself if necessary—and it is always unnerving to have a crowd following you. I marched down the hill, looking and feeling a fool, with the rifle over my shoulder and an ever-growing army of people jostling at my heels. At the bottom, when you got away from the huts, there was a metalled road and beyond that a miry waste of paddy fields a thousand yards across, not yet ploughed but soggy from the first rains and dotted with coarse grass. The elephant was standing eight yards from the road, his left side towards us. He took not the slightest notice of the crowd's approach. He was tearing up bunches of grass, beating them against his knees to clean them and stuffing them into his mouth.

6   I had halted on the road. As soon as I saw the elephant I knew with perfect certainty that I ought not to shoot him. It is a serious matter to shoot a working elephant—it is comparable to destroying a huge and costly piece of machinery—and obviously one ought not to do it if it can possibly be avoided. And at that distance, peacefully eating, the elephant looked no more dangerous than a cow. I thought then and I think now that his attack of "must" was already passing off; in which case he would merely wander harmlessly about until the mahout came back and caught him. Moreover, I did not in the least want to shoot him. I decided that I would watch him for a little while to make sure that he did not turn savage again, and then go home.

7   But at that moment I glanced round at the crowd that had followed me. It was an immense crowd, two thousand at the least and growing every minute. It blocked the road for a long distance on either side. I looked at the sea of yellow faces above the garish clothes—faces all happy and excited over this bit of fun, all certain that the elephant was going to be shot. They were watching me as they would watch a conjurer about to perform a trick.

They did not like me, but with the magical rifle in my hands I was momentarily worth watching. And suddenly I realized that I should have to shoot the elephant after all. The people expected it of me and I had got to do it; I could feel their two thousand wills pressing me forward, irresistibly. And it was at this moment, as I stood there with the rifle in my hands, that I first grasped the hollowness, the futility of the white man's dominion in the East. Here was I, the white man with his gun, standing in front of the unarmed native crowd—seemingly the leading actor of the piece; but in reality I was only an absurd puppet pushed to and fro by the will of those yellow faces behind. I perceived in this moment that when the white man turns tyrant it is his own freedom that he destroys. He becomes a sort of hollow, posing dummy, the conventionalized figure of a sahib.[7] For it is the condition of his rule that he shall spend his life in trying to impress the "natives," and so in every crisis he has got to do what the "natives" expect of him. He wears a mask, and his face grows to fit it. I had got to shoot the elephant. I had committed myself to doing it when I sent for the rifle. A sahib has got to act like a sahib; he has got to appear resolute, to know his own mind and do definite things. To come all that way, rifle in hand, with two thousand people marching at my heels, and then to trail feebly away, having done nothing—no, that was impossible. The crowd would laugh at me. And my whole life, every white man's life in the East, was one long struggle not to be laughed at.

But I did not want to shoot the elephant. I watched him beating his bunch   8
of grass against his knees, with that preoccupied grandmotherly air that elephants have. It seemed to me that it would be murder to shoot him. At that age I was not squeamish about killing animals, but I had never shot an elephant and never wanted to. (Somehow it always seems worse to kill a *large* animal.) Besides, there was the beast's owner to be considered. Alive, the elephant was worth at least a hundred pounds; dead, he would only be worth the value of his tusks, five pounds, possibly. But I had got to act quickly. I turned to some experienced-looking Burmans who had been there when we arrived, and asked them how the elephant had been behaving. They all said the same thing: he took no notice of you if you left him alone, but he might charge if you went too close to him.

It was perfectly clear to me what I ought to do. I ought to walk up to   9
within, say, twenty-five yards of the elephant and test his behavior. If he charged I could shoot, if he took no notice of me it would be safe to leave him until the mahout came back. But also I knew that I was going to do no such thing. I was a poor shot with a rifle and the ground was soft mud into which one would sink at every step. If the elephant charged and I missed him, I should have about as much chance as a toad under a steam-roller. But even then I was not thinking particularly of my own skin, only of the watchful yellow faces behind. For at that moment, with the crowd watching me, I was not afraid in the ordinary sense, as I would have been if I had been alone. A white man mustn't be frightened in front of "natives"; and

[7] Master.

so, in general, he isn't frightened. The sole thought in my mind was that if anything went wrong those two thousand Burmans would see me pursued, caught, trampled on and reduced to a grinning corpse like that Indian up the hill. And if that happened it was quite probable that some of them would laugh. That would never do. There was only one alternative. I shoved the cartridges into the magazine and lay down on the road to get a better aim.

10   The crowd grew very still, and a deep, low, happy sigh, as of people who see the theatre curtain go up at last, breathed from innumerable throats. They were going to have their bit of fun after all. The rifle was a beautiful German thing with cross-hair sights. I did not then know that in shooting an elephant one would shoot to cut an imaginary bar running from ear-hole to ear-hole. I ought, therefore, as the elephant was sideways on, to have aimed straight at his ear-hole; actually I aimed several inches in front of this, thinking the brain would be further forward.

11   When I pulled the trigger I did not hear the bang or feel the kick—one never does when a shot goes home—but I heard the devilish roar of glee that went up from the crowd. In that instant, in too short a time, one would have thought, even for the bullet to get there, a mysterious, terrible change had come over the elephant. He neither stirred nor fell, but every line on his body had altered. He looked suddenly stricken, shrunken, immensely old, as though the frightful impact of the bullet had paralyzed him without knocking him down. At last, after what seemed a long time—it might have been five seconds, I dare say—he sagged flabbily to his knees. His mouth slobbered. An enormous senility seemed to have settled upon him. One could have imagined him thousands of years old. I fired again into the same spot. At the second shot he did not collapse but climbed with desperate slowness to his feet and stood weakly upright, with legs sagging and head drooping. I fired a third time. That was the shot that did for him. You could see the agony of it jolt his whole body and knock the last remnant of strength from his legs. But in falling he seemed for a moment to rise, for as his hind legs collapsed beneath him he seemed to tower upwards like a huge rock toppling, his trunk reaching skywards like a tree. He trumpeted, for the first and only time. And then down he came, his belly towards me, with a crash that seemed to shake the ground even where I lay.

12   I got up. The Burmans were already racing past me across the mud. It was obvious that the elephant would never rise again, but he was not dead. He was breathing very rhythmically with long rattling gasps, his great mound of a side painfully rising and falling. His mouth was wide open—I could see far down into the caverns of pale pink throat. I waited a long time for him to die, but his breathing did not weaken. Finally I fired my two remaining shots into the spot where I thought his heart must be. The thick blood welled out of him like red velvet, but still he did not die. His body did not even jerk when the shots hit him, the tortured breathing continued without a pause. He was dying, very slowly and in great agony, but in some world remote from me where not even a bullet could damage him further. I felt that I had got to put an end to that dreadful noise. It seemed dreadful to see the great beast lying there, powerless to move and yet powerless to

die, and not even to be able to finish him. I sent back for my small rifle and poured shot after shot into his heart and down his throat. They seemed to make no impression. The tortured gasps continued as steadily as the ticking of a clock.

In the end I could not stand it any longer and went away. I heard later   13
that it took him half an hour to die. Burmans were bringing dahs[8] and baskets even before I left, and I was told they had stripped his body almost to the bones by the afternoon.

Afterwards, of course, there were endless discussions about the shooting   14
of the elephant. The owner was furious, but he was only an Indian and could do nothing. Besides, legally I had done the right thing, for a mad elephant has to be killed, like a mad dog, if its owner fails to control it. Among the Europeans opinion was divided. The older men said I was right, the younger men said it was a damn shame to shoot an elephant for killing a coolie, because an elephant was worth more than any damn Coringhee coolie. And afterwards I was very glad that the coolie had been killed; it put me legally in the right and it gave me a sufficient pretext for shooting the elephant. I often wondered whether any of the others grasped that I had done it solely to avoid looking a fool.

WHAT DID THE WRITER SAY, AND WHAT DID YOU THINK?

1. Why did Orwell shoot the elephant?
2. Why did he not want to shoot the elephant?
3. What should he have done instead of shooting it?
4. The experience Orwell describes strengthened his opposition to imperialism. Why?
5. Does the essay have one thesis or two?
6. Why does Orwell, the anti-imperialist, stress his dislike of the Burmese?
7. Is there any indication that his attitude toward the Burmese has changed over the years?

HOW DID THE WRITER SAY IT?

1. Would *courage* have been better than *had the guts* in paragraph 1? In paragraph 2, would *drive a bayonet into a Buddhist priest's stomach* have been better than *a Buddhist priest's guts*? Explain.
2. Where does Orwell directly comment on the meaning of the story?
3. In paragraph 9, what is the intended effect of the sentence, *That would never do?*
4. Why does Orwell describe in such detail the death of the "Dravidian coolie" (paragraph 4)?
5. To a casual reader, the last paragraph may seem a rather weak gathering of irrelevant details. In fact, everything in it ties in effectively to the rest of the essay. How? What would have been lost if the essay had ended with paragraph 13?
6. Vocabulary: *prostrate, labyrinth, squalid, garish, conjurer, sahib, senility.*

[8] Long, heavy knives.

WHAT ABOUT <u>YOUR</u> WRITING?

"If the elephant charged and I missed him," Orwell writes, "I should have about as much chance as a toad under a steam-roller." The comparison works in a number of ways. It successfully communicates the general idea of having no chance at all. It presents the general idea, however, with dramatic, specific language and thus adds to reader interest. It also conveys a strong emotional attitude toward what is being described: the grubbiness of the event, the helplessness of the victim, the ignorance of the attacker.

Comparisons can sometimes add a spark to your own writing. Instead of settling for "I was embarrassed," for example, you might try to finish off the thought with a comparison:

I was as embarrassed as a poolroom hustler hitting the cue ball off the table.

I hadn't been so embarrassed since I was six and my mother caught me playing doctor with Jimmy Fisher next door.

I was so embarrassed it was like having a simultaneous attack of dandruff, noisy stomach, and underarm perspiration.

The two most common kinds of comparisons are similes and metaphors. *Similes* make the comparison explicit by using *like* or *as*.

The friction of the great beast's foot had stripped the skin from his back as neatly as one skins a rabbit.

Metaphors are sometimes defined as similes without the *like* or *as*. The simile "The moon was like a silver dollar" becomes a metaphor when expressed "The moon was a silver dollar." A metaphor can be more sophisticated than that, however, and the term is best defined as a word or phrase ordinarily associated with one context that is transferred to another. Some metaphors have become part of the language—so much so that they are either hopelessly trite or barely recognizable as metaphors.

Life is a rat race.
He ought to come down from his ivory tower.
Keep your paws off me.
She has a good nose for news.
. . . branches of knowledge
. . . key to the problem
. . . legs of a table
. . . hit below the belt

Other metaphors are waiting to be created to add impact, originality, and excitement to your writing.

Cautiously, the psychiatrist started to enter the haunted castle of his patient's mind.

It was the same thing all over again. My whole life had turned into a summer rerun.

His childhood daydreams had gone forever. Facing the fact that success took hard work, he realized that he could not expect to shazam his way to greatness.

Two cautions are necessary. First, use comparisons in moderation; otherwise, your style, instead of becoming enlivened, will bog down through carrying excess baggage. Second, don't be tempted into using the ready-made trite comparisons that fill the language: "as easy as pie," "so hungry I could eat a horse," "like taking candy from a baby," "like a bolt out of the blue," and so on. Trite phrases, by definition, are dead, and good comparisons are intended to be life-giving.

Chapter 10
ARGUMENTATION

In this chapter, argumentation does not refer to fighting or bickering. It refers to the providing of logical reasons in support of a particular point of view. In that sense, of course, this whole book has been about argumentation. It has urged you from the start to form a thesis and devote your primary energies to proving or supporting it.

The readings in argumentation in this chapter have two outstanding characteristics. First, they employ no particular pattern of development consistently; a paragraph that describes may be followed by a paragraph that compares and contrasts and another that explores cause-and-effect relationships. To that extent, the readings here can be viewed simply as readings that refuse to fit neatly into one of the patterns dealt with in previous chapters. This mixture of patterns is a healthy antidote to excessive rigidity of thought; not all subjects lend themselves to only one pattern, and in such cases it's as absurd to write in only one pattern as it would be to play a round of golf with only one club.

The second characteristic of these readings in argumentation is that they rely, to a far greater extent than any others studied so far, on the techniques of formal logic. Formal logic generally combines two ways of thinking: induction and deduction.

Induction is the process of arriving at general conclusions by studying individual cases. All the cats we have seen or read about have whiskers. So far as we can determine, all the cats our friends and acquaintances have seen or read about also have whiskers. We therefore conclude that all cats have whiskers. We haven't come close to surveying all the cats in the world, and to reach our conclusion we must make an *inductive leap*. We work on the unproven assumption that what is true of some or many is true of all. Induction is often the only possible way to approach certain subjects, and it can be extremely convincing. Ultimately, however, the final step in the inductive process must be a leap, an intelligent guess, not proof in the strictest sense of the word.

Doctors use induction when, seeing a child with a fever and a particular kind of rash, they conclude that the child has chicken pox, since all the other children the doctors know with those symptoms have turned out to have chicken pox. (The same symptoms could be those of an obscure tropical disease—just as some cats somewhere may have no whiskers—but the doctors are justified in making their inductive leap.) Customers in a supermarket use induction when they no longer buy milk there. The three most recent times they bought milk it was sour, and by induction they conclude that milk supplies in that store are likely to be of poor quality. Readers use induction when, having been bored by a novelist's three most recent books, they conclude that the novelist is a boring writer.

Skillful induction is mostly a matter of seeing to it that conclusions about a group are drawn only from a study of well-chosen members of that group. Chapter 2 on examples discusses this issue at length (pp. 20–21).

Deduction is the process of arriving at a conclusion by starting with a general premise or assumption instead of with a specific instance. The primary tool in deductive reasoning is the *syllogism,* a three-part argument consisting of two premises and a conclusion.

All Rembrandt paintings are great works of art.
The Night Watch is a Rembrandt painting.
Therefore, *The Night Watch* is a great work of art.

All doctors are quacks.
Smith is a doctor.
Therefore, Smith is a quack.

The syllogism is a tool for analyzing the validity of an argument. You'll rarely find a formal syllogism outside of textbooks on logic. Mostly, you'll find *enthymemes,* abbreviated syllogisms with one or more of the parts unstated.

The Night Watch is by Rembrandt, isn't it? And Rembrandt is a great painter, isn't he?

Look, Smith is a doctor. He must be a quack.

Translating such statements into a syllogism enables the logic to be examined more coolly and clearly than it otherwise could be.

If both premises in a syllogism are true and the reasoning process from one part of the syllogism to the other is valid, the conclusion will be proven. No leap or intelligent guess will be required; the conclusion will be inescapable.

Few arguments worth going into, of course, are open-and-shut cases. The premises are often debatable, to mention just one possible source of difficulty. Argumentation, therefore, usually combines deduction and induction. A deductive argument, for example, will often have to call upon induction to establish the soundness of its premises. A reader has been bored by three books a particular novelist has written and inductively arrives at a conclusion about that novelist's work. That inductive conclusion can now serve, in turn, as the first premise of a syllogism:

> Books by Irwin Shaw are likely to bore me.
> *Rich Man, Poor Man* is a book by Irwin Shaw.
> Therefore, *Rich Man, Poor Man* is likely to bore me.

In addition to relying on formal logic, good argumentation, though it usually does not limit itself to one special rhetorical pattern, usually does require a special pattern of manners. The readers have not yet, in theory, made up their minds and need to be convinced not only that the writer's argument is logical but that the writer is a reasonable, fair-minded person.

Go easy on universals. Qualify when appropriate. Reasonable people can disagree. Logic beats chaos any day, but logic can not create total uniformity of opinions. Be moderate with sweeping generalizations that use—or imply—terms like *all, every, always, never, nobody.* Qualifying terms like *usually, often, perhaps, it seems likely, probably, seldom, rarely, almost* can be helpful in establishing a climate of reason, a sense that the writer is fully aware of the complexities and ambiguities of human experience. Don't assume from these comments that you should not express strongly held views in a strong way or that obvious truths should be expressed with mealymouthed hypocrisy. Assume only that most writers are sometimes tempted to be carried away by enthusiasm for their own ideas into making gross overstatements—and the good writer successfully resists the temptation.

Give consideration to differing opinions. After starting with a cool, impartial presentation of the issue and your way of dealing with it, present any opposition to your ideas fairly. Refute the opposition when you can. When you can't, concede that the opposition has a good point. Argumentation that shows awareness of only one viewpoint will rarely gain a reader's respect.

Be cautious with abuse and ridicule. You may consider some of the opposition's arguments foolish or even dangerous. Moreover, one of the hazards built into any piece of argumentation is that it may commit itself so completely to the precision of logic that it reads as if it were written by a computer instead of by a human being. Still, though there's no law against introducing humor or even passion into argumentation, be careful that such elements do not sabotage the essential logical strengths of your paper. Be particularly careful that any irresistible abuse or ridicule is directed against the ideas of your opponents, not the opponents themselves.

Devote most of your attention toward supporting your view, not advocating it. You're trying to show that your opinion is logical. You're not trying, except in a minor way, to preach or to inspire. The introduction and conclusion will express your basic opinion. By and large, the rest of the paper will discuss your reasons for holding that opinion or for disagreeing with arguments against it.

Some Common Logical Fallacies

Very briefly, here are some of the most common logical fallacies. Good argumentation depends on sound logic, and it may be valuable to have a handy guide to possible pitfalls.

Hasty generalization. Not enough examples or untypical examples. (See pp. 20–21.)

Post hoc, ergo propter hoc. "After this, therefore because of this."

I failed the test after I walked under the ladder; therefore I failed the test because I walked under the ladder.

For further discussion, see p. 103.

Either/or. A writer presents a case as if there were only two alternatives and tries to force the reader to choose between them. Life usually offers more options than that.

Either you're for me or against me.

Either we agree to total disarmament, or we condemn the human race to extinction.

Non sequitur. "It does not follow"—often the result of omitting a necessary step in the thought process or of taking wild emotional flights in which no thought process ever existed.

I despise Professor Jones; so I'm never going to read another book as long as I live.

We all hate war and poverty and racism. Come on, then. Let's seize the administration building and hold the dean for ransom.

Ignoring the question. Instead of dealing with the topic under discussion, the writer or speaker becomes unintentionally sidetracked or deliberately creates a diversion. The question can be ignored in a number of ways. Among them are

"Ad hominem" argument—arguing "to the man," attacking the person who raised the issue rather than dealing with the issue itself.

How dare Congressman Arnold advocate population control when he himself has six children?

Congressman Arnold's failure to practice what he preaches has nothing to do with the merits of population control.

Setting up a straw man—accusing one's opponents of saying something they never said or intended to say and then attacking them for saying it.

You allege this movie has too much sex and violence, but people like you who want censorship are a menace to the basic constitutional rights of free American citizens.

Question begging—assuming the truth of a debatable point and basing the rest of the argument on that shaky assumption.

What shall we do with the medical murderers who perform abortions?

Before deciding what to do with the doctors, the writer must first offer convincing evidence that abortion is murder.

Shifting the burden of proof—as in law, "He who asserts must prove." It is not logical argument to declare

I believe the government is run by secret Martian agents, and nobody can prove that I am wrong.

Argument by analogy. An analogy is an extended comparison. It can be valuable in clarifying a difficult point or dramatizing an abstract idea. *It can never prove anything*. No matter how many suggestive similarities there may be, they can never be more than suggestive since there must also be differences.

Analogy used to clarify or dramatize

Finding a cure for cancer is much like finding a cure for inflation. The exact causes of the diseases are shrouded in mystery; medication carries the risk of unpredictable side effects, but without medication the illnesses grow beyond control; cures are increasingly difficult the longer they are delayed; and the experts always—but always—disagree.

Argument by analogy: analogy used to prove

The Chairman has been unjustly criticized in this country for executing his political opponents in order to create a better society. Surely, one of the oldest truths is that you can't make an omelet without breaking a few eggs. It's too bad the beautiful shells have to be cracked open. There's a terrible mess for a little while. But the final result is well worth the effort, and only fools would waste tears over the sad fate of the poor little eggs. The Chairman has the right recipe for a greater tomorrow, and those who don't understand his techniques should stay out of the kitchen.

The second analogy assumes that a few similarities between breaking eggs and killing political opponents mean that the two actions are alike in all other respects. The writer thus attempts to prove that because one action is justified the other must be justified, too. Argument by analogy ignores all differences. Here, for example, nonhuman things are being compared to humans, nonliving things to living, breaking to killing, and so forth.

Faultily constructed syllogisms.

Introduction of a new term in the conclusion—the two terms in the conclusion must have appeared previously in the premises. Note how the following syllogism introduces a new term in the conclusion and destroys all pretense at logic:

All teachers are cruel.
Mr. Jones is a teacher.
Therefore, Mr. Jones should be fired.

Reasoning from negative premises—*two* negative premises can never lead to any valid conclusion.

No human being is free from prejudice.
Fido is not a human being.
Therefore. . .

Shift in meaning of a term—some syllogisms are rendered invalid because a word has changed in meaning from one part of the syllogism to another.

Only man has a soul.
Susan is not a man.
Therefore, Susan does not have a soul.

In the first premise, *man* referred to the human race. In the second premise, the same word shifted its meaning and referred only to males.

Improper relationship between terms—a well-constructed syllogism establishes relationships that make a particular conclusion inevitable. The following syllogism does not:

Sexists refuse to hire women.
Jones refuses to hire women.
Therefore, Jones is a sexist.

The first premise does not establish that sexists are the *only* ones who refuse to hire women. Jones could theoretically be an ardent supporter of women's rights but be under strict orders—orders he despises—to hire only men. He could be the manager of a men's professional basketball team. Jones could also be the name of a six-week-old puppy. *All* syllogisms constructed with the same relationship between terms as this one will be logically invalid. Even if the conclusion is "true," it will be true by accident, not by logic. (Jones *could* be a sexist, after all.)

Politicians are corrupt.
Simmons is corrupt.
Therefore, Simmons is a politician.

Communists do not believe in God.
She does not believe in God.
Therefore, she is a Communist.

WRITING SUGGESTIONS FOR ARGUMENTATION THEMES

Employing the techniques of formal argumentation, attack or defend one of the numbered statements below.

1. American drivers will never renounce their cars for mass transit systems.
2. Recent reforms have weakened the Roman Catholic church.
3. Taking snapshots with a Polaroid is superior to all other ways.
4. The world's worst bore is ——— .
5. Parents who try to impose their values on young people are the only ones young people respect.
6. The *F* grade should be abolished.
7. The greatest baseball (*or other sport*) player of all time is ——— .
8. The New Math has been an educational disaster.
9. The greatest holiday of all is ——— .
10. Life is a constant process of discovering that older people have been idiots.
11. The worst show on television is ——— .
12. Required English courses should be abolished.
13. Students should have a voice in the hiring and firing of teachers. (See pp. 249–254.)
14. Married couples should not be allowed to have more than two children.
15. Capital punishment should be reinstituted.
16. Cats make better pets than dogs.
17. U.S. Savings Bonds are a poor investment.
18. Cigarette smoking should be made illegal.
19. Automatic advancement to the next grade level must be eliminated from our schools.

Killing for Sport

JOSEPH WOOD KRUTCH

> Joseph Wood Krutch (1893–1970) was a drama critic, professor of literature, columnist, philosopher, and naturalist. He wrote with distinction in all of these roles. Among his many books are the still powerful *The Modern Temper* (1929), *Samuel Johnson* (1944), *Henry David Thoreau* (1948), *The Desert Year* (1952), *The Measure of Man* (1954)—winner of a National Book Award—and *The Great Chain of Life* (1957).
>
> In "Killing for Sport," Krutch's argument is simple and impressive, but is it airtight? Could a lover of hunting find logical grounds on which to attack it?

1   It wouldn't be quite true to say that "some of my best friends are hunters." Still, I do number among my respected acquaintances some who not only kill for the sake of killing but count it among their keenest pleasures. And I can think of no better illustration of the fact that men may be sepa-

rated at some point by a fathomless abyss yet share elsewhere much common ground. To me, it is inconceivable that anyone can think of an animal more interesting dead than alive. I can also easily prove, to my own satisfaction, that killing "for sport" is the perfect type[1] of that pure evil for which metaphysicians have sometimes sought.

Most wicked deeds are done because the doer proposes some good for himself. The liar lies to gain some end; the swindler and the thief want things which, if honestly got, might be good in themselves. Even the murderer is usually removing some impediment to normal desires. Though all of these are selfish or unscrupulous, their deeds are not gratuitously evil. But the killer for sport seems to have no such excusable motive. He seems merely to prefer death to life, darkness to light. He seems to get nothing other than the satisfaction of saying: "Something which wanted to live is dead. Because I can bring terror and agony, I assure myself that I have power. Because of me there is that much less vitality, consciousness and perhaps joy in the universe. I am the spirit that denies." When a man wantonly destroys one of the works of man, we call him "Vandal." When he wantonly destroys one of the works of God, we call him "Sportsman."

The hunter-for-food may be as wicked and as misguided as vegetarians sometimes say, but he does not kill for the sake of killing. The ranchers and the farmers who exterminate all living things not immediately profitable to them may sometimes be working against their own best interests; but whether they are or are not, they hope to achieve some supposed good by the exterminations. If to do evil, not in the hope of gain but for evil's sake, involves the deepest guilt by which man can be stained, then killing for killing's sake is a terrifying phenomenon and as strong a proof as we could have of that "reality of evil" with which present-day theologians are again concerned.

WHAT DID THE WRITER SAY, AND WHAT DID YOU THINK?

1. What is the author's definition of *pure evil?*
2. Can you think of any activities besides hunting that might fit the definition?
3. What separates the sportsman's killing of animals from other kinds of killing?
4. Does Krutch's statement that some hunters are among his "respected acquaintances" weaken his argument?
5. Which elements in Krutch's argument use induction, and which use deduction?

HOW DID THE WRITER SAY IT?

1. What common phrase is alluded to in the first sentence?
2. Where does the author use repetition to intensify the emotional effects of his style?

[1] Symbol.

3. In paragraph 2, why does the author present the thoughts of the hunter as a direct quote?
4. Does the author present his case too one-sidedly? Does he show any awareness that he might be mistaken or at least not completely correct?
5. Vocabulary: *fathomless, abyss, metaphysicians, impediment, gratuitously, wantonly, theologians.*

WHAT ABOUT YOUR WRITING?

At one time or another, nearly every English teacher starts chatting with a student about writing, and more often than seems possible, this kind of scene takes place.

"You write well enough," says the teacher. "But I wonder if you can't try for a little more life in your writing. Don't be so stiff, so formal. Drop in a personal touch now and then."

"A personal touch?" asks the student.

"Well, yes. If you're writing about the generation gap or something like that, don't just come on like a professional sociologist. Start out with an argument you once had with your parents. Then get into the sociology, if you have to."

"You mean I can use *I* if I want to?"

"?"

"We were never allowed to use *I.*"

"?"

It seems that a lot of students had high school teachers who understandably got upset with weasel sentences like "I think that Abraham Lincoln was an important figure in American history" and personal letters like "I remember last week you said in class that Hemingway started his writing career as a newspaper reporter, and I wonder what you think of this idea I came up with." So the teacher made up a rule that prohibited the use of *I.* It's possible to sympathize with the teacher, but the rule has nothing to do with the realities of writing.

Krutch's article on hunting successfully breaks the ice by using *I.* The article is going to rely on logic and cool analysis; it's going to be basically impersonal. Why not first set up a warm, conversational mood? It might help put the reader in a receptive frame of mind and make the logic and philosophy less intimidating. Using *I* in your writing is neither good nor bad in itself, but when *I* works, go ahead.

You're allowed.

Advice on Choosing a Mistress
BENJAMIN FRANKLIN

At one time or another, Benjamin Franklin (1706–1790) did almost everything and was generally outstanding in everything he did. Some of the proverbs in his *Poor Richard's Almanac* have become part of our language: "Early to bed and early to rise," for example. His *Autobiography* is an American literary classic. As ambassador to France, he had a major influence on the success of the American

From *The Papers of Benjamin Franklin*, vol. 3, ed. Leonard W. Labaree, 1961. Letter dated June 25, 1745. Reprinted by permission of the publisher, Yale University Press.

Revolution. He devised and initiated municipal projects in Philadelphia that made it a leader among American cities: the first public lending library, the first city fire department, new methods of street lighting. He did important basic scientific research into the mysteries of electricity. He invented or was among the first to propose daylight saving time, bifocals, the lightning rod, harmonicas, and the famous Franklin stove—a major improvement in home heating for which he refused all personal profit.

"Advice on Choosing a Mistress" was not discovered until 1850 among a collection of Franklin's papers owned by one of his descendants. It remained unpublished for general circulation until 1926. The letter is very likely not addressed to an actual person but is simply an essay masquerading as a letter.

June 25, 1745

My dear Friend,

I know of no Medicine fit to diminish the violent natural Inclinations you   1
mention; and if I did, I think I should not communicate it to you. Marriage is the proper Remedy. It is the most natural State of Man, and therefore the State in which you are most likely to find solid Happiness. Your Reasons against entring into it at present, appear to me not well-founded. The circumstantial Advantages you have in View by postponing it, are not only uncertain, but they are small in comparison with that of the Thing itself, the being *married and settled*. It is the Man and Woman united that make the compleat human Being. Separate, she wants his Force of Body and Strength of Reason; he, her Softness, Sensibility and acute Discernment. Together they are more likely to succeed in the World. A single Man has not nearly the Value he would have in that State of Union. He is an incomplete Animal. He resembles the odd Half of a Pair of Scissars. If you get a prudent healthy Wife, your industry in your Profession, with her good Œconomy, will be a Fortune sufficient.

But if you will not take this Counsel, and persist in thinking a Commerce   2
with the Sex inevitable, then I repeat my former Advice, that in all your Amours you should *prefer old Women to young ones*. You call this a Paradox, and demand my Reasons. They are these:

1. Because as they have more Knowledge of the World and their Minds   3
are better stor'd with Observations, their Conversation is more improving and more lastingly agreable.

2. Because when Women cease to be handsome, they study to be good.   4
To maintain their Influence over Men, they supply the Diminution of Beauty by an Augmentation of Utility. They learn to do a 1000 Services small and great, and are the most tender and useful of all Friends when you are sick. Thus they continue amiable. And hence there is hardly such a thing to be found as an old Woman who is not a good Woman.

3. Because there is no hazard of Children, which irregularly produc'd   5
may be attended with much Inconvenience.

4. Because thro' more Experience, they are more prudent and discreet in   6
conducting an Intrigue to prevent Suspicion. The Commerce with them is therefore safer with regard to your Reputation. And with regard to theirs, if the Affair should happen to be known, considerate People might be rather inclin'd to excuse an old Woman who would kindly take care of a young

Man, form his Manners by her good Counsels, and prevent his ruining his Health and Fortune among mercenary Prostitutes.

7   5. Because in every Animal that walks upright, the Deficiency of the Fluids that fill the Muscles appears first in the highest Part: The Face first grows lank and wrinkled; then the Neck; then the Breast and Arms; the lower Parts continuing to the last as plump as ever: So that covering all above with a Basket, and regarding only what is below the Girdle, it is impossible of two Women to know an old from a young one. And as in the dark all Cats are grey, the Pleasure of corporal Enjoyment with an old Woman is at least equal, and frequently superior, every Knack being by Practice capable of Improvement.

8   6. Because the Sin is less. The debauching a Virgin may be her Ruin, and make her for Life unhappy.

9   7. Because the Compunction is less. The having made a young Girl *miserable* may give you frequent bitter Reflections; none of which can attend the making an old Woman *happy*.

10   8thly and Lastly. They are *so grateful!!*

11   Thus much for my Paradox. But still I advise you to marry directly; being sincerely

Your affectionate Friend.

WHAT DID THE WRITER SAY, AND WHAT DID YOU THINK?

1. Does the letter have two theses or one? Explain.
2. If the letter has two theses, which one is given more logical support?
3. Does the introductory praise of marriage seem genuine or contrived?
4. How might an advocate of young mistresses attempt to refute Franklin?
5. Would it be fair to say that the author is "only interested in sex"?
6. Does the author use inductive or deductive logic?
7. To what extent does Franklin's argument depend on stereotypes of human beings?
8. Should this selection be read as an example of offensive sexism, good fun, or both?

HOW DID THE WRITER SAY IT?

1. Paragraph 1: "Marriage is the proper Remedy." What does the author's word choice suggest about his attitude toward the subject—and perhaps his attitude toward life?
2. Can you think of other comparisons that would make the same point as "the odd Half of a Pair of Scissars"?
3. What is gained by numbering each reason?
4. What determines the order in which the eight reasons are presented?
5. Vocabulary: *diminution, augmentation, mercenary, corporal, debauching, compunction.*

WHAT ABOUT YOUR WRITING?

A short piece of writing will usually state its main idea in the first paragraph—sometimes, for dramatic emphasis, in the last one. Franklin's first paragraph, easily the longest, far from presenting his main idea, appears to attack it. Franklin isn't breaking any sacred rules, however; he's simply using good writing strategy.

Franklin is going to be presenting a thesis, after all, that readers will be likely to find shocking or offensive or at least eccentric. Some people will be bothered by the whole idea of writing so coolly about sex in the first place. Others will find the concept of the charms of old women highly dubious. Franklin knows that for everyone some unconventional notions are going to be coming up. He uses the first paragraph to establish his credentials as a reasonable, fairly ordinary, solid sort of person who can be relied on for his good sense. Then, and only then, is he ready to bust loose. The writer of the first paragraph will not be able to be dismissed as an irresponsible zany.

The more controversial or potentially obnoxious your own views might be to a particular audience, the more important it is to establish at the start your credentials for rationality. Express your awareness of both sides. Grant your opponents any strong points they have—the earlier the better. If you're complaining about unfounded accusations of "police brutality," start out by conceding that some policemen *have* acted terribly and that you're all for punishing them. If you're protesting against police brutality, start out by admitting that some hardened criminals habitually holler "brutality" no matter what the cause and that you're not interested in sticking up for them. Demonstrate your thoughtful recognition of the complexities of life. Then, and on'y then, bust loose with all you've got.

A Six-Year Presidency?

JACK VALENTI

Jack Valenti was special assistant to President Lyndon Johnson from 1963 to 1966. He is now president of the Motion Picture Association of America.

In reading Valenti's article, which appeared originally in *Newsweek,* consider the "pattern of manners" for logical argument as outlined on pp. 236–237. How closely does Valenti follow the pattern?

If the Watergate mess tells us anything, it is that the re-election of a President is the most nagging concern in the White House and that, given the limits of human nature, it is altogether possible that the first item on the agenda of an incoming Administration is its re-election. There is really nothing sinister in this objective—it's the most normal thing in our politics.

But, at the risk of stepping on the droppings of shrewder and wiser philosophers, I think the time has come for changing the rules by which Presidential politics are played. My proposal is a single six-year term for the President with no re-election eligibility.

3   Two of the most respected of all United States senators, Majority Leader Mike Mansfield of Montana and senior Republican George Aiken of Vermont, have both sponsored such an idea. They believe that while we ought not to tinker too much with the constitutional machinery, we can rearrange a bit of the constitutional furniture.

The Judgment of History

4   Consider for a moment the election of a new President under a six-year term. He takes office knowing that he cannot seek re-election, that he will make his place in history, for better or worse, on the deeds and achievements of the next 72 months of his stewardship. He has only to do what he thinks is right, with the sure understanding that he must heed the people, for they are co-authors of the record he will leave to the historians. It is this judgment that most Presidents are keen to certify; they value it far above the Great Gallup Poll in the Sky that measures their popularity rather than their legacy.

5   Should taxes be raised? Should rationing be instituted? Should troops be withdrawn? Should wrongs be righted even though some voters are offended? If the election is a year or two away, you can mark it down as a Major Truth that a first-term President will carefully weigh the effects of whatever he does on his second-term prospects. Kenneth O'Donnell, JFK's closest political aide, wrote some years ago of a conversation President Kennedy had with Senator Mansfield in 1963 during which the senator urged JFK to get the hell out of Vietnam. To which, according to O'Donnell, the President wryly confessed he wanted to do just that, but he had to wait until after the election lest he be swamped at the polling booths.

6   Watergate would never have occurred if Presidential aides were not obsessed with re-election. If they had been comfortable in their tenure, knowing that in six years they would lose their lease—and in that short time they must write their record as bravely and wisely as possible—is it not possible that their arrogance might have softened and their reach for power might have shortened?

7   The counter-arguments to the six-year term are (1) the President must not be freed from considering the political implications of his acts or he becomes isolated from the people, and (2) he is a lame duck the day of his election.

8   Let's consider those two arguments.

Power and Politics

9   Don't we make the President a lame duck now the day he is elected to his second term? Does that hamper him? Of course not. The President has such power that he can wield it sufficiently and with precision to the last

weeks of his tenure. President Johnson signed into law two of the most controversial pieces of legislation of his Administration in the last seven months of his office, the equal-housing and tax reform acts. The powers of appointment, of veto, of budget making, of initiation of programs, of moral suasion—these are all intact, fully armed and borne by him until his successor is sworn in. Lame-duckism is a myth in the Presidency.

A six-year-term President is not isolated and divorced from the daily 10 political marketplace. Any President who wants to pass a bill, build a budget, construct a program, implement a plan, make a treaty, negotiate at a conference must be sensitive to the people and the Congress. He must act within the framework of the separation of powers; he is powerful, but he is not all-powerful. Common sense dictates his actions, and his own sensitivity to his place in history freights his every move. Therefore it follows, quite reasonably, that the President who would write a durable and measurably valuable record must persuade the Congress and the people. .

The Congress and the Supreme Court (the one answerable often to the 11 voters, and the other secure behind lifetime tenure) have only to exercise their power under the Constitution and the insensitive President, opaque to the nation's needs, can be pressured to straighten up and fly right.

We must always remember that a President's noblest stirring is toward 12 his place in history as a Good, perhaps Great, President. If we abort his other objective, his re-election, we reduce the potential for mischief and leave the better angels undisturbed.

We should also factor into our decision the time consumed in the re- 13 election campaign. Some two and a half years after a President is inaugurated, the elephantine apparatus of the Federal establishment moves to provision the re-election caravan. Energy, money and time are thrown into the job of precinct winning.

Why waste this effort and treasure? We no longer have the luxury of slow 14 communications, of ships taking a month to cross the ocean, and the slow seepage of political impact. Today we deal in eight minutes to catastrophe, or the time it takes a MIRVed missile[1] to hurl itself across borders. The stakes in the game have become too high to indulge ourselves in what seemed all right a century, or even three decades, ago.

The Founding Fathers understood the possibility of change: they built 15 the amendment mechanism into the Constitution. We have used this mechanism 26 times, mostly to our great benefit—and we should use it again to bring about the six-year Presidency.

A Hostage to Emergency

Churchill once observed: "The amount of energy wasted by men and 16 women of first-class quality in arriving at their true degree before they begin to play on the world stage can never be measured. One may say that 60,

---

[1] A MIRV (*m*ultiple *i*ndependently targeted *r*eentry *v*ehicle) is a missile with two or more warheads, each of which can be directed at a separate target.

perhaps 70 percent of all they have to give is expended on fights which have no other object but to get to their battlefield."[2]

17   That dusty, wasteful system is no longer acceptable in a world living on the nerve edge of disaster. The Presidency today is hostage to emergency. Every moment devoted to getting re-elected squanders the most precious resources of the Presidency—and the nation.

WHAT DID THE WRITER SAY, AND WHAT DID YOU THINK?

1. Does Valenti blame presidents for worrying so much about re-election?
2. What is a *lame duck?*
3. Under the current system, a president can have only two terms in office. Are presidents' second terms characterized by less interest in politics and more in great issues?
4. Does the author explain why he chooses one six-year term rather than one four-year or eight-year term?
5. Where does Valenti cite authorities (see pp. 163–164) to support his argument? Are the citations helpful?
6. Does the author give adequate treatment to opposing arguments? Can you think of any he does not mention?
7. Why does Valenti not propose one-term limits for congressmen?

HOW DID THE WRITER SAY IT?

1. Valenti uses several interesting figures of speech. Explain the meaning of *stepping on the droppings of shrewder and wiser philosophers.* Explain *while we ought not to tinker with the constitutional machinery, we can rearrange a bit of the constitutional furniture.* Explain *leave the better angels undisturbed.*
2. What is the purpose of the reference to the Founding Fathers in paragraph 15?
3. Point out any trite phrases in this selection.
4. Vocabulary: *stewardship, legacy, wryly, tenure, opaque.*

WHAT ABOUT <u>YOUR</u> WRITING?

Valenti's article begins with a topical reference to Watergate. A topical reference is one pertaining to current events, personalities, problems, and so on. Topicality presents some obvious opportunities for any writer—together with some not-so-obvious dangers.

Valenti's reference to Watergate—a front-page newspaper story day after day when the article was written—is intended to make his concern with the comparatively abstract idea of a six-year presidency more immediate and therefore more interesting to his audience. Perhaps, too, the reference makes the article more reassuring: before getting into the intricacies of political theory and constitutional amendments, Valenti begins by mention-

---

[2] Winston Churchill first became prime minister of England when he was in his middle sixties.

ing an issue everyone knows something about. Moreover, the mention of Watergate serves to create a picture of the writer not as a dreamy philosopher, but as one aware of and troubled by the burning topics of the day.

At the same time that it can work so well, topicality also raises some disturbing questions. Will the topical reference be understood or felt with any real force a few months or a few years later? Will readers in 1979 and beyond feel that Valenti's proposal of 1974 was based on an overreaction to a bygone scandal rather than reasoned concern for the future of the country? Even if the proposal is sound, will the topical reference automatically create a dated effect for future readers so that they associate the proposal, good as it is, with ancient history? None of these questions can be answered with any certainty, of course, but the writer ought to ask them.

Topicality can certainly help your writing from time to time. Your reference to a current television show or movie, a politician, a sports figure, a trial can enliven your paper and impress your audience. Just remember that topicality has its dangers. It can give a bogus contemporary feel that distracts a reader's attention from the real subject. It can date the paper and the ideas—sometimes overnight. Television shows are canceled; politicians retire or get defeated; athletes become newscasters. Today's pleased recognition becomes tomorrow's vacant stare. Today's fad becomes tomorrow's footnote.

For comments on references and allusions in general, see pp. 204–205.

Student Evaluations Re-Evaluated

IRENE R. KIERNAN

Irene R. Kiernan is a sociology professor at Kingsborough Community College in Brooklyn, New York. Her article appeared in a journal for community college teachers.

Let me begin with three demurrers. First, the idea of student evaluations appears to be a good one. Second, this paper refers solely to student evaluations of faculty in two-year colleges. Third, the sample reported is limited to 10 two-year colleges, in and around the New York metropolitan area. The method of study followed scientific regulations. Spot checks suggest that experiences over the country with regard to student evaluations are similar to the results here reported.   1

Some four or five years ago, largely in response to student pressure, and with many misgivings, faculty and administrators at many colleges accepted a demand that students be given "a voice" in the appointment, reappointment, and promotion deliberations of their colleges. As a vehicle for the "voice," some colleges instituted the questionnaire form of student evaluation. Formerly, evaluations by students were solely the property of the faculty member for his or her personal information and guidance. Student evaluations are still the property of the teacher, but if the individual wants to be reappointed, or promoted, these evaluations must be reviewed by   2 students and by various faculty committees. Questions raised concerning this procedure form the basis of the discussion presented here.

1

3   How are student evaluations used? Do they really give students a "voice" in college policy concerning appointments, reappointments, and promotions? If so, how much of a voice?

4   Student evaluations of faculty members have been collected and used in some manner in all of the two-year colleges studied. The extent to which they are used varies from one college and from one department within a college to another. At one extreme, a college committee based its judgment of teaching excellence on student evaluations. At the other extreme, a college committee ignored student evaluations completely, although the form for gathering them and collecting statistical data was observed. Most colleges followed practices somewhere in between the two extremes. It seems highly probable that, and certainly students and faculty interviewed believe that, when the student evaluations support the prior affirmative or negative decision of the college committee, they are used. Otherwise they are ignored or minimized. In one case, 85% of the student evaluations were positive; about 10% were mixed, and 5% were negative. The 5% negative evaluations outweighed the 85% positive ones, since the faculty did not wish to promote their colleague anyway.

2

5   When are evaluations administered? In almost all the colleges there is a regular but variable time set aside for student evaluations. Variable timing raises intriguing points. If a teacher knows he or she is to be evaluated any time after mid-semester, what effect will this have on grading? Since nearly all teachers know that research evidence shows that faculty who give good grades are likely to receive good student evaluations and *vice versa,* it certainly must be a temptation for a teacher to avoid giving student evaluations just after mid-semester, or to avoid giving poor grades if there is no choice over timing of evaluations.

3

6   How can an undergraduate judge a teacher's knowledge of his field? All students and faculty interviewed for this study indicated that beginning college students cannot usually judge breadth or depth of a teacher's knowledge of his subject. A beginning mathematics, psychology, nursing, merchandising or any other major simply is not in a position to estimate in any way whether the facts given in class lectures are in conformity with current findings in the field; whether they are idiosyncratic to the teacher; whether they represent his own bias or the sum of many thinkers in his field; or even whether or not they are false. Despite this, in almost every student evaluation, students are asked to answer this question.

4

Do students realize there is a body of scientific facts to be mastered?   7
Often in the behavioral or social sciences and related fields students do not
understand this. Partly because of their unfamiliarity with the fields, and
partly because of misinterpretation of the value of opinions in classroom
discussions, students think social science is a matter of "common sense"
and that their opinions on a topic are as valid as any other "opinion."
Teachers in technical subjects, such as art and design, are troubled by the
same problem; most students must master basic concepts and techniques
before they can be creative.

When students do not understand or do not accept these facts, the teacher   8
reaps a negative personality evaluation based on the student's ignorance.

5

Again, related to the same topic, questionnaires often ask whether or not   9
the teacher gives students the benefit of other thinking in the field. Interviews show that students usually do not know about the vast variety of
views in a discipline. How much reading do we expect of two-year college
students, as another way of exposing them to various outlooks? A question
which asks whether or not a teacher expounds viewpoints other than his or
her own invites students to give subjective answers, based on conjecture
rather than facts.

6

What does a "yes" or "no" answer mean? Some questionnaires ask   10
straightforward questions to which one might expect a straightforward response: for example, does this teacher go too fast? Too slow? Is he or she
clear? Do you understand the lectures? Assignments? Expectations? Regarding clarity of a teacher's presentation, has the student who writes "no"
just received a poor grade, and blamed this on the teacher for not explaining
clearly? Does it mean the student did indeed understand what the teacher
requested or required, but the student did not want to conform with the
demands? What percentage of students who say "no" means that the
teacher did not explain clearly?

Suppose 90% of the students in class say they understand the teacher all   11
or most of the time, and 10% say they never understand him or her? Could
it not be that this says something about the students themselves? Do they
always pay attention? Are they absent frequently? Do they come in after
the beginning of a class and thereby miss part of the explanation so that
they do not understand the rest of the lecture?

Is their grasp of standard American English full or limited? Can they read   12
with ease and write clearly? Are they able to conceptualize in those classes
where such an ability is essential? Do they take advantage of a teacher's
office hours to clarify specific points which they did not understand? Do
they expect a teacher to be able to clarify a point immediately after class,

in a ten-minute break when the teacher must get to another class within that time, and perhaps rush three or four blocks to get there?

7

13   Are good teachers friendly and poor teachers arrogant? For years now we have been hearing about the faults and failings of teachers—not so much their human faults but their inhumane qualities. Teachers have sometimes been painted as ogres, waiting to impose the strictures of the "establishment" on innocent young people. While keeping in mind that some teachers may be professionally unsuited, poorly trained, and even psychiatrically disturbed and hostile toward students, should it not be kept in mind that students are also people and can suffer the same emotional problems as teachers?

14   In evaluating evaluations, therefore, what percentage of student evaluations should be discounted to compensate for those students who are hostile toward teachers in general, or this teacher in particular? How many students are friendly? How many students are arrogant? How can one judge this from a student evaluation?

15   Over 50% of students in our sample reported incidents when they committed vengeful acts by giving hostile evaluations, seldom connected with academic matters or ability to teach. Such responses, geared to the personality questions, sometimes reflected a social class or racial prejudice.

8

16   Are we not allowing students to make unsubstantiated and anonymous charges via unsigned student evaluations? Student evaluations of teachers are uniformly anonymous. Students must be protected, of course, from vengeful acts of retaliation by teachers. But this does not mean that in turn they should be encouraged by others to make charges anonymously. There appears to be no good educational reason for this anonymity and many good reasons why we should not be teaching students that they can make charges against anyone anonymously. Our catalogs say we try to teach students the American values, values of assuming innocence until guilt is proven, and of due process, while we do not practice these values and indeed encourage students to ignore them.

9

17   How does subject matter which a teacher must handle affect the evaluation he receives? Let us use sociology and the teaching of social class as an example. It is well-known that the average American reports himself to be a member of the middle class. If Americans admit to believing any social class system exists, they claim to be middle class. At the same time we know that community college students come largely from blue collar families, as contrasted to the professional family background of four year college students. Thus, when the sociologist talks about social class, the social stigma presently attached to blue collar status, the hardening of social class lines, and difficulties or even the myth of social mobility, many community

college students experience this information as a "put down." They wish to move up. They hear the faculty member telling them of the difficulties they will encounter. They truly feel the faculty member is hostile to them, unfriendly, and discouraging, and considers himself or herself "better than us." Unaware of their own projection, they take out anger and frustration, accumulated over years in a home which nurtures such thoughts, by giving the teacher a negative evaluation.

10

And how do we account for racial, ethnic, and sex biases of students in evaluating teachers? This problem will become more and more evident if the Civil Rights Act is successful in placing women and other minority group members in high prestige positions in colleges. A white, male student who is worried about his future career and the competition he may face from women, Blacks, Jews, Puerto Ricans, Chicanos, American Indians or others not seriously considered competition in his father's day may have a very difficult time objectively evaluating the woman or minority group teacher. Women teachers frequently complained they find they are condemned for the very conduct which students not only tolerate but admire in men: the man is "strong" and is liked, while the woman behaving in the same way is "unfeminine" and is disliked. How is this taken into consideration in an evaluation? What proportion of students hold racist/sexist views? If the proportion is about the same as in the general population, how can we protect minority group members and women?   18

11

All these points lead to the question of how valid any present student evaluations are. Is liking the teacher an evaluation of the teacher's excellence? Present student evaluations appear to measure only one thing: whether or not students like their teacher. The Rodin and Rodin study indicates that students rate most highly those faculty members from whom they learn the least. They point out that the only objective method of evaluating teacher effectiveness is whether or not the students have learned. The subjective methods of evaluation find out whether or not students like the teacher. Who has measured that liking equals learning? Without such a measure, who can say that popularity means effective teaching?   19

Logically, then, we reach our final point. Student evaluations of faculty fall under the definition of "tests" as defined by the American Psychological Association and the Equal Employment Opportunities Commission Guidelines concerning appointment, reappointment, and promotion of faculty members. The policy statement of the Department of Health, Education, and Welfare says that all tests used in matters relating to faculty, and in particular to minority group faculty members, must be validated before they are used. It is the responsibility of the college to define what they intend to test (e.g. teacher effectiveness as measured by student learning) and to assure that these tests validly measure what they claim to measure. None   20 of the student evaluations used in any of the colleges studied have been validated. They do not comply with Equal Opportunity Commission regulations and all faculty members may challenge their use in any employment related question.

21   In summary, this paper has presented 11 questions which must be raised in the use of student evaluation of community college teachers. Ten questions deal with political, sociological, and psychological aspects of the student evaluations currently in use. The last question concerns a legal matter, one of using unvalidated tests which may have the effect of discriminating against women and minority group members in matters of employment.

WHAT DID THE WRITER SAY, AND WHAT DID YOU THINK?

1. Which objections to student evaluations strike you as most valid and least valid?
2. Do you think the objections are as applicable to evaluations in high schools and four-year colleges as in two-year colleges? What does the author think?
3. Can changes eliminate the objections to student evaluations, or is the system itself at fault?
4. What does the author think is the only fair and realistic way to evaluate a teacher? Explain why you agree or disagree.
5. According to the author, what do student evaluations really evaluate instead of teaching ability?
6. If teachers were sufficiently cynical and calculating, what could they do to increase their chances of getting a good evaluation?
7. Should student evaluations be abolished? If not, how much weight should be given to them?

HOW DID THE WRITER SAY IT?

1. What does the author do in the introduction to create the impression of objectivity and impartiality?
2. What is the thesis? Is it ever directly stated?
3. Which problem with student evaluations seems to upset the author most?
4. Which problem does the author have most trouble explaining?
5. Most readers would agree that the conclusion is remarkably dull. Does it serve any useful purpose other than providing a dry summary?
6. Does the author show adequate awareness of the arguments in favor of student evaluations?
7. Does the author rely mainly on induction or deduction?
8. Vocabulary: *demurrers, idiosyncratic, conceptualize, ogres, strictures, stigma.*

WHAT ABOUT YOUR WRITING?

On pp. 118–119 this text discussed the question-and-answer technique of developing a theme. Kiernan employs this technique in a number of sections of "Student Evaluations

Re-Evaluated." Notice, for example, paragraphs 5, 6, and 7–8. In paragraphs 11 and 12, she also uses questions in another way. These paragraphs consist of a series of *rhetorical questions*.

A rhetorical question is a question that either expects no reply or clearly calls for one desired reply. The author, like the reader, knows perfectly well that some students who complain about an instructor's lack of clarity may simply not have paid attention or come to class late or seldom bothered to come to class at all. Flat statements and direct accusations by the author, however, might sound crude or hostile. Rhetorical questions, in this case, help avoid the problem and still make the point.

In moderation, rhetorical questions can also be a powerful device for establishing a dramatic atmosphere, especially in conclusions. Rhetorical questions of this kind must be handled with restraint, or they become forced and artificial, but a good writer should feel free to use them.

> Can all these blunders really be honest mistakes? Isn't it possible that we've let ourselves be victimized again? And isn't it time to act?

> We pay American producers of oil, then, about half of what we pay foreign producers. Is that fair? Is that smart? Is that even sane?

> Is life so dear, or peace so sweet, as to be purchased at the price of chains and slavery? Forbid it, Almighty God! I know not what course others may take; but as for me, give me liberty, or give me death.

A Modest Proposal

JONATHAN SWIFT

Jonathan Swift (1667–1745) still has the power to inspire, to shock, and to offend. Active in politics, dean of St. Patrick's Cathedral (Church of England) in Dublin, Swift is the master of satire in English literature, as seen in *A Tale of a Tub* (1704), *The Battle of the Books* (1704), "An Argument Against Abolishing Christianity in England" (1708), *Gulliver's Travels* (1726), and, in the majesty of its full title, "A Modest Proposal for Preventing the Children of Poor People in Ireland from Being a Burden to Their Parents or Country, and for Making Them Beneficial to the Public" (1729). The fury, hatred, and cruelty in much of Swift's satire often make readers overlook his passionate and idealistic commitment to human welfare. Also too often overlooked is his muscular, unornate prose style, especially remarkable in an age sometimes given to forced elegance.

"A Modest Proposal" is an attack on British oppression and exploitation of Ireland. As you read, distinguish between what is said and what is meant.

It is a melancholy object to those who walk through this great town[1] or travel in the country, when they see the street, the roads, and cabin doors, crowded with beggars of the female sex, followed by three, four, or six children, all in rags, and importuning every passenger for an alms. These mothers, instead of being able to work for their honest livelihood, are forced

[1] Dublin.

to employ all their time in strolling to beg sustenance for their helpless infants, who, as they grow up, either turn thieves for want of work, or leave their dear native country, to fight for the Pretender in Spain, or sell themselves to the Barbadoes.[2]

2   I think it is agreed by all parties that this prodigious number of children in the arms, or on the backs, or at the heels of their mothers, and frequently of their fathers, is in the present deplorable state of the kingdom a very great additional grievance; and therefore whoever could find out a fair, cheap, and easy method of making these children sound and useful members of the common-wealth, would deserve so well of the public as to have his statue up for a preserver of the nation.

3   But my intention is very far from being confined to provide only for the children of professed beggars; it is of much greater extent, and shall take in the whole number of infants at a certain age, who are born of parents in effect as little able to support them, as those who demand our charity in the streets.

4   As to my own part, having turned my thoughts, for many years, upon this important subject, and maturely weighed the several schemes of other projectors, I have always found them grossly mistaken in their computation. It is true, a child just dropt from its dam, may be supported by her milk for a solar year with little other nourishment, at most not above the value of two shillings, which the mother may certainly get, or the value in scraps, by her lawful occupation of begging; and it is exactly at one year old that I propose to provide for them in such a manner, as, instead of being a charge upon their parents, or the parish, or wanting food and raiment for the rest of their lives, they shall, on the contrary, contribute to the feeding and partly to the clothing of many thousands.

5   There is likewise another great advantage in my scheme, that it will prevent those voluntary abortions, and that horrid practice of women murdering their bastard children, alas! too frequent among us—sacrificing the poor innocent babes, I doubt,[3] more to avoid the expense than the shame—which would move tears and pity in the most savage and inhuman breast.

6   The number of souls in this kingdom being usually reckoned one million and a half, of these I calculate there may be about two hundred thousand couples whose wives are breeders; from which number I subtract thirty thousand couples, who are able to maintain their own children, although I apprehend there cannot be so many, under the present distresses of the kingdom; but this being granted, there will remain an hundred and seventy thousand breeders. I again subtract fifty thousand, for those women who miscarry, or whose children die by accident or disease within the year. There only remain an hundred and twenty thousand children of poor parents annually born: The question therefore is, How this number shall be reared,

---

[2] The Pretender was James Francis Edward Stuart (1688–1766), son of the deposed Catholic king of England, James II. He claimed the British throne and was supported by most of Catholic Ireland. Many Irishmen tried to escape from their poverty by hiring themselves out as indentured servants in the Barbadoes and other West Indies islands.

[3] I think.

and provided for: which, as I have already said, under the present situation of affairs, is utterly impossible by all the methods hitherto proposed; for we can neither employ them in handicraft or agriculture; we neither build houses (I mean in the country) nor cultivate land: They can very seldom pick up a livelihood by stealing till they arrive at six years old, except where they are of towardly parts,[4] although, I confess, they learn the rudiments much earlier; during which time they can however be properly looked upon only as probationers; as I have been informed by a principal gentleman in the county of Cavan,[5] who protested to me, that he never knew above one or two instances under the age of six, even in a part of the kingdom so renowned for the quickest proficiency in that art.

I am assured by our merchants, that a boy or a girl before twelve years old, is no saleable commodity, and even when they come to this age, they will not yield above three pounds, or three pounds and a half crown at most, on the exchange; which cannot turn to account either to the parents or kingdom, the charge of nutriment and rags having been at least four times that value.   7

I shall now therefore humbly propose my own thoughts, which I hope will not be liable to the least objection.   8

I have been assured by a very knowing American of my acquaintance in London, that a young healthy child well nursed is at a year old a most delicious nourishing and wholesome food, whether stewed, roasted, baked, or boiled; and I make no doubt that it will equally serve in a fricassee, or a ragout.   9

I do therefore humbly offer it to publick consideration, that of the hundred and twenty thousand children, already computed, twenty thousand may be reserved for breed, whereof only one fourth part to be males; which is more than we allow to sheep, black cattle, or swine; and my reason is that these children are seldom the fruits of marriage, a circumstance not much regarded by our savages; therefore one male will be sufficient to serve four females. That the remaining hundred thousand may, at a year old, be offered in the sale to the persons of quality and fortune through the kingdom; always advising the mother to let them suck plentifully in the last month, so as to render them plump and fat for a good table. A child will make two dishes at an entertainment for friends; and when the family dines alone, the fore or hind quarter will make a reasonable dish, and seasoned with a little pepper or salt will be very good boiled on the fourth day, especially in winter.   10

I have reckoned upon a medium that a child just born will weigh 12 pounds, and in a solar year, if tolerably nursed, increaseth to 28 pounds. I grant this food will be somewhat dear,[6] and therefore very proper for landlords, who, as they have already devoured most of the parents, seem to have the best title to the children.   11

Infant's flesh will be in season throughout the year, but more plentiful in   12

[4] Advanced talents.
[5] An especially poor district of Ireland.
[6] Expensive.

March, and a little before and after; for we are told by a grave author, and eminent French physician,[7] that fish being a prolific diet, there are more children born in Roman Catholic countries about nine months after Lent than at any other season; therefore, reckoning a year after Lent, the markets will be more glutted than usual, because the number of popish infants is at least three to one in this kingdom: and therefore, it will have one other collateral advantage, by lessening the number of papists among us.

13   I have already computed the charge of nursing a beggar's child (in which list I reckon all cottagers, laborers, and four-fifths of the farmers) to be about two shillings per annum, rags included; and I believe no gentleman would repine to give ten shillings for the carcass of a good fat child, which, as I have said, will make four dishes of excellent nutritive meat, when he hath only some particular friend or his own family to dine with him. Thus the squire will learn to be a good landlord, and grow popular among his tenants; the mother will have eight shillings net profit, and be fit for work till she produces another child.

14   Those who are more thrifty (as I must confess the times require) may flay the carcass, the skin of which artificially dressed will make admirable gloves for ladies, and summer boots for fine gentlemen.

15   As to our city of Dublin, shambles[8] may be appointed for this purpose in the most convenient parts of it, and butchers we may be assured will not be wanting; although I rather recommend buying the children alive and dressing them hot from the knife, as we do roasting pigs.

16   A very worthy person, a true lover of his country, and whose virtues I highly esteem, was lately pleased in discoursing on this matter to offer a refinement upon my scheme. He said that many gentlemen of this kingdom, having of late destroyed their deer, he conceived that the want of venison might be well supplied by the bodies of young lads and maidens, not exceeding fourteen years of age nor under twelve; so great a number of both sexes in every country being now ready to starve for want of work and service; and there to be disposed of by their parents if alive, or otherwise by their nearest relations. But with due deference to so excellent a friend, and so deserving a patriot, I cannot be altogether in his sentiments; for as to the males, my American acquaintance assured me from frequent experience, that their flesh was generally tough and lean, like that of our schoolboys, by continual exercise, and their taste disagreeable, and to fatten them would not answer the charge. Then as to the females, it would, I think with humble submission, be a loss to the publick, because they soon would become breeders themselves: And besides it is not improbable that some scrupulous people might be apt to censure such a practice (although indeed very unjustly) as a little bordering upon cruelty, which, I confess, hath always been with me the strongest objection against any project, how well soever intended.

[7] François Rabelais (c. 1494–1553) in *Gargantua and Pantagruel*.
[8] Slaughterhouses.

But in order to justify my friend, he confessed, that this expedient was   17
put into his head by the famous Psalmanazar,[9] a native of the island For-
mosa, who came from thence to London, about twenty years ago, and in
conversation told my friend, that in his country when any young person
happened to be put to death, the executioner sold the carcass to persons of
quality, as prime dainty, and that, in his time, the body of a plump girl of
fifteen, who was crucified for an attempt to poison the Emperor, was sold
to his Imperial Majesty's prime minister of state, and other great mandarins
of the court, in joints from the gibbet, at four hundred crowns. Neither
indeed can I deny, that if the same use were made of several plump young
girls in this town, who, without one single groat to their fortunes, cannot
stir abroad without a chair, and appear at a play-house and assemblies in
foreign fineries which they never will pay for, the kingdom would not be
the worse.

Some persons of a desponding spirit are in great concern about that vast   18
number of poor people, who are aged, diseased, or maimed, and I have
been desired to employ my thoughts what course may be taken, to ease the
nation of so grievous an encumbrance. But I am not in the least pain upon
that matter, because it is very well known, that they are every day dying,
and rotting, by cold, and famine, and filth, and vermin, as fast as can be
reasonably expected. And as to the young labourers, they are now in almost
as hopeful a condition. They cannot get work, and consequently pine away
for want of nourishment, to a degree, that if at any time they are accidentally
hired to common labour, they have not enough strength to perform it, and
thus the country and themselves are happily delivered from the evils to
come.

I have too long digressed, and therefore shall return to my subject. I think   19
the advantages by the proposal which I have made are obvious and many,
as well as of the highest importance.

For *first,* as I have already observed, it would greatly lessen the number   20
of papists, with whom we are yearly over-run, being the principal breeders
of the nation, as well as our most dangerous enemies, and who stay at home
on purpose with a design to deliver the kingdom to the Pretender, hoping
to take their advantage by the absence of so many good Protestants, who
have chosen rather to leave their country, than stay at home, and pay tithes
against their conscience to an Episcopal curate.

Secondly, the poorer tenants will have something valuable of their own,   21
which by law may be made liable to distress and help to pay their landlord's
rent, their corn and cattle being already seized, and money a thing unknown.

Thirdly, whereas the maintenance of an hundred thousand children, from   22
two years old and upward, cannot be computed at less than ten shillings
apiece per annum, the nation's stock will be thereby increased fifty thousand
pounds per annum, besides the profit of a new dish introduced to the tables

[9] George Psalmanazar (c. 1679–1763) was a Frenchman who pretended to be a Formosan
and wrote a popular, completely fictional account of the supposed customs of his native land.

of all gentlemen of fortune in the kingdom who have any refinement in taste. And the money will circulate among our selves, the goods being entirely of our own growth and manufacture.

23   Fourthly, the constant breeders, beside the gain of eight shillings sterling per annum by the sale of their children will be rid of the charge of maintaining them after the first year.

24   Fifthly, this food would likewise bring great custom[10] to taverns, where the vintners will certainly be so prudent as to procure the best receipts[11] for dressing it to perfection, and consequently have their houses frequented by all the fine gentlemen who justly value themselves upon their knowledge in good eating; and a skillful cook, who understands how to oblige his guests, will contrive to make it as expensive as they please.

25   Sixthly, this would be a great inducement to marriage, which all wise nations have either encouraged by rewards or enforced by laws and penalties. It would increase the care and the tenderness of mothers toward their children, when they were sure of a settlement for life to the poor babes, provided in some sort by the public, to their annual profit instead of expense. We should soon see an honest emulation among the married women, which of them could bring the fattest child to the market. Men would become as fond of their wives during the time of their pregnancy as they are now of their mares in foal, their cows in calf, their sows when they are ready to farrow; nor offer to beat or kick them (as is too frequent a practice) for fear of a miscarriage.

26   Many other advantages might be enumerated. For instance, the addition of some thousand carcasses in our exportation of barreled beef, the propagation of swine's flesh, and improvement in the art of making good bacon, so much wanted among us by the great destruction of pigs, too frequent at our table; which are no way comparable in taste or magnificence to a well-grown, fat, yearling child, which roasted whole will make a considerable figure at a lord mayor's feast or any other public entertainment. But this and many others I omit, being studious of[12] brevity.

27   Supposing that one thousand families in this city would be constant customers for infants' flesh, besides others who might have it at merry-meetings, particularly at weddings and christenings, I compute that Dublin would take off annually about twenty thousand carcasses; and the rest of the kingdom (where probably they will be sold somewhat cheaper) the remaining eighty thousand.

28   I can think of no one objection that will possibly be raised against this proposal, unless it should be urged that the number of people will be thereby much lessened in the kingdom. This I freely own, and 'twas indeed one principal design in offering it to the world. I desire the reader will observe that I calculate my remedy for this one individual kingdom of Ireland, and for no other that ever was, is, or, I think, ever can be upon earth. Therefore let no man talk to me of other expedients: of taxing our absentees at five

[10] Trade.
[11] Recipes.
[12] Concerned with.

shillings a pound: of using neither clothes, nor household furniture, except what is of our own growth and manufacture: of utterly rejecting the materials and instruments that promote foreign luxury: of curing the expensiveness of pride, vanity, idleness, and gaming in our women: of introducing a vein of parsimony, prudence and temperance: of learning to love our country, wherein we differ even from Laplanders, and the inhabitants of Topinamboo:[13] of quitting our animosities, and factions, nor act any longer like the Jews, who were murdering one another at the very moment their city was taken:[14] of being a little cautious not to sell our country and consciences for nothing: of teaching landlords to have at least one degree of mercy towards their tenants. Lastly, of putting a spirit of honesty, industry, and skill into our shop-keepers, who, if a resolution could now be taken to buy only our native goods, would immediately unite to cheat and exact[15] upon us in the price, the measure, and the goodness, nor could ever yet be brought to make one fair proposal of just dealing, though often and earnestly invited to it.

Therefore I repeat, let no man talk to me of these and the like expedients,   29
till he hath at least some glimpse of hope, that there will ever be some hearty and sincere attempt to put them in practice.

But as to myself, having been wearied out for many years with offering   30
vain, idle, visionary thoughts, and at length utterly despairing of success, I fortunately fell upon this proposal, which as it is wholly new, so it hath something solid and real, of no expense and little trouble, full in our own power, and whereby we can incur no danger in disobliging England. For this kind of commodity will not bear exportation, the flesh being of too tender a consistence, to admit a long continuance in salt, although perhaps I could name a country, which would be glad to eat up our whole nation without it.

After all, I am not so violently bent upon my own opinion, as to reject   31
any offer, proposed by wise men, which shall be found equally innocent, cheap, easy, and effectual. But before something of that kind shall be advanced in contradiction to my scheme, and offering a better, I desire the author or authors, will be pleased maturely to consider two points. *First,* as things now stand, how they will be able to find food and raiment for a hundred thousand useless mouths and backs. And *Secondly,* there being a round million of creatures in human figure throughout this kingdom, whose whole subsistence put into a common stock would leave them in debt two millions of pounds sterling, adding those who are beggars by profession, to the bulk of farmers, cottagers and labourers, with their wives and children, who are beggars in effect; I desire those politicians, who dislike my overture, and may perhaps be so bold to attempt an answer, that they will first ask the parents of these mortals, whether they would not at this day think it a great happiness to have been sold for food at a year old, in the manner I prescribe, and thereby have avoided such a perpetual scene of misfortunes

[13] Jungle region of Brazil.
[14] Reference to the fall of Jerusalem, as described in the Bible.
[15] Impose.

as they have since gone through, by the oppression of landlords, the impossibility of paying rent without money or trade, the want of common sustenance, with neither house nor clothes to cover them from the inclemencies of the weather, and the most inevitable prospect of entailing the like or greater miseries upon their breed for ever.

32   I profess, in the sincerity of my heart, that I have not the least personal interest in endeavoring to promote this necessary work, having no other motive than the public good of my country, by advancing our trade, providing for infants, relieving the poor, and giving some pleasure to the rich. I have no children by which I can propose to get a single penny; the youngest being nine years old, and my wife past childbearing.

WHAT DID THE WRITER SAY, AND WHAT DID YOU THINK?

1. "A Modest Proposal" is an ironic essay: the author deliberately writes what he does not mean. What is the real thesis? Is there more than one?
2. Is the essay only an attack on something? Does Swift ever present any serious proposals for improving conditions? If so, where?
3. What is the character of the "projector" of the proposal? Don't confuse him with Swift.
4. Are there any flaws in the logic? Could you refute the proposal by using logic? What assumptions about life and morality does the projector make before.the logical argument begins?
5. What people or groups are singled out as special targets for Swift's attack?
6. Are the Irish presented completely as innocent victims, or are they also to blame?
7. Where does Swift's own sense of bitterness and rage come closest to emerging from beneath the cool irony?
8. Would it be possible to read this essay as a seriously intended proposal?

HOW DID THE WRITER SAY IT?

1. When does the reader start to realize that the essay is ironic? Before or after the actual proposal is made in paragraph 10?
2. Comment on the word choice in *a child just dropt from its dam* (par. 4), *two hundred thousand couples whose wives are breeders* (par. 6), *a boy or a girl before twelve years old, is no saleable commodity* (par. 7).
3. Comment on the word choice in *people might be apt to censure such a practice . . . as a little bordering on cruelty* (par. 16) and *they are every day dying, and rotting, by cold, and famine, and filth, and vermin, as fast as can be reasonably expected* (par. 18).
4. What is the purpose of the last paragraph?
5. Which parts of the essay are *not* ironic?
6. Vocabulary: *importuning, alms, prodigious, dam, raiment, proficiency, nutriment, collateral, repine, mandarins, desponding, tithes, curate, emulation, brevity, parsimony, animosities, factions, effectual, sustenance.*

WHAT ABOUT **YOUR** WRITING?

Verbal irony in its simplest form is saying the opposite, or near opposite, of what is meant. It can be seen at a primitive level when someone says, "Nice weather we're having" during a thunderstorm, and at the level of genius in "A Modest Proposal."

Nearly any subject can lend itself to the ironic approach, and you may want to consider trying your hand at an ironic paper. Successful irony has structured into it a strong element of humor and dramatic tension—tension between the surface statement and the underlying reality. With its special slant, it can also break through an audience's resistance toward reading another piece on a frequently discussed subject. It can often present familiar ideas in a fresh and exciting way.

A writer opposing capital punishment, for example, may be concerned about coming through as a shallow idealist who thinks that all murderers are poor misunderstood victims of society. Using irony, the writer might be able to avoid the problem by pretending to be a bloodthirsty advocate of capital punishment, urging public executions, death by torture, and any other hideous ideas that come to mind. A writer supporting capital punishment, on the other hand, concerned about coming through as an unfeeling brute, might pretend to be the simple-minded idealist, arguing ironically that if only society had provided more playgrounds and Boy Scout troops, the murderer would have become a priest or ecologist.

In writing an ironic essay, watch out for two pitfalls:

Don't let the reader misunderstand. Exaggerate enough so that the reader knows what side you're really on.

Don't lose the ironic tone. Don't let your true feelings enter directly. The worst enemy of an effective ironic paper is sincerity. Beware, in particular, of the last paragraph that introduces a "but seriously, folks," or "what I really mean to say" element. If the irony isn't clear long before that, the whole paper probably needs to be reworked.

Critics often distinguish between verbal irony and two other kinds. _Irony of fate_ refers to events that turn out differently from a normal person's expectations. A man compulsively afraid of germs has his whole house sterilized, fills his medicine chest with every known drug, and dies before he's thirty by tripping over a discarded bottle of medicine and breaking his neck. Most short stories with surprise endings employ irony of fate. _Dramatic irony_ occurs when a literary character says or does something without realizing its significance, but the audience or reader does realize it. The hero of a melodrama beats up some villains, turns to the audience, says "Virtue triumphs again," and does not see another villain sneaking up behind him with a club.

Sarcasm is verbal irony used in an extremely bitter and personal fashion: "You really have a big heart, don't you?"

Index